THE STORY OF

One Hundred Great Composers

OTHER BOOKS BY

HELEN L. KAUFMANN

◇◇◇

From Jehovah to Jazz

The Story of Music in America

The Home Book of Music Appreciation

The Story of One Hundred Great Composers

The Little Dictionary of Musical Terms

The Little Guide to Music Appreciation

The Little Book of Music Anecdotes

[IN COLLABORATION WITH EVA VB. HANSL]

Minute Sketches of Great Composers

Artists in Music of Today

THE STORY OF *One Hundred Great Composers*

HELEN L. KAUFMANN

Grosset & Dunlap
PUBLISHERS
NEW YORK

PRINTED IN THE UNITED STATES OF AMERICA

Acknowledgments

THE AUTHOR ACKNOWLEDGES her indebtedness for the facts in this volume to Groves' *Dictionary of Music and Musicians*, Oscar Thompson's *International Cyclopedia of Music and Musicians*, Paul Lang's *Music in Western Civilization*, and Bauer & Peyser's *Music Through the Ages;* for the pronunciation of names to Webster's *Unabridged Dictionary;* and for editorial assistance to her good friends Russell Ames and Arthur Loesser.

Contents

Author's Acknowledgment v
Index of Composers ix
Foreword xiii
The People and Their Music xv
Story of One Hundred Great Composers 1
The Unknown Composer 226
Some Definitions 228
Appendix
The Work of One Hundred Great Composers 235

Index of Composers

Albéniz, Isaac (1860–1909) 153
Bach, Johann Sebastian (1685–1750) 28
Bach, Carl Philipp Emanuel (1714–1788) 34
Bartók, Béla (1881–1945) 195
Beethoven, Ludwig van (1770–1827) 49
Bellini, Vincenzo (1801–1835) 65
Berlioz, Hector (1803–1869) 68
Bizet, Georges (1838–1875) 114
Bloch, Ernest (1880) 193
Boccherini, Luigi (1743–1805) 42
Borodin, Alexander (1833–1887) 108
Brahms, Johannes (1833–1897) 106
Bruch, Max (1838–1920) 112
Bruckner, Anton (1824–1896) 97
Byrd, William (1543–1623) 5
Carpenter, John Alden (1876) 189
Chausson, Ernest (1855–1899) 139
Chavez, Carlos (1899) 219
Cherubini, Maria Luigi Carlo Zenobio Salvatore (1760–1842) 47

Index of Composers

Chopin, Frédéric François (1810–1849) 73
Copland, Aaron (1900) 222
Corelli, Arcangelo (1653–1713) 13
Couperin, François (1668–1733) 18
Debussy, Claude (1862–1918) 162
Delius, Frederick (1862–1934) 160
Donizetti, Gaetano (1797–1848) 64
Dukas, Paul (1865–1935) 171
Dvořák, Antonin (1841–1904) 120
Elgar, Sir Edward (1857–1934) 140
Enesco, Georges (1881) 197
Falla, Manuel de (1876–1946) 190
Fauré, Gabriel Urbain (1845–1924) 132
Foster, Stephen Collins (1826–1864) 101
Franck, César (1822–1890) 92
Franz, Robert (1815–1892) 87
Gershwin, George (1898–1937) 215
Glinka, Michael Ivanovitch (1803–1857) 66
Gluck, Christoph Willibald (1714–1787) 36
Gounod, Charles François (1818–1893) 89
Granados, Enrique (1867–1916) 173
Grieg, Edvard (1843–1907) 127
Handel, George Frederick (1685–1759) 26
Harris, Roy (1898) 217
Haydn, Franz Joseph (1732–1809) 39
Herbert, Victor (1859–1924) 146
Hindemith, Paul (1895) 211
Humperdinck, Engelbert (1854–1921) 135
Indy, Vincent D' (1851–1931) 133
Ives, Charles Edward (1874) 184

Kern, Jerome David (1885–1945) 204
Lassus, Orlandus (Orlando di Lasso) (1530–1594) 3
Leoncavallo, Ruggiero (1858–1919) 144
Liszt, Franz (1811–1886) 78
Loeffler, Charles Martin (1861–1935) 155
Lully, Jean Baptiste (1632–1687) 10
MacDowell, Edward (1861–1908) 157
Mahler, Gustav (1860–1911) 148
Mascagni, Pietro (1863–1945) 165
Massenet, Jules Emile Frédéric (1842–1912) 123
Mendelssohn, Felix Bartholdy (1809–1847) 70
Meyerbeer, Giacomo (1791–1864) 59
Milhaud, Darius (1892) and "Le Six" 208
Monteverdi, Claudio (1567–1643) 7
Moussorgsky, Modest Petrovich (1835–1881) 115
Mozart, Wolfgang Amadeus (1756–1791) 44
Offenbach, Jacques (1819–1880) 91
Palestrina, Giovanni Pierluigi da (1524–1594) 1
People and Their Music xi
Pergolesi, Giovanni Battista (1710–1736) 32
Prokofieff, Serge (1891) 206
Puccini, Giacomo (1858–1924) 142
Purcell, Henry (1659–1695) 15
Rachmaninoff, Sergei (1873–1943) 179
Rameau, Jean Philippe (1683–1764) 20
Ravel, Maurice (1875–1937) 186
Rimsky-Korsakoff, Nicolas Andreievitch (1844–1908) 129
Rossini Gioacchino Antonio (1792–1868) 61
Rubinstein, Anton Gregorovitch (1829–1894) 104

Index of Composers

Saint-Saëns, Charles Camille (1835–1921) 110
Scarlatti, Alessandro (1659–1725) 23
Scarlatti, Domenico (1685–1757) 23
Schönberg, Arnold (1874) 181
Schubert, Franz (1797–1828) 56
Schumann, Robert (1810–1856) 76
Scriabin, Alexander Nicolaievitch (1872–1915) 175
Shostakovich, Dmitri (1906) 224
Sibelius, Jean (1865) 169
Smetana, Bedřich (1824–1884) 95
Some Definitions 228
Sousa, John Philip (1854–1932) 137
Still, William Grant (1895) 213
Strauss, Johann Junior (1825–1899) 99
Strauss, Richard (1864–1949) 166
Stravinsky, Igor (1882) 199
Sullivan, Sir Arthur (1842–1900) 125
Szymanowski, Karol (1883–1937) 201
Tchaikowsky, Peter Ilitch (1840–1893) 117
Unknown Composer (The) 226
Vaughan-Williams, Ralph (1872) 177
Verdi, Giuseppe (1813–1901) 84
Villa-Lobos, Hector (1884) 203
Wagner, Richard (1813–1883) 81
Weber, Carl Maria von (1786–1826) 53
Wolf, Hugo (1860–1903) 150

Foreword

THE MUSIC OF THE ONE HUNDRED COMPOSERS in this little book is heard today in the concert hall and opera house, over the radio and on the gramophone. It is everywhere. To listen, knowing something of the personality and problems of the men who wrote it, is to enjoy it tenfold. "Tell me the story of your life" has marked the beginning of many a beautiful friendship. The stories of composers' lives create such friendships, not only for the men, but also for the music in which they expressed themselves, and it is with the hope of introducing every reader to many such new friends that this book has been written.

To quote the English composer Henry Purcell, "The author has no more to add, but his hearty wishes, that his Book may fall into no other hands but theirs who carry Musical Souls about them; for he is willing to flatter himself into a belief, that with such his labours will seem neither unpleasant nor unprofitable."

The People and Their Music

WHEN THE FIRST CAVEMAN saw his mother-in-law being chased by a saber-toothed tiger, he probably grunted sounds of pleasure in honor of the event. His children and children's children added their sounds to his, and established traditional noises for other happenings in their lives. Gradually words and melodies emerged. One or two individuals would start a song, others would finish it. The process began long before certain men made the writing of music their business. It has resulted in a great mass of unwritten music, which passes from one to another in a group, and from group to group. This is folksong—the spontaneous expression of the people. Ballads like *Frankie and Johnny*, Negro spirituals and Indian tribal chants are an important part of American culture, and increasingly students of music are patiently assembling and recording them.

Folksong need not, like an antique, be a hundred years old to be good. It is being created here and now, everywhere and all the time. The process begun so long ago never stops. These songs have become a descriptive musical history of the people, told in the people's language. It contains their characteristic expression as nations, as groups within nations, as smaller groups within those. No wonder, then, that professional composers thankfully draw their material from folksong. It is a never-ending source of supply, a staff of life to their music. It invests their concepts with a group personality more powerful than their own or any single individual's. Folksong can exist without benefit of composer, but the converse is not true. And so folksong becomes an inspiration to great writers, and the people from whom it emanates become the greatest composer of them all.

◇◇◇◇◇◇◇◇◇◇◇◇◇◇◇◇◇◇◇◇◇◇◇◇◇◇◇◇◇◇◇◇

Giovanno Pierluigi da Palestrina

(dä päl′äs-trē′nä)

b. PALESTRINA, ITALY, 1525 *d.* ROME, ITALY, FEB. 2, 1594

FROM THE MOMENT WHEN, at the age of eleven, Giovanno Pierluigi da Palestrina became a choir boy at Santa Maria Maggiore in Rome, until he died, the church was a permanent backdrop for the drama of his life,—now it was the Sistine Chapel, now a simple country place of worship, but always a house of God.

After some years of study in Rome, he became organist and choirmaster in Palestrina, his home town, was married at twenty, and returned to Rome with his family. In gratitude for his appointment to the Capella Giulia there, he wrote a honeyed dedication to Pope Julius III for his *First Book of Masses*. Unfortunately Julius died, and a later pope Paul IV abruptly dismissed the young man from the college of singers of the papal chapel, on the ground that he was married, a crime not censured up to that time. Though a small pension accompanied the dismissal, Palestrina suffered the sixteenth century equivalent of a nervous breakdown. He continued composing, however, and serving as choirmaster in various churches.

With the accession of Pope Pius IV, fortune smiled again, and so did Palestrina. In the dedication of his *First Book of Motets* in 1563, he wrote: "The function of music in the church is the seasoning of devotion by the added delight of sweetness of song and variety of harmony. The sharper blame therefore do those deserve who misemploy so great and splendid a gift of God in light or unworthy things, and thereby excite men, who of themselves are inclined to all evil, to sin and misdoing."

So well did his music embody that pious belief that a commission appointed by the Council of Trent to purify the church service in 1564 left Palestrina's compositions untouched, and bestowed special praise on the glorious *Marcellus Mass*, written some time previously. His townsfolk put on a festival for his fiftieth birthday. He marched in a procession, with the people behind him, all singing his music. This was a proud moment in his career.

Within four years, death claimed his wife, two sons, and two grandchildren. In his grief, he contemplated becoming a monk, and had his head shaved in a tonsure, but thought better of it. Instead, he remarried, and in directing his new wife's thriving fur business made enough to enable him to publish sixteen collections of his own music. The combination of piety and business ability was marked in Palestrina throughout his life; there was nothing of the dreamy, impractical artist about him despite his idealism. From 1571 on, he lived in Rome as director of the Capella Giulia, and composed peacefully for Mother Church until his death. In all the long list of masses, madrigals and motets, there is not one that is cheap or unworthy. Purity and clarity, comparative brevity and simplicity, polyphony used with judicious reserve, the banishing of secular elements from his music,—these are the qualities which won him the title Princeps Musicae—Prince of Music—which is engraved on his tombstone.

◇◇◇◇◇◇◇◇◇◇◇◇◇◇◇◇◇◇◇◇◇◇◇◇◇◇◇◇◇◇

Orlandus Lassus (Orlando di Lasso)

(dē läs′sō)

b. MONS, BELGIUM, ABOUT 1530 *d.* MUNICH, GERMANY, JUNE 14, 1594

THE FLEMISH ORLANDUS LASSUS was almost the musical twin of the Italian Palestrina. Not only did they look alike, with pointed beards and serious deepset eyes, but they held choirmaster jobs successively at the same church, and died in the same year. Unlike his "twin," Lassus did not concentrate wholly on church music, and secular writings brought his grand total to twelve hundred and fifty, a formidable sixty volumes.

He was very much a man of the world. He consorted with kings and princes, and was as popular at court as in chapel. In 1570 the Emperor Maximilian of Bavaria gave him a patent of nobility, and a year later Pope Gregory bestowed on Lassus the Papal Order of the Golden Spur in recognition of a volume of masses dedicated to him. Although Palestrina was accounted a good business man, Lassus cashed in on his talents even more successfully. This was decidedly pleasant for the wife he took to himself in 1558, and for the four sons and two daughters who blessed their union. So was his habit of traveling, which took him from Belgium to Italy, Germany and France.

Lassus' religious writings were serious, meditative, almost somber, as witness his moving setting of the *Seven Penitential Psalms*, whereas in those designed for the world and the flesh, if not for the devil, he of course released a lighter mood. He understood the instruments of his day,—the lute, viol and dulcimer—and wrote for groups of singers as though their voices were these instruments, instead of following a purely vocal line. While Palestrina's compositions were characterized by pure, graceful melody, Lassus' displayed more variety, greater depth, more abrupt and massive architecture; the former can be compared with Raphael and Mozart, the latter with Michael Angelo and Bach. The two men together represent the highest point attained in sixteenth century polyphonic writing.

◇◇◇◇◇◇◇◇◇◇◇◇◇◇◇◇◇◇◇◇◇◇◇◇◇◇◇◇◇◇◇◇◇◇◇◇◇

William Byrd

(bûrd)

b. LINCOLN, ENGLAND, ABOUT 1543 — *d.* ESSEX, ENGLAND, JULY 4, 1623

A CATHOLIC in the Protestant England of Queen Elizabeth had to be careful to keep his head, in every sense of the phrase. William Byrd, Master of Musicke, succeeded in living to be eighty and dying in one piece. By writing for the Protestant Church a Great Service and a Short Service, and for the Papists three masses, besides madrigals, anthems, and hymns, he remained in the good graces of both.

He had friends at court, too, when he needed them. Having been granted by the Queen the exclusive right, with his colleague Thomas Tallis, to print and sell music in her domain, he found it an honor which paid no cash dividends, so he sent her a respectful S O S, and received a lease on a substantial manor in Gloucestershire. He took up residence there, and rode daily on horseback to the Chapel Royal in London to discharge his duties as organist to the Queen.

It is strange that a man "of himselfe naturally disposed to Gravitie and Pietie" should all his life have been plagued by lawsuits, but the records show that he spent almost as much time in the magistrates' court as in the organ loft. He fought tooth and nail to secure his disputed title to Stondon Place in Essex, to which he removed in 1593, and in the end he had his way, lived there with his family until his death, and left it to them free and clear.

But he left a far more valuable heritage, for today he is acknowledged as one of the most versatile, original, and creative composers of all time. In his position, he was called upon for music for every sort of occasion, and rose nobly to the challenge, inventing new types of composition as need arose. He composed a number of songs with string quartet accompaniments, actually the first vocal solos in which instruments played the part purely of accompaniment. Introduced as a novelty into several plays, they proved a history-making innovation. He produced chamber music also,—dance suites for violins, violas and celli, instead of for the old-fashioned "case of viols." The virginal, favorite keyboard instrument of the day, he exploited in pieces of exquisite charm. "In form and style," says Edward Lockspeiser, "he set an entirely new standard in keyboard composition, the influence of which was felt far beyond England."

◇◇◇◇◇◇◇◇◇◇◇◇◇◇◇◇◇◇◇◇◇◇◇◇◇◇◇◇◇◇

Claudio Monteverdi

(mŏn′tā-vâr′dē)

b. CREMONA, ITALY, BAPTIZED MAY 15, 1567

d. VENICE, ITALY, NOV. 29, 1643

EVEN AFTER THREE CENTURIES, the music of Monteverdi glows with the passionate genius of a musical prophet. He was far ahead of his day in his conception of music as a dramatic, expressive art, and in the realization of that conception.

He enjoyed a thorough musical education with Ingegneri in Cremona, from whom he learned rules of composition with which he often disagreed. In his *First Book of Madrigals*, published when he was fifteen, there are already premonitions of musical revolt which did not, however, deter the Duke of Mantua from taking him as singer and violinist into the ducal orchestra. Presently another patron, Duke Vincenzo I, annexed him to his suite, and with him the young man saw something of the world before settling in Mantua. He had in the meantime married

Claudia Cataneo, a charming and accomplished harpist.

At Vincenzo's behest, Monteverdi wrote his first opera, *Orfeo*, performed in 1607, in which he employed every device that occurred to him to lift the orchestra from the duenna-like neutrality of pure background to active participation in the action and mood of the drama. Instead of the dry recitativos common to the opera of the day, lovely melodies were given to the singers. Short song-like passages were also interpolated in the orchestral score. In this, his first attempt, he spurned the cut and dried, and, with the dramatic madrigal in mind, made the opera a living thing. But the year that witnessed the success of *Orfeo* was also the year of the death of his wife. He was prostrated. *Lasciatemi morire* (*Let me die*), probably his most sublime aria, is from the opera *Arianna*, composed the following year. The poignant intensity of this cry of grief still moves to tears those who hear it.

When his patron Vincenzo died, Monteverdi went as choirmaster to St. Mark's Cathedral in Venice,—a city where all the arts flourished and invited a Monteverdi to flourish with them. Many of his madrigals and masses, almost as famous as his operas, were composed there. His outstanding opera of this period was *Il Combattimento di Clorinda e Tancredi* (*The Battle of Clorinda and Tancred*), in which the composer had practically to bludgeon the orchestra violinists into playing *tremolo* and *pizzicato* to produce the emotions of excitement and suspense. This was the first time they had been expected to do so.

In 1630, a plague which was ravaging Europe reached Venice. Monteverdi vowed to make a pilgrimage if he was spared, and did even better, for he took priestly orders. During the following decade, he composed several operas,—so his letters tell us,—most of which have been lost. Two, *Il Ritorno d'Ulisse in Patria* (*Ulysses' Home-Coming*) and *L'Incoronazione di Poppea* (*The Coronation of Poppea*) remain in part. The youth and vitality of *L'Incoronazione* are remarkable, emanating as they do from a seventy-four-year-old churchman.

Monteverdi's vision embraced all the arts converging on one,—the opera. In trying to make that vision a reality, he blazed a trail followed by composers in every land for centuries after.

Jean Baptiste Lully

(lü'lē')

b. FLORENCE, ITALY, NOV. 29, 1632 *d.* PARIS, FRANCE, MARCH 22, 1687

A MISCHIEVOUS LITTLE ITALIAN BOY in Florence three centuries ago used to play hookey from his father's mill at Carnival time when the strolling players passed by, because they allowed him to strum the guitar and play the violin with them. At one of the Carnivals, the Duc de Guise was so amused by the monkey-faced youngster that he took him back to the French court as a kitchen scullion to Mlle. de Montpensier, where, when Mademoiselle discovered his talent, she took him into her band as a violinist. Six years later he repaid her kindness by lampooning her in a comic song, and, enraged, she handed him over to her cousin, King Louis XIV, then a lad in his teens.

In the triple capacity of ballet-dancer, composer for the court entertainments, and violinist in the Vingt quatre Violons du Roi (King's twenty-four Violins), he had the King's ear in every sense. He persuaded the monarch to allow him to form his own string orchestra, which speedily surpassed the twenty-four in brilliancy of execution and quality of programs. For the royal entertainments at Versailles, he devised ballets and spectacles, wrote music, played it, danced and acted indefatigably for his "Roi Soleil." As Instrumental Composer to the King, Composer to the King's Chamber Music, and Music Master to the Royal Family, he collected a pay envelope in keeping with these highsounding titles. When he was married, the Royal Family witnessed his contract, as though he were their own son.

Lully took his first step toward the opera in 1664, when, working with the playwright Molière on a series of comedy ballets, he insistently emphasized the musical end of the collaboration. When an opportunity was presented by the failure of two lesser men to establish an opera house, he craftily secured from his King their patent, and became Dictator of the opera in Paris. In 1673 he produced his first French lyrical tragedy, *Cadmus et Hermione.*

Sole artistic as well as financial director of L'Académie Royale, he conducted the orchestra, stage-managed the performances, and coached the performers. Correct phrasing and declamation were his passion. He eliminated many flourishes customarily extemporized by the singers, though much of the rococo still remained. In the ballet, he replaced stately court airs with lively allegros, and engaged artists who would dance as fast as he piped, adding men to the hitherto all-feminine corps de ballet. He wrote entertaining orchestral overtures to his operas, livened their recitatives with an expressive accompaniment, made of the recitative itself a piece of exquisite declamation, and interpolated charming light airs. *Theseé*, *Isis*, *Atys*, *Phaeton*, *Armide*, *Roland*, operas written to please a king, were equally pleasing to the king's subjects. Lully's absolute rule established France as a great musical power.

While conducting his Te Deum in celebration of the King's recovery from an illness, Lully accidentally struck his foot with the heavy baton. Bloodpoisoning ensued, and he died at the height of his power and success. Brilliant, unscrupulous, overweeningly ambitious, a master of intrigue, he was not a good man. But none denies his greatness in music.

Arcangelo Corelli

(kô-rĕl'lē)

b. FUSIGNANO, ITALY, FEB. 12, 1653 *d.* ROME, ITALY, JAN. 10, 1713

THE FAMOUS VIOLIN MAKER, Anton Stradivarius, evolved the perfect instrument just in time to place it in the hands of Arcangelo Corelli, the greatest violinist of his day. Corelli loved above all things the instrument that most resembles the human voice, and composed for it melodies that sing like the voice itself. He perfected the concerto grosso, which means "big altogether," a piece for several instruments (in which Corelli usually included a violin), with orchestral accompaniment. Though written for the church, these concerti had an operatic flavor that savored pleasantly of Monteverdi and Lully. Among the first and best of the solo sonatas written for the violin were Corelli's; Bach's and Handel's followed their lead. Corelli's *La Folia*, a noble theme with variations which is the delight of all violinists, is known as the final essence of classical Italian violin music.

Corelli lived frugally, though he created richly. After he had been trained in counterpoint by

Matteo Simonelli and in violin by Bassani, he traveled in Germany and visited Paris. Lully is said to have made life so uncomfortable for this potential rival that Corelli cut short his stay, but the fact has not been proven. In any event, he went home to Italy when he was about thirty-two, and passed the remainder of his life in Rome under the protection and in the palace of his patron, Cardinal Ottoboni.

Amiable, gentle, unusually modest, he was well loved. He composed both church and secular music, conducted on Mondays concerts that were the musical event of the week in Rome, and amassed a fortune that he never spent. Pupils came in great numbers, among them Geminiani and Locatelli, who acquired considerable reputations. Corelli was simple to the point of parsimony. He walked where others rode, wore plain, almost shabby clothes in the midst of silks and satins, ate and drank sparingly at tables groaning with food. Next to the violin, paintings were his passion; a malicious commentator said that "Corelli liked nothing better than seeing pictures without paying for it, and saving money." Nevertheless he was the owner of a fine collection of paintings, in the purchase of which he took the advice of the leading artists of the day.

In 1708, he visited the court of Naples, where he heard the orchestra, under Alessandro Scarlatti, play one of his concertos so well that he cried out approvingly "They play well in Naples." But when he himself played, the king, obviously bored, left before the end, and Corelli in his nervousness made a mistake which he repeated after Scarlatti had called it to his attention. Mortified and humiliated, he continued to brood over his failure after his return to Rome. When he found a new violinist in favor there, it was the last straw. He lost interest in life, and died because he could not bear to live.

◇◇◇◇◇◇◇◇◇◇◇◇◇◇◇◇◇◇◇◇◇◇◇◇◇◇◇◇◇◇

Henry Purcell

(pûr′sĕl)

b. LONDON, ENGLAND, ABOUT 1659

d. THERE, NOV. 21, 1695

HENRY PURCELL looked like a Florentine prince, was hail-fellow-well-met in tavern and taproom, wrote for the church and also for the stage and salon, was in fact a most likeable young man, as well as a "very great Master of Musick."

He took to music young, for at six he became a choirboy in the Chapel Royal, and at fourteen "Keeper, mender, maker, repayrer and tuner of the regalls, organs, virginalls, flutes and recorders and all other kind of wind instruments, in ordinary, without fee, to his Majesty." The following year he was made tuner of the organ of Westminster Abbey, at a salary equivalent to ten dollars per annum, and he later became organist there. As a stripling of eighteen, he was composer to the King's violins, as valuable a training as was the oldfashioned stock company for an actor, since it gave him practice in his art before a considerable public.

He came of age in all ways at one time. At twenty-one he delivered a *Song to Welcome Home His Majesty from Windsor*, first of the many official odes he was asked to emit, like a slot machine, when the proper coin was inserted. Incidental music to a tragedy, *Theodosius or The Force of Love*, marked his first appearance as a theater composer. He was married that year, too.

Except for his appointment as organist at the Chapel Royal and other churches, his compositions are the chief events of his life. Incidental music to *The Fairy Queen*, *King Arthur* and *The Tempest* brought him fame. His anthem, *They That Go Down to the Sea in Ships* still tempts bassos to essay its low D, and the songs *Arise, ye subterranean winds*, and *I attempt from love's sickness to fly* are pleasing to the ears of today. His greatest work for the voice, the opera *Dido and Aeneas*, was commissioned by a young ladies' seminary at Chelsea and performed by the young ladies themselves. Purcell was a master of English declamation. He did not "write down" to his amateurs, but gave them the best he had, with the result that there are those who declare *Dido and Aeneas* to be the one great English opera, its exquisite aria, *When I am Laid in Earth* a landmark in English music. His instrumental writings are not handicapped, as were many of his songs, by vulgar or frivolous words. The *Fantasias* and *Sonatas for Strings* exemplify the best of French and Italian influence on Purcell's uncompromising Englishness.

Almost his last anthem, *Thou Knowest, Lord, the Secrets of our Hearts*, written for the funeral of Queen Mary in 1694, was described by one who was there as "so rapturously fine and solemn and so Heavenly in Operation" that it "drew tears from all." Six months later it again drew tears when it was sung for the composer's burial in Westminster Abbey.

François Couperin

(kōō′-pĕ-răn′)

b. PARIS, FRANCE, NOV. 10, 1668 *d.* THERE, SEPT. 12, 1733

AS CORELLI WAS THE MASTER of the violin, François Couperin, called Le Grand (The Great) was the master of the harpsichord. He studied his instrument tenderly, recognized its limitations as well as its excellences, and in composing for it took account of both. J. S. Bach and Handel were not too proud to study his great treatise, *L'art de toucher le Clavecin* (*The Art of Playing the Harpsichord*), nor to apply its teachings.

Of a large family of musical Couperins, François was the most illustrious. Like Lully, he lived most of his life in the luxurious court of Louis XIV, where he succeeded his teacher, Jacques-Denis Thomelin, as organist of the Royal Chapel. He became music teacher to the royal family, and also composed and performed pieces in the "little chamber concerts" held for the King on Sundays. He wrote some organ pieces and religious vocal music, but the harpsichord was his true love.

Couperin borrowed from Corelli the idea of the trio sonata. He wrote a few in the brilliant

Italian manner and tried them successfully under an Italian alias on his French audience. Since Italian works were then all the rage, he wanted to be sure of a favorable reception before revealing his identity as the composer. Then, in 1726, he published a large folio of these sonatas for two violins and harpsichord, entitled *Les Nations* (*The Nations*). As time went on he brought out four books of *Pièces de Clavecin* (*Harpsichord Pieces*), a "world picture book" which contains much of his finest writing. Some of these pieces have been transcribed for the piano. Many he christened with names like *La Voluptueuse*, *La Séduisante*, *La Belle Nanette*, the music being as voluptuous, seductive, and descriptive of beautiful Nanette as he could make it. These character pieces afforded a welcome change from the dance suites of the time, for they were poetic, imaginative, and tenderly conceived, and gave off welcome glints of humor. Couperin confessed, "I love that which stimulates me much more than that which overwhelms me," and he composed accordingly. During the last three years of his life, the younger of his two daughters took his place as clavecinist to the King, the first woman to be so honored.

The coat of arms bestowed upon him by his monarch depicts the sun, his King, shining benignly upon a golden lyre, himself, from a cloudless blue sky studded with silver stars. It is pleasantly emblematic of his life, warmed and nourished by the sun of royal favor.

Jean Philippe Rameau

(rà'mō')

b. DIJON, FRANCE, OCT. 23, 1683 *d.* PARIS, FRANCE, SEPT. 12, 1764

A LITTLE BOY OF SEVEN who could play the harpsichord well and read at sight anything that was put before him was a rarity even in a family of musicians, so Papa Rameau permitted Jean Philippe to study the organ, violin and harpsichord, but headed him for the law as a livelihood. However, his teachers soon rejected so disinterested a pupil, so he shook the dust of the law books from his fingers and contentedly taught himself harmony. Then an adolescent love affair necessitated a disciplinary trip to Italy, which gave him an opportunity to hear something of the music of his Italian contemporaries, though his stay was not long enough for a thorough study.

On his return to France, he supported himself here and there as organist. Meanwhile he made a thorough study of the philosophy and science of sound, and embodied his conclusions in a book, *Traité de l'Harmonie* (*Treatise on Harmony*), which he took to Paris in 1722 to be published. It clarified, simplified and amplified the existing rules, and established a complete system upon which rests the modern science of harmony. Moreover, it marked its author as an original thinker and musical genius, one of the greatest in France. "Soyez raisonnable" ("be reasonable") was his motto in music, as it would have been had he followed the law.

In Paris, the pedagogue of forty married a girl of eighteen, and divulged his secret ambition to compose for the stage. He found a patron in the artist-manager La Popelinière. When his first opera, *Hippolite et Aricie*, was produced in 1733, half the French public were mad over it, the other half were mad with it. He continued the formality of the Lully opera, but employed richer orchestration, piquant rhythms and harmonies and fresh, pleasing melodies. Although married to a singer, he never wrote as successfully for the voice as for instruments, his libretti were poor, and his indifference to declamation fatal. A later commentator described him as a symphonic dramatist.

The Lullistes of his own day, led by Rousseau, called him by much worse names, which were hurled back at them by the Ramistes, led by Voltaire, who wrote, "It would be desirable that in the measure in which the nation's taste improves Rameau's style should dominate it." *Castor et Pollux*, *Les Fêtes d'Hébè* (*The Festival of Hebe*), and *Les Indes Galantes* (*The Gallant Indies*) were the most successful of his many operas. Though historically important they are never sung, but their overtures are still played; so too are his charming harpsichord pieces.

When Pergolesi's *La Serva Padrona* (*The Maid Mistress*) was produced in Paris in 1752, Rameau again became a storm center, this time for the enmity between French classicists and Italian romanticists. He made many enemies, but he was too firmly entrenched at court to be dislodged. He became a member of the Académie, and drew a pension from the king, for whom during his last twenty years he composed ballets and court entertainments. He was about to receive a patent of nobility when typhoid fever ended his drama of clash and conflict.

The Scarlattis

(skär-lät′-tĕ)

ALESSANDRO SCARLATTI

b. PALERMO, SICILY, 1659 — *d.* NAPLES, ITALY, OCT. 24, 1725

DOMENICO SCARLATTI

b. NAPLES, ITALY, OCT. 26, 1685 — *d.* THERE, 1757

ALESSANDRO, Papa Scarlatti, was the first great master of the Neapolitan opera. He left a hundred and fifteen operas, instrumental pieces, many cantatas and oratorios, and much church music. He conducted the orchestra of the King of Naples, and was a famous teacher also—a serious, exacting, somewhat crabbed pedagogue. Historians agree upon his importance as a link in the chain of the opera's development, and many of his arias are still sung, but his fame is overshadowed by that of his son and prize pupil.

Domenico, as gay and lighthearted as his father was dignified, is, in fact, the most important Italian composer of his century. After dutifully writing a few operas in the style of his respected parent, Domenico escaped to his true medium, the harpsichord. For that instrument he had a passion which he expressed in over six hundred compositions. Many of them, transcribed for the piano, are among the glories of its literature. The *Esercizi* which he induced his pupils to practice for the good of their techniques are now dignified with the name of sonatas on concert programs, though to most of his works he gave no names.

There is good reason for the popularity of these pieces. They are, for the most part, short, piquant and dance-like, while their dazzling rapid runs in thirds and sixths, their arpeggios and involved counterpoint afford an opportunity for a magnificent display of virtuoso technique. Domenico reveled in their difficulties, even when he grew so fat from high living that he had to reach across his stomach to get at the keyboard, and when his favorite effect, the rapid crossing of hands, constituted a physical challenge. He still played so superbly that he is considered one of the founders of the piano style that has been perfected by Chopin, Liszt and others.

Early in his career, his patron, Cardinal Ottoboni, pitted him against Handel in a harpsichord contest at his palace. Both played so well that neither was adjudged the winner, but Scarlatti crossed himself reverently when Handel's name was mentioned thereafter, and the two men became fast friends. Domenico, as cultured as he was fat, rolled jovially around the world gathering inspiration. In Rome, he supplied operas for the private theater of the Polish Queen Marie and was musical director of St. Peter's. He was cembalist to the Italian opera in London and to the King of Portugal in Lisbon, concertized in Dublin and was music master to the Spanish princesses in Madrid. Twanging guitar effects, the tunes of Spanish muleteers and peasants in his works are a souvenir of those Spanish days and nights. Scarlatti said that he "thought there was scarce any other rule worth the attention of a man of genius than that of not displeasing the only sense (hearing) of which music is the object."

He lived lustily, spending as he went, and gambled away all that he accumulated. When he died he left a large family, a pile of debts, and no assets except his compositions. Even these were not printed during his life. The manuscripts were scattered here and there, to be collected, in part, almost a century after his death, but no approximately complete edition appeared until 1910.

George Frederick Handel

(hăn′d'l)

b. HALLE, GERMANY, FEB. 23, 1685 *d.* LONDON, ENGLAND, APRIL 14, 1759

OF GEORGE FREDERICK HANDEL OF ENGLAND, born Georg Friedrich Händel of Germany, an English critic wrote, "He did bestride our musical world like a Colossus." The description was apt, for George was a huge, fleshy man, who ate, drank and composed music all on a grand scale.

His father intended him for the law, but permitted him to take lessons from the best teacher in Zachau in harmony and counterpoint, violin, oboe and harpsichord. He was eighteen when his father died, and without hesitation he dropped the law and turned to music. He served an apprenticeship in various places, including the Hamburg Opera, where a duel with a jealous rival who wanted his place at the harpsichord gave rise to the story that his life had been saved by a button which deflected the point of his adversary's sword.

He went to Italy in 1706, and for three years he absorbed Italian music, which powerfully influenced his own style of writing. He hobnobbed.

too, with Corelli and the Scarlattis. Then his opera *Rinaldo* made such a hit in London that he decided to remain there. The famous *Water Music* he wrote for a Thames boating party given by his Majesty King George is said to have effected a reconciliation with that monarch after a disagreement, and to have clinched Handel's determination to make London his home. And so this international German who wrote like an Italian became a naturalized Englishman in 1726, though he never lost his German accent.

During the ten years from 1720 to 1730, Handel was to London what Lully had been to Paris. At the Royal Academy of Music he directed, engaged the singers, and wrote fifteen successful operas. His first important oratorio, *Esther*, the pastoral cantata *Acis and Galatea*, and the book of *Harpsichord Suites* date from this period. But lean years were to follow. *The Beggar's Opera*,—spicy, satirical, and off-color—came to London and charmed audiences away. Italian opera was lampooned in the press, and Handel with it. He had to regain his lost prestige. He decided to do so by way of the oratorio.

The English passion for oratorio is largely due to Handel. Every year from 1738 to 1751, he produced at least one. The *Messiah* is *The* modern oratorio, not only because of the custom of rising and stretching in the seventh inning, when the *Hallelujah Chorus* is sung, but because its magnificent choruses, soaring arias and orchestral accompaniment are truly thrilling. Handel's oratorios, more dramatic than any previously written, were like operas, save that they were given without scenery and costumes. Had they and his operas not made him famous, his many fine instrumental works, especially the *Concerti Grossi*, would surely have done so.

When he died, after seven years of blindness, he was buried in Westminster Abbey with that ceremony which England bestows upon her favorite sons. His influence endured well into the nineteenth century.

◇◇◇◇◇◇◇◇◇◇◇◇◇◇◇◇◇◇◇◇◇◇◇◇◇◇◇◇◇◇◇

Johann Sebastian Bach

(bäk)

b. EISENACH, GERMANY, MARCH 21, 1685 *d.* LEIPZIG, GERMANY, JULY 22, 1750

JUST AS EVERY YOUNG AMERICAN DREAMS that some day he may become president of the United States, so may every music teacher think of himself as a potential Bach, for to his contemporaries this great man was a provincial pedagogue and organist like hundreds of others. His significance as a composer was not fully appreciated until passing years had revealed the immortal quality of the compositions which Mendelssohn made known, three quarters of a century after Bach's death.

In Eisenach, musical Bachs grew on every tree. When Johann Sebastian was ten, he went to live with his older brother, who prepared him to earn his living in music. He held several organist jobs, notably one in Arnstadt, from which he played truant for four fruitful months to sit at the feet of the organist Buxtehude in Lübeck. He traveled many weary miles on foot for this privilege; the Arnstadt elders scolded him for his prolonged absence; but Bach profited greatly.

With his young wife, Maria Barbara, he settled at Weimar in 1708 under the patronage of Duke Wilhelm Ernst. This was his "organ period"; the *Preludes*, *Fugues and Toccatas*, the rich *Orgelbüchlein* (*Little Organ Book*), and many others stem from long hours at the Weimar organ, which he had to repair with his own hands to make it fit to play upon. His reputation as a performer grew to such dimensions that, when a contest was arranged in Dresden with the distinguished Marchand, that gentleman was afraid to compete and left town before the contest could take place.

After nine years, Bach was invited to Cöthen, a more congenial berth than the chilly court of Weimar. Prince Leopold, his new patron, maintained and himself played in an excellent little orchestra, which proved as great an inspiration as had been the organ in Weimar. Bach wrote for it the *Brandenburg Concertos*, the great *Suites*, and many more. For his own children (he eventually had twenty, of whom six survived), he produced the *Little Preludes and Symphonies*, dear to all piano students. These were idyllic years, but the spell was broken by the death of Bach's wife, and Prince Leopold's marriage at the same time to a court lady who "didn't like music nohow." Bach left Cöthen, to become cantor of the Thomasschule in Leipzig. He was expected to teach singing and instrumental music, Latin, and Luther's Catechism; to rehearse the singers of four churches; to lead the choir at funerals and weddings; to conduct a cantata every Sunday, and to write cantatas and oratorios as they were needed. A second wife, the gentle Anna Magdalena, made a home for him in Leipzig from 1723 until his death.

But friction as to his duties and privileges arose with annoying frequency. He wrote his sublime music for the church because it was his job, but doubtless also because it helped to restore his own serenity after petty disputes. Cantatas composed for every Sunday service, masses, Passions and oratorios, loaded his shelves. Most of his Clavier works were written for clavichord or harpsichord; he was nearly sixty before he ever saw a modern piano. He employed an immensely resourceful musical vocabulary, which utilized every known device and added a few besides, to make, of polyphonic writing particularly, a vitaminized source of musical sustenance. Most important, his writings have a spiritual power, a solid strength and sincerity that cannot be traced to technique, but to the inspiration of pure genius.

"Old Bach is here," cried Frederick of Prussia when J. S. came to court to visit Carl Philipp Emanuel. Forthwith J. S. tried every piano and organ in the palace, improvised a six-part fugue on the king's own theme, and when he returned to Leipzig, bound and sent it to the king,—the famous *Musikalische Opfer* (*Musical Offering*). Shortly after that, while working on *The Art of the Fugue*, he was stricken with blindness. An operation aggravated his condition, a paralytic stroke was the final calamity, and the invitation of his magnificent chorale, *Komm, Süsser Tod* (*Come, Sweet Death*) was accepted.

Giovanni Battista Pergolesi

(pĕr-gō-lā'zē)

b. JESI, ITALY, JAN. 4, 1710 — *d.* POZZUOLI, ITALY, MARCH 16, 1736

A SHORT LIFE AND A MERRY ONE, which brought laughter and merriment to others, was Giovanni Battista Pergolesi's. He was the only son of poor people, and attended the Conservatorio dei Poveri (Conservatory for the Poor) in Naples. The handsome stripling, who played the violin with a flourish, was much petted, and after graduation had no difficulty in finding a teaching job, a patron, and time to compose. Several light comic operas, violin sonatas, and a mass won him a measure of recognition. Following the successful performance of his first serious opera, *San Guglielmo d'Aquitania*, he celebrated by sowing a crop of wild oats that caused headshaking and raised eyebrows even in those tolerant days. Maria Spinelli, a lady of gentle birth, became a nun for love of him, when her brothers threatened her with death if she refused to marry a more reputable suitor. There are other equally romantic stories.

Pergolesi loved life, lived it to the hilt during

his twenty-six years, and conveyed it to his music in the form of radiant vitality. His best known work, *La Serva Padrona* (*The Maid-Mistress*) was written as a light intermezzo between the acts of a long and serious opera, long since forgotten. Studded with charming melodies, having unusual life and color, and a form and technique since recognized as typically Italian, the two-act intermezzo, mildly received in its day, exerted an appreciable influence on succeeding writers of light opera.

When a more ambitious attempt, *L'Olimpiade*, was produced, only to be received with catcalls and overripe fruit, Pergolesi was overcome with disappointment. He returned to the writing of church music, and also produced one comic opera, *Il Flaminio*, which was very successful. But he fell ill, and retreated to the Capuchin monastery at Pozzuoli to take the baths. Here he died of tuberculosis, his end doubtless hastened by past profligacies.

The *Stabat Mater*, which the composer Bellini described as "divina poema del dolore" (divine poem of suffering) does bolster his slim claim to fame. It may have been composed during his last illness or earlier. Characteristically he tossed off, almost on his deathbed, a *Scherzo fatto ai Cappucini di Pozzuoli*, a coarsely humorous piece at the expense of his hosts, a last ribald chuckle.

◇◇◇◇◇◇◇◇◇◇◇◇◇◇◇◇◇◇◇◇◇◇◇◇◇◇◇◇◇◇◇◇◇◇

Carl Philipp Emanuel Bach

(bäk)

b. WEIMAR, MARCH 8, 1714 *d.* HAMBURG, DEC. 14, 1788

CARL PHILIPP EMANUEL, second son of Johann Sebastian Bach, was a powerful personality with no inferiority complex. Though his prudent parent trained him for the law, he followed the call of his blood, and when he was twenty-four became harpsichordist at the court of Frederick the Great in Prussia. He was there when "Old Bach" paid his historic visit.

Young Bach did not need to take a back seat on that occasion, for as a performer he too was superb. He has been called the father of modern piano playing, and the creator of clavier technique. His *Versuch über die Wahre Art das Klavier zu Spielen* (*Text-book of Piano Technique*) has served many pianists, including Mozart and Beethoven.

When the Seven Years' War caused music at the Prussian Court to be temporarily discontinued, C. P. E. went to Hamburg, where he speedily became the largest frog in the musical puddle. He enjoyed the support of the five principal churches, whose music he directed, and moreover had free rein to play his own compositions in concerts whenever he wished. Cheerful, lively, and full of fun, he made his home a musical center for his own community, and neither he nor his reputation traveled far afield during his life. When Haydn, who admired him greatly, came to call on him in 1795, he had already been dead seven years without the news' having traveled beyond Hamburg!

He is now gaining recognition as an innovator He led the way in clarifying the sonata form whicl Haydn further improved. He wrote more expressively for the piano than any previous composer, actually initiating the personal style which Beethoven perfected, even marking sudden contrasts of loud and soft as Beethoven did. In writing for the voice, he produced numerous art songs, anticipating by some years Schubert, the master of the art song. By the time he died he had not only proved himself the worthy son of an illustrious father, but artistic father of the equally illustrious composers,—Haydn, Beethoven and Schubert,—who followed him.

Christoph Willibald Gluck

(glo͝ok′)

b. WEIDENWANG, GERMANY, JULY 4, 1714 *d.* VIENNA, AUSTRIA, NOV. 15, 1787

IT SEEMS STRANGE that deliberate, classic melody of the type of *Orfeo* and *Alceste* should have issued from a full-blooded choleric man like Gluck, but while this German father of the French opera, who lived in Vienna, knew how to make the most of the Viennese wine, women, and song, he also knew how to keep unsullied his ideal of pure music.

He was the son of a Bavarian game-keeper, received his early education in a Jesuit school, and continued his studies in Prague, Milan, and Vienna. The writing of opera was his earliest obsession. Yet his compositions until he was almost forty were in no way remarkable, although *Antigono* in 1756 won for him the papal order of Knight of the Golden Spur. When he visited London, and gave his famous "concert on the musical glasses with orchestra," he expressed great admiration for Handel, which, however, was not reciprocated, for to the Great Bear is attributed the ungracious comment on

Gluck, "He knows no more counterpoint than mine cook."

After his marriage, at thirty-six, his luck changed. When *La Clemenza di Tito* was produced in Naples, in 1752, its composer was hailed by Italian audiences as "the divine German." Upon his return to Vienna, he was engaged as opera director at the court of the Empress Maria Theresa. Since she demanded French opéra comique and Italian pastorals, Gluck learned, during his ten years at her court, to temper his opera to her shorn taste. He clung, however, to his growing conviction that by applying to the opera the principles of classic Greek art, he might improve it.

Orfeo ed Euridice, produced in 1762, was the first flowering of this belief. It is difficult to write dispassionately of its lovely music. Within it, cloaked in deceptive simplicity, are all the elements of the modern music drama. *Alceste* is the next of the so-called reform operas. In it, Gluck wrote animated recitative to replace the "recitativo secco" (dry recitative) of Italian opera, and supplied not only expressive overtures, but orchestral accompaniments that are rich in comparison with the few scattered chords of the Italian tradition. In his lengthy preface to this opera, Gluck expressed his intention "to reduce music to its proper function, that of seconding poetry by enforcing the expression of the sentiment and the interest of the situations, without interrupting the action, or weakening it by superfluous ornament." In *Paride ed Elena* and *Armide* he further developed his thesis.

Not until 1773 did Gluck move to Paris at the behest of Marie Antoinette, his former pupil at the court of Maria Theresa. Upon his arrival he supervised the production of *Iphigénie en Aulide* (*Iphigenia in Aulis*) at the Paris Opera, and composed some "chicken-feed" for court entertainments. A quarrel with the Neapolitan composer Piccini, maliciously fomented by the press, created a teapot tempest. Gluck, who commuted as he could from Paris to Vienna, remained in Vienna until the excitement subsided. In 1778 he witnessed in Paris the last of his masterpieces, *Iphigénie en Tauride* (*Iphigenia in Tauris*), then retired again to Vienna. Here he spent his declining years, happy despite several apoplectic strokes, for he was the honored center of the city's musical activity, and this was to him as incense to the gods of his tragedies. The efforts of Lully and Rameau, of Monteverdi, Scarlatti and Handel, all contributed to his, and to the gradual development which resulted in grand opera as we know it.

Franz Joseph Haydn

(hī′dn)

b. ROHRAU, AUSTRIA, MARCH 31, 1732 *d.* VIENNA, AUSTRIA, MAY 31, 1809

THE CIRCUMSTANCE of his father's being a wheelwright and his mother a cook had much to do with the earthy peasant quality of Haydn's music; his early life was in a small village where dancing on the green was a daily occurrence, where people sang folksongs for the sheer joy of it, and where his own father, though not a musician, doubtless whistled as he worked. Before Haydn's music was born, these prenatal influences shaped it. They endured, though he left his village at the age of six.

The boy received his first training from a cousin, who paid more attention to his "weak but pleasing voice" than to his hungry young body. At the Vienna Choir School from his eighth to his seventeenth year, he was hardly better off. When he was dismissed, his luggage consisted of two secondhand harmony books, a shabby coat and a couple of shirts, which he carried gratefully to the attic refuge his friend Spangler offered him. For a while, he valeted the boots and wig of an

Italian composer, Porpora, happy because the master corrected his exercises and tossed him the bone of an occasional lesson. Gradually he picked up pupils, and finally a job in the modest establishment of a Count von Fürnberg, which provided him with the incentive to write eighteen string quartets. At twenty-seven, he became music director to Count Morzin, who employed a small orchestra for which Haydn composed his *First Symphony*. In that fateful year, he committed the error of marrying the older sister of the girl he loved, a shrew whose shrill tirades did music a service, for to escape them he locked himself in his study and worked.

In 1761, he became musical man-of-all-work to the wealthy and cultured Count Esterhazy. He wrote, rehearsed, and produced all the Esterhazy entertainments in town and country for thirty smooth-flowing years. Every morning, he sat at his desk in a black satin suit with immaculate ruffles, and did his daily dozen in music. While with the Esterhazys he wrote five masses, eleven operas, sixty symphonies, forty string quartets, and so on. He occasionally visited Vienna, where Mozart, who became his close friend, dedicated to him his first six quartets, the young Beethoven was his pupil, and the ladies loved him.

When the English concert manager Salomon invited him to England, Esterhazy the Magnificent had died, and Haydn was glad of the change.

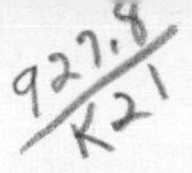

He was fifty-eight, yet his new works aroused the English to such enthusiasm that he said wryly, "It is England that has made me famous in Germany." England revived his interest in oratorios and he added to those he had already composed two more,—*The Seasons* and *The Creation*,—completed when he was almost seventy.

The French occupation of Vienna in May 1809, a tragedy for all patriotic Austrians, shocked him unspeakably. Within a month, he quietly breathed his last.

Papa Haydn accomplished permanent things. He clearly defined, as it was to be used from then on, the sonata form previously employed by C. P. E. Bach. He "house-cleaned" the orchestra, pruning unnecessary instruments and elements. He made his string quartets the models for all. And he laughed into music his own bubbling joy of living; his peasant love of nature and his fellow-man, and his innate nobility.

Luigi Boccherini

(bôk'kâ-rē'-nê)

b. LUCCA, ITALY, FEB. 19, 1743   *d.* MADRID, SPAIN, MARCH 28, 1805

ALTHOUGH THE SUGARY MINUET which Boccherini wrote for the ladies of the Spanish court has caused his name to be associated with the dance, his fame rests more solidly upon the substantial chamber music with which he supplied his royal patrons. His trios and quartets were patterned so closely upon Haydn's that he was jestingly nicknamed "the wife of Haydn," but he made at least one improvement on his model. Since he played the cello himself, he refused to write the tum-ti-tum accompaniment which Haydn considered suitable for that bass-voiced instrument, assigning to it instead very respectable solos and subsidiary melodies. By that token, he is the quartet cellist's favorite composer. His gift was lyric, a trifle delicate for symphonic writing, but ideal for chamber music.

His father was a double-bass player, who taught him the elements of music, then sent him to Rome to study violin, cello and composition with Abbate Vanucci. A joint concert tour with the violinist Manfredi, during which he published his first six string quartets, Opus I, brought him an agreeable reputation and many new friends. In 1769, he was invited to the court of Charles IV in Madrid, where he settled down with a contract first to supply the king's brother, the Infante Luis, and later the monarch himself, with chamber music, opera and symphony ad lib. His facility was enormous. He could do his stint with no effort at all, and have plenty of time left in which to enjoy the easy luxury of the Spanish court. When he and the king had a falling out because Boccherini, always cocky, overreached himself, he transferred his activities to the Court of Friedrich Wilhelm of Prussia, for a ten-year interim of the simple life at a modest salary.

Wilhelm died, and Boccherini returned confidently to the scene of his former triumphs. To his chagrin, he found no patron in all Madrid desirous of the services formerly so prized. The French consul Lucien Buonaparte gave him a few commissions, but when Buonaparte returned to France, Boccherini was left without regular employment. He was reduced to all kinds of expedients for keeping body and soul together. Orders to make guitar arrangements for amateurs were thankfully received. He sank lower and lower; poverty and illness were the companions of his old age, until, at sixty-two, death mercifully set him free.

◇◇◇◇◇◇◇◇◇◇◇◇◇◇◇◇◇◇◇◇◇◇◇◇◇◇◇◇◇◇◇◇◇◇

Wolfgang Amadeus Mozart

(mō′-tsärt)

b. SALZBURG, AUSTRIA, JAN. 27, 1756 *d.* VIENNA, AUSTRIA, DEC. 5, 1791

EVERY PIECE MOZART WROTE bears the mark of the unique genius that caused Haydn to say to Mozart père, "I declare to you upon my honor that I consider your son the greatest composer I have ever heard." "Sounds and sweet airs that give delight and hurt not" crowded his mind, giving him no peace until he put them on paper. The result is an incredible number of works designed to soothe, caress, comfort and charm. He wrote that "passions, whether violent or not, must never be expressed in such a way as to excite disgust, and even in the most terrible situations, must never cease to be *music*."

His years as an infant prodigy were probably his happiest. He was born of the handsomest couple in Salzburg—his father, Leopold, an accomplished musician. The talented three-year-old, listening to his sister's lessons on the harpsichord, learned to play, and, at five, to compose little pieces of his own. His reward was that he became probably the most-kissed child in Europe.

Wherever Leopold took him and his sister Nannerl,—and they made triumphal tours in Austria, Hungary, and Germany, and visited Brussels, Paris, and London,—their success was phenomenal.

He first visited Italy when he was only thirteen. He lost his heart to Italian opera, two later visits confirmed his passion, and his own operas are more Italian than German. The influence of the Italian aria is noticeable in his instrumental compositions as well.

After his travels he returned to Salzburg, and became concertmaster in the orchestra of the kindly archbishop there. But the archbishop died, and was succeeded by the haughty Hieronymus. When Mozart again wished to go on a tour, Hieronymus refused permission in an ugly scene wherein the young man was actually kicked out of the room by the steward. Mozart left Salzburg forever.

Chaperoned by his mother, he traveled again. In Mannheim, he encountered the finest orchestra in Europe, and there too he met the Weber family. A few months later, his mother died in Paris, and Mozart, now a young man of twenty-two, was on his own for the first time in his life! He went to Vienna, and married Constanze Weber, much against his father's wishes. In Vienna, he and Haydn enjoyed a friendship which was a mutual admiration society.

His patron, Emperor Joseph II, was not as appreciative as Haydn. When Mozart's charming opera, *Die Entführung aus dem Serail* (*The Escape from the Seraglio*) swept Vienna off its feet in 1782, Joseph only remarked that it had too many notes. A niggardly monarch, he gave poor Mozart so few commissions that the composer scrawled bitterly on a record of his income: "Too much for what I produce; too little for what I could produce."

Financial difficulties became yet more serious. Constanze's health was poor, and she was a bad manager. Mozart made a fortunate deal with Lorenzo da Ponte, by which he secured Da Ponte's excellent libretti for *Le Nozze di Figaro* (*The Marriage of Figaro*), *Don Giovanni*, and *Cosi fan Tutte* (*Thus do all Women*), operas which have become immortal. Other works added to his renown, but still not sufficiently to his income. He wrote his last opera, *Die Zauberflöte* (*The Magic Flute*) when he was ill and depressed, but he controlled his depression and made of it a sparkling comedy.

Then a *Requiem Mass* was commissioned by a stranger whose mysterious manner convinced the sick man that he was a visitant from another world. It was not completed when Mozart became seriously ill of malignant typhus, and died. Where his mortal remains lie buried is unknown; his immortal works have place in the hearts and minds of all true musicians, who echo Rossini's "There is only one Mozart."

Luigi Cherubini

(kā′-rōō-bē′nē)

b. FLORENCE, ITALY, SEPT. 14, 1760 *d.* PARIS, FRANCE, MARCH 15, 1842

NAMED CHERUBINI, but definitely no cherub, Luigi Maria is remembered as a difficult, dictatorial pedagogue. With a baton tipped with iron, he ruled the French Conservatoire for twenty years. His pupils there, who included Halévy, Auber, Berlioz, and César Franck respected and feared him.

He was a strange phenomenon—this boy born in sunny Florence, with so little sun in his soul—a musical efficiency expert, German model. The early training he received from his father and other teachers was so dry that it apparently contained none of the joy of music. But the boy derived from it a habit of industry, and a backlog of knowledge to which he added continuously, so that, in later years, he was recognized as one of the most learned musicians in Europe. His *Cours de Contrepoint* (*Counterpoint Course*), has clarified many important contrapuntal difficulties.

He passed through the usual three periods of composition. In the beginning, he concentrated on sacred music and light opera. In his maturity, he wrote grand operas which became the backbone of French opera of his time. They were among those patronized by the citoyens and citoyennes during the French Revolution, when, as Mme. Cherubini remarked, "In the morning the guillotine was kept busy, and in the evening one could not get a seat at the theater." Today only the overtures to *Lodoiska*, *Medée Les Deux Journées* (*The Water Carrier*) and *Anacreon* are known. These operas, classic in spirit, aimed to put down the mighty prima donna by exalting orchestration and dramatic interest, a technique which found great favor in France, and even more in Germany.

When the composer visited Vienna in 1805, he spent a great deal of time with Beethoven, shouting into deaf but attentive ears his unflattering opinion of Napoleon. Beethoven generously pronounced Cherubini the greatest composer of the day, may even have been influenced to write *Fidelio* by *Les Deux Journées*, and admittedly derived inspiration for his overture to *Egmont* from *Medée*.

During his third period, Cherubini, like many others, returned to the church. As musician and superintendent of the King's Chapel (Louis XVIII), and director of the Conservatoire, he was easily able to bar the wolf from his door while composing his *Requiem in C minor* and other religious works.

His crotchety eighty-two years covered an eventful era. Mozart was a child of four when Cherubini was born. When he died, Victoria had come to the throne of England, and Wagner had already written *Rienzi* and *The Flying Dutchman.* For a man who hated change, he had to put up with a great deal of it. And, strange as it seems, he was himself indirectly responsible for some of the change, since he stimulated the development of French opera, and influenced such German composers as Beethoven, Mendelssohn, Schumann and Wagner.

Ludwig van Beethoven

(bā'-to-vĕn)

b. BONN, GERMANY, DEC. 16, 1770

d. VIENNA, AUSTRIA, MARCH 26, 1827

"I KNOW THAT I AM AN ARTIST," murmured the dying Beethoven in the most magnificent of understatements. He was in truth the greatest artist of them all. His majesty of soul gave its own nobility to his music, while his force and his vision democratized and liberated it, making it serve all times, all places, and all peoples. Yet his beginnings were humble.

His father started him at the piano when he was four, and kept him steadily at it. While still in his teens, he was forced to become head of the family, for Beethoven senior drank more and more, and earned less and less. When he was twenty-two, he went to Vienna to seek his fortune, a pockmarked, rather clumsy young man in provincial clothes. But nobody "laughed when he sat down at the piano"; his improvisations amazed all Vienna. Lessons in composition with Haydn he supplemented by working with Schenck and, later, with Albrechtsberger and Salieri. He made friends too with jolly fat Schuppanzigh, whose chamber group performed many of his string quartets.

Before 1800, he had published works modeled upon Haydn and Mozart, but already touched with the power and beauty that are Beethoven. He was barely thirty when the first symptoms of deafness appeared, and despite doctoring, grew gradually worse. The despair in his diary and in the Heiligenstadt Testament, a letter to his brothers, is heartbreaking. Yet, during the years from 1800 to 1815 before he became totally deaf, eight of his nine symphonies were completed, also five piano concertos, the opera *Fidelio*, and other masterpieces. He spent a great deal of time in the beautiful suburbs of Vienna, and as he roamed alone, dropping in for beer and sausages at some cozy village inn, he jotted down musical ideas in notebooks always at hand. These have been, fortunately, preserved. They record the working habits of a genius who reviewed his inspiration for months, sometimes years, before giving it finished form.

In the midst of all his activities, Beethoven found time to address a mysterious letter to an "Immortal Beloved" whose identity has never been revealed. Nevertheless, he remained a bachelor, and when his brother died, commending to Ludwig's care his only son Karl, he dismissed forever the thought of marriage. For Karl was a ne'erdowell who gave him no peace for eleven years, and was finally banished in disgrace from Vienna in 1826.

The last five great piano sonatas, the *Ninth Symphony*, and the later string quartets represent the climax of Beethoven's genius during this troubled later period. That he should have stamped up and down, singing aloud, forgetting to eat or sleep while creating so greatly is understandable when one listens to his music. "He found the art of music narrowed to the pastime of a special class of society. He made it broadly human. He left it superhuman," says Robert Haven Schauffler. He took the sonata, symphony and concerto, consolidated in form by C. P. E. Bach, Haydn and Mozart, and transmuted them into "grandiose, great and mad music" of unprecedented scope and variety. He emphasized self-expression, the warm personal note presaged by C. P. E. Bach and Mozart. He made the piano and the symphony orchestra more expressive than ever before. When rules interfered with free and beautiful sound, he changed the rules. A revolutionist who created faster than he destroyed, a democrat in the truest sense, he is the touchtone by which others are evaluated.

It took more than one disease to kill this Titan. He died of dropsy, cholera and jaundice, complicated by pneumonia. This last he caught driving home in an open carriage from a visit on behalf of the unworthy Karl. Just before he died, he shook his clenched fist at the storm raging outside, in a gesture that symbolized his life of protest.

Carl Maria von Weber

(fŏn vā′bĕr)

b. EUTIN, GERMANY, DEC. 18, 1786 *d.* LONDON, ENGLAND, JUNE 5, 1826

THE HERO OF GERMAN ROMANTIC OPERA was not a hero to his father, who forced the sickly child to practice the piano and violin for hours on end, in the hope of developing a prodigy. "If Mozart, why not Carl Maria?" was the argument which deprived the boy until his twelfth year of a home life, an education, and companionship. He remained a strolling player until his mother's death broke up the family troupe. Then he entered the choir-boys' school in Salzburg, where he had lessons from Haydn's younger brother, Michael. Later, Abt Vogler topped off his musical education in Vienna.

Carl was a charming but dissolute youth, with a talent for getting into hot water. While he was secretary to the Duke of Württemberg in Stuttgart, some funds entrusted to his keeping disappeared, and he and his father, though adjudged innocent, were banished. He went to Mannheim, then to Darmstadt, where, with Meyerbeer and a few others, he formed the Harmonic Society. An excellent conductor, a remarkable pianist, and an acceptable singer until an accidental drink of nitric acid deprived him of his voice, he spent his youth as a roving German troubadour of easy morals. In 1813, he became director of the opera in Prague, and three years later, took a similar position in Dresden. A liaison with an unscrupulous prima donna very nearly ruined him, but after he married Caroline Brandt, who loved and understood him, he settled down to serious work.

In Germany, as elsewhere, Italian opera was all the rage, and Weber realized that he would have to re-educate the public to listen willingly to a German product. His three romantic operas, which put Germany on the operatic map, were his means of re-education. *Der Freischütz* (*The Enchanted Huntsman*), and *Euryanthe* are fairy tales of a kind very common in sentimental Germany of the early 1800's. After Weber had conducted *Der Freischütz*, he wrote happily, "Greater enthusiasm there cannot be"; it captured the German heart. *Euryanthe* was somewhat less successful, but the overtures of both are still popular on symphony programs all over the world.

Weber originated the Leitmotif before Wagner thought of it. Bravura showmanship and restless originality characterized his orchestral scores. He practically revolutionized classic instrumentation, blending strings and woodwinds as they never had been blended before, creating effects which Berlioz and Wagner later elaborated upon. He was the John Barrymore of the musical scene, a Barrymore of exaggerated poses, elocutionizing, and Thespian flourishes, whose service to the drama was unquestioned.

At thirty-seven, he learned to speak English in order to execute a commission to write an opera in English, *Oberon*. He went reluctantly to London, knowing that he had not long to live. He survived the season, conducted the first twelve performances as agreed, and died soon after of combined tuberculosis, exhaustion and home-sickness.

His songs and piano works—the *Concertstück*, concertos and variations—have been unduly overshadowed by the operas. They form a by no means negligible part of the German romantic music which for years dominated world music.

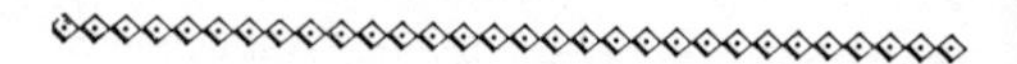

Franz Peter Schubert

(shōō′bĕrt)

b. LICHTENTHAL, AUSTRIA, JAN. 31, 1797

d. VIENNA, AUSTRIA, NOV. 19, 1828

"FRANZL" WAS THE MOST TALENTED, if not the handsomest of the thirteen children of a village schoolmaster and a cook. When, stammering, shabby, and unprepossessing, he applied for a scholarship to the Konviktschule in Vienna, the haughty Salieri, pupil of Gluck, friend of Haydn and teacher of Beethoven, admitted him grudgingly. As clear-voiced choir-boy and violinist in the school orchestra he became acquainted with works of Haydn, Mozart, Cherubini, and Beethoven, and remarked that Mozart's *G minor Symphony* "shook me to the depths without my knowing why." He picked up harmony and composition, and "sometimes put his thoughts into notes," thanks to his friend Spaun, who gave him the precious manuscript paper he was too poor to buy for himself.

His schooling completed, he unwillingly became a teacher in his father's school, but when musical notations took the place of corrections in his pupils' exercise books, he was soon encouraged to withdraw, and he did. Barring visits to friends, and a short engagement at Count Esterhazy's in Hungary, he sat writing in a poor little hall bedroom in Vienna, from six in the morning till well into the afternoon. Then, songs and string quartets under his arm, he sallied forth to a friend's house or a convivial inn, to try them. When he had finished his great song, *Der Erlkönig* (*The Erlking*), he played it for his cronies with the ink hardly dry upon the paper. Professor Ruziczka, instructor at the Konviktschule, quieted the ensuing hubbub of criticism with "If Franzl wrote it, it must be right. His ideas come straight from Heaven."

He lacked money and influence, but he had devoted friends,—Schober, Mayrhofer, Grillparzer, Carl Maria von Weber. Despite one or two mild love affairs, he never married. The year 1815, when he was but eighteen, was his year of years. He wrote one hundred and forty-four of his six hundred songs—among them *Der Tod und das Mädchen* (*Death and the Maiden*), *An die Musik* (*To Music*), *Kennst Du das Land* (*Do you Know the Land*), *Der König von Thule* (*The King of Thule*)—to poems by Goethe and other great poets. In his art songs, the music altered with the meaning and followed the line of the poetry, while the accompaniment, which followed both, did all that harmony could to create the sought-after-mood. For Schubert, a man possessed by melody, art song was an ideal form, and he made himself master of it. Even his symphonies and chamber music are instrumental song-fests, which have much of the appeal of folk songs. Yet not till ten years after his death, when Schumann found in Vienna pieces till then unknown, and Mendelssohn performed them, was much attention paid to him as a composer. Had he not lived so close to Haydn, Mozart and Beethoven, he might have been sooner recognized, but during his lifetime his genius was overshadowed by theirs.

Shyly he worshipped Beethoven from afar. But when Beethoven lay on his deathbed, Schubert, too overcome for speech even then, visited him, and was a torch-bearer at the funeral, which preceded his own by twenty short months. When, at thirty-one, he succumbed to typhus, Beethoven's was the name he called in his delirium. On his tombstone, placed as close as possible to his idol's, was inscribed, "Music has buried here a rich treasure, but fairer hopes."

Giacomo Meyerbeer

(mī′ĕr-bār)

b. BERLIN, GERMANY, SEPT. 5, 1791   *d.* PARIS, FRANCE, MAY 2, 1864

AN OPERA COMPOSER more imitative than original, who wrote with bombastic grandeur and yet with a certain beauty, Giacomo Meyerbeer, born Jakob Liebmann Beer, is known to all who follow the opera.

The son of a banker, he inherited great wealth, which might well have induced him to remain a dilettante, but, after lessons with the best masters, he settled down to a serious professional career. Infatuated with the Italian operas of Rossini, he determined to "go Italian." Weber, whom he met when he visited Germany, advised him to "go German" instead. Whereupon he solved his problem by moving to Paris in 1826, and "going French."

His first outstanding success, *Robert le Diable* was hailed in Paris as a right-little-tight-little combination of German technique, Italian melody, and French wit. In New York, where opera was in its infancy, its performance was a huge success. His next, *Les Huguenots*, an opera of

Gone-with-the-Wind length, always has to be cut before it is performed, but people like it anyway. It is known as the opera in which "Catholics and Protestants kill each other, while a Jew makes the music to it." After he became director of the Royal Opera in Berlin, he induced Jenny Lind to appear frequently under his baton, and basked in the glory she reflected. He deserted Berlin long enough to witness the première of *Le Prophète* in Paris in 1849, and to rejoice when its finest aria, *Oh, mon fils* (*Oh, my son!*) brought down the house.

His was no fine free careless rapture of composition. He was a carefully schooled, industrious composer, who dominated French opera for a few years and influenced its composers.

Gioacchino Rossini

(rôs-sē′-nê)

b. PESARO, ITALY, FEB. 29, 1792 *d.* PARIS, FRANCE, NOV. 13, 1868

WHEN ROSSINI BENT TO KISS THE HAND OF NAPOLEON, it was withdrawn with a benign "No ceremony between emperors." The melodious operas of his Italian guest appealed to the Little Corporal as much as the precise Germanic works of Cherubini irritated him. Napoleon was not alone in his appreciation, for Rossini swam into Paris on an overwhelming wave of popular enthusiasm. To him goes much of the credit for the hold of Italian opera not only on his own country, but on Germany, France, England and the United States. He produced thirty operas between his eighteenth and his thirty-seventh birthdays, not one thereafter.

His mother was an opera singer, his father town trumpeter, nicknamed Vivazza for his gaiety. At ten, Gioacchino, so handsome that he was known as "the angel," was a choir-boy, and two years later he became the cembalist in the opera house. His one-act opera, *La Cambiale de Matrimonio* (*The Marriage Contract*) was produced in 1810. This contains an extraordinary stage American, the first one in opera, a Mr. Slook who puts his feet on the table, keeps his hat on in the house, and gives away a million dollars. Several rollicking comedies followed. When his first serious opera, *Tancredi di Siracusa* (*Tancred of Syracuse*) found favor, he was as deluged with offers from impresarios as a movie star. *Il Barbiere di Seviglia* (*The Barber of Seville*), produced when he was twenty-six, marked him with a big star on the Italian operatic map.

During the prodigiously active first half of his life, he traveled with his wife Isabella from one opera house to another, selling as fast as he wrote them scores upon which the ink was barely dry. He was drawn through the streets of towns by cheering admirers harnessed to carriages; even England, France and Germany deserted their native composers to flock to his standard. In Vienna he visited Beethoven, and was humble despite his own recent triumphs.

When he returned to Paris in 1824, he became director of the Theâtre Italien, and assumed other responsibilities which also paid him well. He was the Rockefeller of composers, never in want. Into his opera *William Tell* he put six months of concentrated labor which resulted in severe insomnia, nervousness and eye-strain. It was his last opera. Even after a long rest in Bologna, he seemed to have no further desire to compose. He wrote only one big work after this, the florid but moving

Stabat Mater. For the rest: when Isabella died, he married again, and settled in Paris, where his salons became famous for good food, witty conversation, and the charming little pieces he wrote to entertain his guests. During this period, he met Mendelssohn in Frankfurt, and discussed with him, pessimistically, the future of opera.

But there is nothing pessimistic about his own comic operas. They are permeated with comedy, provocative, now of deep uncontrollable laughter, now of the quiet smile that responds to delicate satire. He wrote music which characterized the personages of the drama, and he also gave them lyric solos, much as Mozart did, therefore he was known as "the Italian Mozart." Like Monteverdi, he used his orchestra most expressively, with due attention to impressive overtures; witness the Overture to *William Tell*.

Rossini was generous in his appreciation of Mozart and Beethoven, and described Bach as "a miracle of God." He gave thought also to those who had not scaled the heights, and when he died he bequeathed his large fortune as a Rossini Foundation for their care.

Gaetano Donizetti

(dō′-nê-dzĕt′-tê)

b. BERGAMO, ITALY, NOV. 25, 1797 — *d.* THERE, APRIL 8, 1848

A COMPOSER WHO KNEW HIS ROSSINI had need to fear no lack of appreciation in the Italy of the 1820's. Donizetti cast a shrewd eye upon his compatriot, and picked him for a model when he started writing on his own. When he entered the army to escape practicing law, his ultimate aim was to become a composer. He succeeded very quickly for he wrote in barracks an opera, *Zoraïde de Granata*, which proved a sensation, and after he had been carried in triumph through the streets of Rome following its première, he received permission to change his uniform permanently for an opera cloak.

Possessor of a facile talent, which resembled Rossini's in that it was prolific and produced easily singable tunes, he lacked the dramatic sense, originality, brilliance, and strength of his model. Of the sixty-five operas Donizetti tossed off as nonchalantly as one lights a cigarette, two of the comedies—*L'Elisir d'Amore* (*The Elixir of Love*) and *Don Pasquale*, and one tragedy, *Lucia di*

Lammermoor, known for its mad scene and much abused sextet—deserve honorable mention.

Donizetti taught on the staff of the Naples Conservatory, and became well-known throughout Europe, in which he traveled extensively. He had become a popular, rather than a significant figure, when he died of paralysis, at fifty-one.

◇◇◇◇◇◇◇◇◇◇◇◇◇◇◇◇◇◇◇◇◇◇◇◇◇◇◇◇◇◇

Vincenzo Bellini

(bĕl-lē′-nē)

b. CATANIA, SICILY, NOV. 1, 1801 *d.* PUTEAUX, NEAR PARIS, SEPT 24, 1835

BELLINI WAS DONIZETTI'S GREAT FRIEND, and like him followed the star of Rossini. Of his eleven operas, *La Sonnambula*, *I Puritani*, and *Norma* are revived for the charming melodies, admirably suited for vocal display, and for a poetic quality that was tenderly noted by Chopin, at whose candle-light musicales in Paris Bellini was a welcome guest. A tendency to write languishing music might have been counteracted in time. But the young composer died suddenly at thirty-four, while on a visit to Paris, when his life's work was barely begun.

Michael Ivanovitch Glinka

(glĭng′-kä)

b. SMOLENSK, RUSSIA, JUNE 2, 1803 *d.* BERLIN, GERMANY, FEB. 15, 1857

LIKE A TYPICAL HERO of an old Russian novel, the orphan Glinka was reared by his grandmother on her country estate, in a hot-house luxury which made of him a delicate semi-invalid. But her aristocratic teachings did not vitiate his inherent sense of kinship with the serfs on the land, any more than his later travels in many lands destroyed the Russian flavor of his compositions.

He received desultory instruction in piano, violin, and voice, just enough to make him a fair amateur, although at ten he wrote in a letter, "Music is my very soul." At twenty-four, however, he was ordered to Italy for his health, and improved the shining hour while there by studying composition. He made friends with Bellini and Donizetti, and was for a while carried away by their Italian opera, but on sober second thought decided that it was too soft and sensuous to serve him as a model. In pursuit of more knowledge, he traveled to Vienna and Berlin before returning to St. Petersburg, where he was married in 1835.

The following year witnessed the production of

his first great opera, *A Life for the Tsar*. The audience of lords and ladies at the Imperial Opera pronounced it "the music of coachmen," to which Glinka heatedly retorted, "What matter, since the men are superior to their masters?" Because the opera had a typical Russian folk-hero, a full quota of patriotic sentiment, and fresh spontaneous music, it was sure to succeed. It did in fact mark a fresh departure, the birth of a genuinely Russian school of music.

Russlan and Ludmilla, his second opera, was completed in a mood of depression after his separation from his wife. It met with an indifferent reception, and the disgruntled composer sought distraction abroad. In Paris Berlioz reviewed his music favorably, and Glinka then became the Frenchman's advocate in Russia. From every country he assimilated as much as he could without the sacrifice of his own individuality, and he returned regularly to St. Petersburg to renew his national inspiration. His output was small but significant and includes songs, piano pieces and chamber music, orchestral works and operas. The last may be called epoch-making, in that they permitted the music of his country to take a distinctive place in the Europe of his day; they earned from Liszt for their composer the title of Prophet Patriarch of Russian music. Today they are dear to Soviet Russia because of their prophetic championing of the right to happiness of serfs and peasants.

Hector Berlioz

(bĕr'lē-ôs')

b. COTE-ST. ANDRÉ, FRANCE, DEC. 11, 1803

d. PARIS, MARCH 8, 1869

THE RED HAIR that distinguished Hector Berlioz from other people in his provincial village crowned an unruly spirit. His father insisted that he become a country doctor, but he finally fought free of the narrow tyranny of his home, and entered the Paris Conservatoire.

With Cherubini, then director, he had repeated run-ins, and was actually chased around the library tables by that irate pedagogue after crossing him in an argument. The originality of his youthful musical ideas—which already ran to blaring brasses, harmonic experiments, and intimate personal revelations—was heartily distasteful to the tight-lipped Cherubini, who blackballed the young man three years running for the Prix de Rome, and without pity saw him almost starve to death between disappointments.

During these student years, Berlioz fell madly—truly madly—in love with Henrietta Smithson, a stodgy English actress some years his senior. When she rejected him, after a wooing compounded of distracted emotional scenes and threats of suicide, he retaliated with the *Symphonie Fantastique* (*Fantastic Symphony*). It marked an epoch in orchestral composition. It was narrative music, with interpretative notes supplied by the composer. This was a new departure. Its melodies were appealing, but the like of its orchestration had not before been heard. The tympani and brasses were a challenge to his beloved and to the ears of the public. In 1833, Henrietta, at last, accepted the challenge, but in winning he lost her, for the marriage was unhappy, and culminated in divorce.

He finally won the Prix de Rome, after the *Symphonie Fantastique* had been praised by Liszt, but he returned to Paris, homesick, before the term was up. His acute intelligence served him in the writing of caustic music criticism, and this augmented his income. Success came to him, but not in Paris. *Roméo et Juliette*, *Benvenuto Cellini*, and *La Damnation de Faust* were apathetically received at home, to be applauded to the echo elsewhere. He traveled in Russia, England, and Germany. Mendelssohn, Schumann and Liszt were his advocates in Germany; Chopin befriended him in Paris.

Possibly they recognized in this striking figure the culmination of Romantic music in France. He was an artist of immense creative power who had the gift of grandiloquence. He underlined and enlarged everything in the interest of greater expressiveness. In his *Traité de l'Instrumentation*, he suggested an ideal orchestra of five hundred pieces, instead of the usual eighty, but he also suggested many practical changes which led to decisive improvement of the symphony orchestra.

His last years were most unhappy. His second wife died suddenly in 1862. His only son Louis, of whom he wrote "We love each other like a couple of twins," was lost at sea. The press attacked his works, and his last opera, *Les Troyens*, was hissed off the stage of Paris in 1863. He wrote "I am alone. Every hour I say tc Death 'When you like.'" He made one last trip to Russia in 1867, and came back to Paris to die.

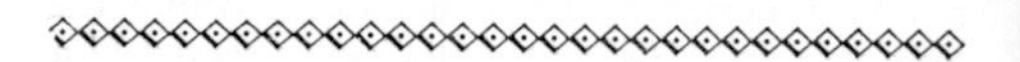

Felix Bartholdy Mendelssohn

(mĕn′dĕl sōn)

b. HAMBURG, GERMANY, FEB. 3, 1809 *d.* LEIPZIG, GERMANY, NOV. 4, 1847

ON FEW DOES FORTUNE SMILE so tenderly as it did on Felix "the happy" Mendelssohn. The loving kindness of wise parents provided the best tutors money could buy. The rambling Mendelssohn house and garden in Berlin became a musical rendezvous as soon as the boy Felix started to wield a baton over a youthful orchestra he assembled on Sundays. He played piano, organ and viola, and composed music too for these parties. The fairy measures of the *Midsummer Night's Dream Overture* which he wrote at seventeen still weave an enchanted spell.

At twenty, as a result of one of these amateur performances, he conducted professionals in a revival of Bach's long neglected St. Matthew Passion. Fired by its beauty, he did all he could from then on to open people's ears to the genius of Bach. The formation of the Bach Gesellschaft (Bach Association) in 1850, after Mendelssohn's death, was largely the result of his efforts.

He traveled widely, attracting like a a magnet the best music and musicians wherever he went. Handsome, one of the finest pianists of his time, and an accomplished linguist, he was dearly beloved, especially in London, which he much preferred to Paris. His letters are charming, and give a vivid picture of his wanderings.

When he became conductor of the Gewandhaus Orchestra in Leipzig, he duplicated on a large scale the Sunday musicales of his youth. Rossini and Chopin visited him, Ferdinand David was his concert master, Schumann and he became close friends, and here he conducted Schubert's *C major Symphony*, discovered by Schumann in Vienna. He organized and headed the first German Conservatory of Music in Leipzig, to which he attracted a brilliant staff of teachers, and he traveled regularly from Leipzig to Berlin and Dresden to conduct the court orchestra. His home life with his wife and five children was happy.

Of his music Heifetz, the violinist, has said, "If it is conceivable that the music of Mendelssohn can die, then all music can die." Wonderfully polished and fluent, it is accused of having little depth, but its effortless orderly sparkle and flowing melody can compensate for any real or fancied lack. The *Italian*, *Scottish* and *Reformation Symphonies* and the *Fingal's Cave Overture* are imaginative program music at its best, the oratorio *Elijah* is one of the great choral works of literature, the songs and piano pieces and singing violin concerto hold their own in any company. In perpetuating the ideals of Mozart and Bach, in developing contemporary composers and reviving neglected ones of the past, he did music an inestimable service. His attributes, personal and professional, are so lovable that even at this date the thought of his early death is painful.

◇◇◇◇◇◇◇◇◇◇◇◇◇◇◇◇◇◇◇◇◇◇◇◇◇◇◇◇◇◇◇◇◇◇

Frédéric Chopin

(shô′-păn′)

b. ZELAZOWA-WOLA, POLAND, MARCH 1, 1809

d. PARIS, FRANCE. OCT. 17, 1849

THOUGH CHOPIN STARTED LIFE as a happy, healthy little boy, who played dolls with his sisters in the garden of their home near Warsaw, in later years he became the perfect type of the sensitive, suffering artist. Perhaps he lived too intense an inner life during his youth; at eight he was hailed in Warsaw as a second Mozart, at eighteen he suffered his first nervous breakdown, and was never robust thereafter.

Nevertheless, as soon as he was recovered he announced that the piano virtuoso's was the life for him. On a trial trip to Vienna, he gained encouraging comment on his youthful works and his playing, and he decided that he would like to live in so charming an environment. At his farewell party in Warsaw, Elsner, his former teacher at the Warsaw Conservatory, presented him with a silver goblet filled with Polish soil, as though forewarned that his favorite pupil would never see Poland again. Hardly had Chopin arrived in Vienna, prepared to remain, when Warsaw was at war with Russia. He found himself an undesirable alien, ill, lonely, and with little money. His concert, from which he had expected everything, was a failure. Then Warsaw surrendered, a tragedy recorded by Chopin in the thunderous Revolutionary Étude, Opus 10, No. 12. He left Vienna and went to Paris shaken in mind and body.

But his spirits soon revived, for Paris was kind. Prince Radziwill took him to a soirée where his playing—intimate, delicate, and elegant—brought him the promise of enough piano pupils to enable him to pay for his white kid gloves and fitted frock-coats. Cherubini and Rossini, Mendelssohn and Liszt gave him professional advice; Delacroix the painter, Heine the poet, Bellini and Berlioz, Maria Malibran and Pauline Viardot-Garcia became his friends. They sat enthralled at the candlelight musicales, where his incredibly fleet fingers and inspired pedalling brought new meaning to piano music. Life was good, even though he was an exile.

Then Marie Wodzinska, one of the many girls of his heart, married another man, and Chopin sought sympathy in the masculine arms of George Sand, the novelist (Madame Dudevant). She nursed him through a long illness, and accompanied him to Majorca for the restoration of his body and the completion of his twenty-four marvelous piano *Preludes*. Later, they had neighboring apartments during the winter in Paris, and he visited her for whole summers at her home in Nohant, and wrote music between attacks of illness. In 1846 their relationship was broken by a quarrel. Chopin left Nohant forever. He never saw George Sand again, and he composed no more.

When the Revolution of 1848 shook Paris, he took refuge in London. But he was over-lionized and under-paid, the fogs aggravated the weakness of his lungs, and after a short time he crept back to Paris to die. The Polish soil he had cherished all these years was buried with him.

Chopin "spoke piano" with a unique vocabulary. Though he sometimes worked over one page of a composition for months, the finished product appears free and spontaneous. He introduced numerous short pieces into piano literature; with his name are associated the mazurkas and polonaises, nocturnes, ballades, scherzos and impromptus that made him famous. He "composed confessions," and was in fact the creator of a romantic idiom for the piano which has served many composers since.

Robert Schumann

(shōō′män)

b. ZWICKAU, GERMANY, JUNE 8, 1810

d. ENDENICH, GERMANY, JULY 29, 1856

IN ROBERT SCHUMANN'S LIFE, as in his friend Mendelssohn's, generous encouragement to other artists went hand in hand with his own creative activity; but whereas success came to Mendelssohn, Schumann fought a losing fight against frustration, poverty, and melancholia.

When, at his mother's request, he studied law, first at the University of Leipzig, then at Heidelberg, his repressed musical ambitions strained his nervous system. Then, once he had entered on his chosen career, he let himself in for sleepless nights by falling in love with Clara Wieck, the daughter of his piano teacher, much against Papa Wieck's wishes. The course of true love, which ran anything but smooth, was enlivened by code-messages in the form of inpassioned piano pieces. Clara's father whisked her away to Dresden, forbidding her to see or communicate with her persistent suitor. Result: Robert married her when she was eighteen and he thirty. The marriage was favorable to his art, for Clara was one of the finest pianists in Europe, and an outstanding interpreter of his works.

Before this, he had destroyed his chances to be a pianist by practicing with a contraption of his own invention designed to strengthen the fourth finger, which instead deprived him of its use. He compensated by composing, before he was thirty, many of his most brilliant piano pieces. The *Papillons*, *Carnaval*, *Fantasiestücke*, the tender *Kinderscenen* (*Scenes of Childhood*), *Kreisleriana*, *Symphonic Études* and *Noveletten* are all of this youthful period. Sir Hubert Parry wrote, "Schumann loved to dream with the pedal down."

When he was twenty-three, he founded a magazine, *Die Neue Zeitschrift für Musik* (*The New Journal of Music*), of which he was the editor and chief contributor. In his warfare against the lowering of musical standards, he supported such struggling young composers as Chopin, Mendelssohn and Brahms, as well as the honored dead, Beethoven, Bach, and Mozart.

When Clara was away on concert tours, his genius did not burn, but each return was signalized by a burst of musical eloquence. During the first year of married bliss, 1840, he wrote over a hundred beautiful songs; in 1841, the eldest of his five children was born, and he turned to the symphony to express his happiness; 1842 was his chamber music, 1843 his choral year. On each phase he concentrated with such fervor that in 1844 he suffered a severe nervous breakdown.

The family moved to Dresden, where he tried to teach, but black moods of depression accompanied by complete prostration attacked him increasingly. In 1850 he moved again, to Düsseldorf, where he conducted the orchestra and chorus. Here too he felt himself a failure. The compositions of these years—the *Rhenish Symphony*, *Manfred Overture*, and chamber music, lack the luster of happiness of his earlier writing. Even the presence of Brahms, who had become the Schumanns' devoted friend, could not cheer him. A despairing attempt to drown himself in the Rhine necessitated his removal to a private sanatorium, where, two years later, he died.

◊◊◊◊◊◊◊◊◊◊◊◊◊◊◊◊◊◊◊◊◊◊◊◊◊◊◊◊◊◊◊◊◊◊◊

Franz Liszt

(lĭst)

b. RAIDING, HUNGARY, OCT. 22, 1811

d. BAYREUTH, GERMANY, JULY 13, 1886

THOUGH HE WAS A PUNY CHILD who had almost died at birth, Franz Liszt lived to make his final bow from the platform at seventy-five. His successes as a touring child pianist were phenomenal. In Vienna, Salieri and Czerny taught him for love, and Beethoven kissed him approvingly, though Cherubini refused him at the Conservatoire on the ground that he was not French. When his father died, the sixteen-year-old settled in Paris, to teach, study, and Live with a capital L. The romantic post-Revolutionary Paris of Chopin and George Sand, of Balzac, Flaubert, and Victor Hugo moulded his character and his ideals. In 1834 he fell violently in love with the novelist Daniel Stern (the Comtesse d'Agoult) and they had three children. To her in Geneva he returned from brilliant concert tours which took him to all parts of the world. Everywhere his technique, improvisation, and gypsy magnetism moved audiences to hysterical adulation. He was a one-man musical circus.

He became visiting court artist in Weimar in 1843, and five years later director of the opera. There he wrote twelve symphonic poems, the *Hungarian Rhapsodies*, the *Faust* and *Dante* symphonies. He had broken with Mme. d'Agoult, and his new love, the Polish princess Sayn-Wittgenstein, urged him constantly to more ambitious efforts. During eleven crowded years of teaching, conducting and composing, he made Weimar a Mecca for musicians. His kindness to the students who thronged his salon was as unremitting as his generosity to "causes"—the relief of flood sufferers, the erection of a statue in Bonn to Beethoven, the publication of Scarlatti's works. More than that, he made himself the champion of new music;

composers flocked to lay their scores at his feet, forming a School of the Future that exerted a far-reaching influence. He conducted Wagner's neglected *Lohengrin*, *Flying Dutchman*, and *Tannhäuser*, Berlioz' *Benvenuto Cellini*, Weber's *Euryanthe*, and others now famous. The encouragement these performances afforded the struggling composers was incalculable. They brought adverse criticism along with the glory, however, and when the criticism became too insistent to be ignored, he relinquished his opera post, in 1859.

From then on, he divided his working time between Budapest, Weimar, and Rome. He donned the picturesque abbé's robe, and wrote oratorios and requiems for the good of his soul. During his last years, he still played concerts for idolizing audiences, and still clung to his princess, though permitting himself ample amorous excursions on the side.

While on a visit to Bayreuth to his daughter Cosima, wife of Wagner, he caught bronchitis, and died after a short illness. He was buried in Bayreuth with the dramatic ceremony appropriate to a great showman.

Liszt was a daring innovator. Though he did not actually invent the symphonic poem, he perfected it, and his narrative pieces in one movement, such as *Les Préludes* and *Mazeppa*, found many imitators. His brilliant piano transcriptions of songs and operas, and the *Hungarian Rhapsodies* are show-off pieces, to be sure, but of their kind they are superb. Even those who find his music banal or flashy cannot deny its originality and intense emotional appeal; it is an unfailing rabble-rouser. Unequaled as a pianist, he is a worthy if uneven composer.

◇◇◇◇◇◇◇◇◇◇◇◇◇◇◇◇◇◇◇◇◇◇◇◇◇◇◇◇◇◇◇◇

Wilhelm Richard Wagner

(väg′nẽr)

b. LEIPZIG, GERMANY, MAY 22, 1813

d. VENICE, ITALY, FEB. 13, 1883

WHETHER OR NOT ONE APPROVES of the Führer of nineteenth century opera, Wagner, there is no denying his overpowering and far-reaching influence. He did wonders with the orchestral score as developed from Monteverdi, through Mozart, Weber and Beethoven. He added instruments, doubled those in use, and combined tones in new harmonies of great variety and richness. The recurrent Leitmotif in voice and orchestra added interest. The libretti, which he wrote himself, were poetic, and fitting to the music. His operas, though overlong, repetitious and romantic almost to absurdity, are still the high point of nineteenth century music drama.

Wilhelm Richard Wagner

Wagner had a passion for the stage from the time his stepfather introduced him as a little boy to the fascinating world behind the footlights. At school in Dresden and Leipzig he studied the plays of two S's, Shakespeare and Schiller, the music of two B's, Bach and Beethoven, and from Theodor Weinlig, Cantor of the Thomasschule in Leipzig he received a thorough technical grounding in music. His first music drama, *Die Feen*, composed when he was twenty, was an experiment along Beethoven-Mozart-Weber lines; his second, *Das Liebesverbot* (*Forbidden Love*), based on Shakespeare's *Measure for Measure*, followed the Rossini-Donizetti model.

In 1836 he married Minna Planer, who might, by the facetious, be called Minna Com-planer, for she audibly failed to find in his artistic eminence compensation for poverty and insecurity, and for his open infidelities. While conducting opera in Riga, he composed *Rienzi*, the first "Wagnerian" opera. Then, following a quarrel with the management, he made his difficult way from Russia to Paris, where he tried unsuccessfully through Meyerbeer for a production at the Opéra. While waiting, he wrote *The Flying Dutchman*, which, with *Rienzi*, was produced in Dresden. An appointment at the Royal Court of Saxony followed in 1843, but during the fateful year of 1848, he threw in his lot with the revolutionaries, was outlawed from Dresden, and had to flee to Switzerland.

In Zürich, new friends, Mathilde and Otto Wesendonck, offered him a charming "refuge on a green hill." He appreciatively made love to Mathilde, who inspired *Tristan* and part of the *Ring* cycle. His Minna resented the intimacy, which was further complicated by the visits of Cosima Liszt, wife of Von Bülow. So again they packed, and moved to Paris. When officially pardoned for their revolutionary indiscretion, they went to Germany. Young King Ludwig appointed Wagner royal director of music in Munich, with an ample subsidy. He worked steadily at his cycle of four operas, *Der Ring der Nibelungen* (*The Ring of the Nibelungen*), which contains *Rheingold*, *Die Walküre*, *Siegfried*, and *Götterdämmerung*. But true to form, he soon again became a storm center, and, at Ludwig's reluctant request, left Munich for Switzerland, without Minna. He settled at Triebschen, near Lucerne. Cosima and their three children joined him there permanently, and he completed *Die Meistersinger* and *Siegfried* and started *Götterdämmerung*.

His voluminous literary works show that this Titan in a beret was a man of brilliant intellect and extreme sensitivity, who lived in a constant state of excitement. His intermittent periods of creation he described as "exaltation." He was conceited, selfish, and insincere, an opportunist who exploited his friends, and played upon their love as he did upon the instruments of the orchestra.

On his fifty-ninth birthday, the cornerstone of the Festspielhaus (Festival Theatre) was laid in Bayreuth, and a home, Wahnfried, was presented to him by his admirers. Festivals of his works were held annually at the Festspielhaus after the première of Parsifal in 1882, until the New Order in Germany discouraged visitors. After the triumph of Parsifal, Wagner went with his family to Venice to rest, and died there a few weeks later. He is buried in the garden of Wahnfried.

◇◇◇◇◇◇◇◇◇◇◇◇◇◇◇◇◇◇◇◇◇◇◇◇◇◇◇◇◇◇◇◇◇◇◇◇

Giuseppe Verdi

(vâr′dê)

b. LE RONCOLE, ITALY, OCT. 10, 1813 — *d.* MILAN, ITALY, JAN. 27, 1901

GIUSEPPE VERDI dreamed of writing an opera from the time he became a church organist, at the age of eleven. He left this post to study music in Milan, a move made possible by his patron, Barezzi, with whose daughter Margherita the lad had played piano duets. He married her in 1836, and shortly thereafter composed his first opera, *Oberto*, which was so successful that his future seemed assured. But shortly after its performance, his wife and two babies died of an undiagnosed malady, the opera he forced himself to complete in order to fill a contract was a failure, and he vowed never to write another.

In order to rouse him, the impresario Merelli asked him for an opinion of the book, *Nabuco* (*Nebuchadnezzar*), as opera material. Verdi unwillingly took the volume home, and threw it on a table. The book fell open, he read a few lines, and began to write music, as Merelli intended he should. Therewith he embarked on the career which eventually made him the Grand Old Man of Italian opera. In modern slang, he was a "natural." Operatic melody welled from him inexhaustibly, while thanks to his sense of theater, his accompanying dramas escaped the ridiculousness which so often mars grand opera. From *Oberto*, written in his twenties, to *Falstaff*, completed when he was eighty, his characteristic integrity and intensity persisted; as he wrote his thirty operas, his powers of expression broadened and deepened. Old age brought no slackening, but the added subtle wisdom that sometimes is the fruit of experience. He was compared with, and accused of imitating, Wagner, to the embitterment of his later years, but his Italian lyricism seems to bear little relationship to the thunderings from Bayreuth.

Verdi's early operas, *I Lombardi*, *Ernani* and *Attila* struck a note of defiance against the Austrian oppressors of his people, and their choruses, virile and aggressive, served well in anti-Austrian demonstrations. During the Revolution of 1848 he was in Paris, eagerly following the movement for independence. With *Rigoletto*, *Il Trovatore* and *La Traviata* he struck his full operatic stride. While Italy was at war with Austria, he became a senator, until a commission to write an opera, *La Forza del Destino*, brought him back to the footlights. He was obliged by his profession to travel a great deal, but he returned whenever he could to his peaceful farm outside Busseto, where he showed himself to be an able farmer and administrator.

By the time he wrote *Aïda*, commissioned by the Khedive of Egypt, Verdi was fifty-six. Again a libretto released his inspiration. He could not resist the story as it was suggested to him by the French Egyptologist, Mariette Bey. *Aïda* is often named as his greatest opera. The live elephants used in the production, the authentic costumes and musical instruments copied from ancient Egyptian tombs made an attractive picture, and his music made a "Celeste Aida" of the whole. Two others, *Otello* and *Falstaff* complete the list of operas, to which his Manzoni *Requiem Mass*, *Stabat Mater*, and other church music add a balancing religious touch.

In memory of his second wife, he founded a Home for Musicians at Milan, similar to the Rossini foundation. A Verdi Museum, and a concert hall in that city, where he lies buried, are further Verdi memorials.

◇◇◇◇◇◇◇◇◇◇◇◇◇◇◇◇◇◇◇◇◇◇◇◇◇◇◇◇◇◇◇◇◇◇◇◇

Robert Franz

(fränts)

b. HALLE, GERMANY, JUNE 28, 1815 *d.* HALLE, OCT. 24, 1892

THIS "POLYPHONIC SCHUBERT," so called because he wrote art-songs as lyrical as Schubert's, but with polyphonic accompaniments, was the special friend of mezzo-sopranos, all of his songs being written for their range. His was a somewhat limited gift, for aside from arrangements of the works of other composers, he wrote only songs. Furthermore, he excluded from them everything dramatic, realistic, or unpleasant. Characterized by purity, dignity and reticence, Franz' songs are distinctly "dated." There are three hundred and fifty, among the best known *Die Lotosblume*, *Auf dem Meere* (*On the Sea*) and *Mädchen mit dem rothen Mündchen* (*Maiden with the Rosy Lips*).

In the beginning, he learned piano and organ against his parents' wishes. He finally won their consent to two years of study in nearby Dessau, but when that was over, he suffered a long period of unemployment because no musical job was offered him, and he would accept no other. Finally, a set of songs he sent to Schumann in 1843 was highly praised by that discerning critic in the *Neue Zeitschrift*. Liszt, Mendelssohn and other composers chimed in. The city of Halle decided to give him a job. He was made organist at the Ulrichskirche, director of the Singakademie, later musical director of Halle University. In 1868 he was obliged to retire because of increasing deafness complicated by nervous disorders. His friends came to the rescue with a benefit performance which netted him and his family enough for living expenses until his death.

◇◇◇◇◇◇◇◇◇◇◇◇◇◇◇◇◇◇◇◇◇◇◇◇◇◇◇◇◇◇◇◇◇

Charles Gounod

(gōō′-nō′)

b. PARIS, JUNE 17, 1818   *d.* PARIS, OCT. 13, 1893

CHARLES GOUNOD, composer of the opera *Faust*, almost became a priest, instead of a composer. He was dissuaded by his worldly friends, Pauline Viardot-Garcia, and the gay Fanny Mendolssohn, favorite sister of Felix. Nevertheless, his five years of preparation for the priesthood contributed to his musical career, for in the course of them he diligently studied the works of Schumann and Berlioz and acquired an excellent knowledge of orchestration. Attractive Charles Gounod, son of an artist and a musician, followed the usual course of the French composer;—the Conservatoire, Prix de Rome, and a trip abroad. His musical models were Bach, Palestrina, Mozart, Rossini and Weber, his preparation for his career was thorough, his general education that of a man of high culture.

His first opera, *Sapho*, was not a success. He became choral conductor at the Theatre Orphéon, for which he wrote *Le Médecin Malgré Lui* (*The Physician Against His Will*), which achieved a mild renown. *Faust* was next (1859). A sentimental grand opera, it exactly suited the French bourgeoisie, who clasped it ecstatically to their comfortable bosoms. They did not become aware of its existence as soon as they might have, however; after its first few months at the Opéra Comique in Paris, it was withdrawn, not to be produced again until ten years later. When its success in other cities convinced the timid souls at the Paris Opéra that it should be readmitted, it became the most popular opera in the repertoire, a universal and enduring success. *La Reine de Saba*, *Philémon et Baucis*, *Roméo et Juliette*, and *Mireille*, tuneful and well orchestrated as they were, never attained the popularity of *Faust*. Though this opera presented no startling departures from the accepted formula—perhaps because of that very fact—it gave and has continued to give complete satisfaction to vast audiences.

Gounod visited London from 1870 to 1875, while the Franco-Prussian War was going on. He emulated Handel and Mendelssohn in writing oratorios, of which the best known are *The Redemption* and *Death and Life*. At the end, the priest in him triumphed over the pagan, and the erstwhile gay bachelor, aged seventy-five, blind and paralyzed, composed as his last piece a *Requiem*. He died shortly after its completion, and was buried in the cemetery at St. Cloud.

Jacques Offenbach

(ô′făn′bak′)

b. OFFENBACH-ON-RHEIN, GERMANY, JUNE 20, 1819 — *d.* PARIS, FRANCE, OCT. 5, 1880

THIS COMPOSER CHANGED HIS NAME from Levy to Offenbach, his residence from Germany to France, his raiment from the sober garb of a cantor's son to the elegant costume of a Parisian dandy. His style of writing and he himself became, in fact, more French than the French. The ninety elegant, satirical operettas he produced in twenty-five years made him the favorite composer of Napoleon III's Second Empire.

He was prepared for his career by study at the Paris Conservatoire and by a job at the same time in the orchestra of the Opéra Comique. Later he became conductor at the Théatre Français, and managed various theatres, including the Bouffes Parisiens, where many of his operettas were produced. In his book, *Notes d'un Musicien en Voyage*, he describes a tour to the United States in 1876, and takes many a sly dig at the provincialism, the "blue Sundays," and the musical barbarism of American small towns.

Les Contes d'Hoffman (*Tales of Hoffman*), which

he did not live to see produced, is his best known. However, *La Vie Parisienne* (*Parisian Life*), *La Belle Hélène* (*Beautiful Helen*), *Barbe Bleue* (*Bluebeard*), and others are often revived, and always give pleasure. Their cleverness, supple orchestration and impudent satire give them a Gilbert and Sullivan character which has created an Offenbach cult in France and pre-Hitler Germany.

◇◇◇◇◇◇◇◇◇◇◇◇◇◇◇◇◇◇◇◇◇◇◇◇◇◇◇◇◇◇

César Franck

(frångk)

b. LIÉGE, BELGIUM, DEC. 10, 1822 *d.* PARIS, FRANCE, NOV. 8, 1890

AN UNOBTRUSIVE LITTLE MAN, whose sleeves and trouser-legs were always a bit too short, César Franck looked like anything but the saviour of French music. In the organ loft of his church, he was a male St. Cecilia, whose marvelous improvisations held listeners spellbound, but in the halls of the Paris Conservatoire he was a music-teacher, with no outward evidence of the greatness of spirit and profound knowledge that were his.

During his boyhood at Liége, he did so well at the conservatory that Cherubini admitted him to the Paris Conservatoire when he was fourteen, and even instituted a special award for the lad who at his entrance examination not only wrote a fugue on a given theme, but transposed it. However, when he was graduated, Cherubini refused him permission to compete for the Prix de Rome, because of his Belgian birth.

His father wanted him to become a pianist, but César, strengthened by marriage in 1848, went his own way as composer and teacher. He and his bride had to climb over the barricades erected in the streets by the revolutionaries to get to church to be married. She was a thrifty housewife, to whom he handed over all his fees. There is a story of his having secretly put by a few francs for a trip to Bayreuth, and of her having found and spent them on the household. He did not go to Bayreuth, nor any farther afield than the omnibus ride from his house to the church, to his private pupils and to the Conservatoire.

He was fifty when he was made professor of the organ at the Conservatoire. His pupils—D'Indy, Chausson and other composers afterward well known—reverently received from "Père Franck" the themes for exercises which he produced from the wellworn notebook in his pocket. He worked systematically at his own compositions from five to seven A.M. Before he was fifty, he had completed an oratorio, *Ruth;* a symphonic poem *Re-*

demption; the *Prelude, Fugue and Variations* for piano, and much church music. Between 1874 and 1890, his output was bigger and better: four symphonic poems, the *D minor symphony*, the *Variations Symphoniques* for piano and orchestra, several oratorios, including *Les Béatitudes*, chamber music, piano and organ works.

He might have remained unknown, had it not been for the Société Nationale de la Musique (National Society of Music), and his devoted pupils, who organized a Franck festival in 1887. Indifference or derision marked the reception of his works. Gounod described the *D minor symphony* as "the affirmation of incompetence pushed to dogmatic lengths"; nevertheless it became the most important symphony in French musical literature.

Franck's music was mystical and ecstatic. It lacked the sensuousness of the French music of his day, though it was by no means devoid of passion. Its "squirming chromatic meanderings" are balanced by delicacy and symmetry. As an organist, Franck was compared by Liszt with J. S. Bach, and as a writer, too, he is comparable.

He was struck by an omnibus a month after the first public performance of his string quartet. Pleurisy developed, and shortly afterward he died, and was buried in the cemetery of Montparnasse.

Bedřich Smetana

(smĕ′tänä)

b. LITOMYSL, BOHEMIA, MARCH 2, 1824 *d.* PRAGUE, MAY 12, 1884

CZECHO-SLOVAKIA has fallen upon evil days, but its spirit lives triumphant in the music of Bedřich Smetana, its first national composer. This son of a brewer played first violin in a Haydn quartet at the age of five, made a piano appearance in public while still a schoolboy, and started to compose as soon as his father permitted him to leave his law-books and go to Prague to study music. As the permission was not accompanied by any visible means of support, young Bedřich at first often had to tighten his belt against the pangs of hunger. When, after some months, he became music master to the family of Count Thun, he was at least assured of three meals a day. The warm friendship of Clara and Robert Schumann, and the support of Liszt, who financed a music school in Prague which Smetana directed, helped him materially, and stimulated his musical ambitions. To such friends as these he confided his hope that Bohemia, then in revolution, would shake off the Austrian yoke and become a free nation.

In 1848 he married Katerina Kolar, who became his assistant in the music school at Prague. Three years in the free air of Gothenburg, Sweden, from 1856 to 1859 afforded a breathing spell during which he conducted the new Philharmonic orchestra, gave piano recitals, and put by a little money. He also composed three symphonic poems patterned on Liszt's,—*Richard III*, *Wallensteins Lager*, and *Hakon Jarl*. But his wife became ill, and died in Dresden on the way home to Prague. A couple of years later, he married again, returned to Gothenburg and Stockholm, and toured in Germany, Holland and Sweden before he finally settled in Prague, where he became Director of the new National Opera house.

His operas were produced there one after another. *Brandenburgers in Bohemia*, *The Bartered Bride*, *Dalibor*, *Libusǎ*, *Two Widows*, are so strongly national that they suffer a certain loss when translated, yet the *Bartered Bride* has wound her fluttering peasant ribbons around the hearts of music lovers of every land. *Ma Vlast*, an orchestral epic in six cantos, is a saga of Bohemia, rich in folksong.

In 1874, the composer became wholly deaf. Unlike Beethoven, he was not forewarned by a gradual lessening of his powers; his affliction came suddenly, following a period of ill health and overwork. In his autobiographical string quartet, *Aus Meinem Leben* (*From My Life*), a shrill, long drawn high note represents the distracting sounds he heard in his deafness. Literally driven mad by them, he died in an insane asylum a few months after his sixtieth birthday. He is the acknowledged founder of a Czech national music, his works "the best medium for a Czech to become conscious of his national character."

◇◇◇◇◇◇◇◇◇◇◇◇◇◇◇◇◇◇◇◇◇◇◇◇◇◇◇◇◇◇◇◇

Anton Bruckner

(bro͝ok′nẽr)

b. ANSFELDEN, AUSTRIA, SEPT. 4, 1824 — *d.* VIENNA, AUSTRIA, OCT. 11, 1896

BRUCKNER LIVED to be three score and ten. He was forty-one, when, having made Wagner's personal acquaintance at the première of *Tristan* in Munich, he became an intimate friend and disciple. Wagner described him as the only real symphonist since Beethoven, a tribute which did him little good in view of the unpopularity of the speaker at the time. Bruckner left nine symphonies—the ninth unfinished—in which he paid Wagner the compliment of employing the Wagnerian idiom to a marked degree. He left, too, a string quartet, three masses and a *Te Deum*, and much other sacred music.

Anton Bruckner

He was the eldest of the eleven children of a poor village schoolmaster, and had more responsibilities than advantages, but he somehow managed to prepare himself to become an organist, teacher, and composer. He earned his daily bread in the organ loft of the Cathedral of Linz, a job he received as the result of a competition which he entered with no anticipation of winning. It gave him courage to make music his profession. After years of struggle, he became a professor at the Vienna Conservatory, and earned enough to supply the simple needs of his monastic celibate existence, and to permit him to compose at ease.

His symphonies, characterized as "the monumentalization of his organ improvisation," require from an hour to an hour and three quarters to perform, and there is not a smile in a carload. Pious, mystical, deeply and fearfully earnest, they are most admired by those who prefer their serious music straight. During his lifetime, he was compared to his disadvantage with Brahms, who was nine years his junior and as anti-Wagner as Bruckner was pro. Since his death, there has been an increasing realization that he was really born out of his time. A medieval priest like Bruckner did not belong in the nineteenth century, though in his own suffering way he managed to reflect something of the period he lived in.

Johann Strauss, Junior

(shtrous)

b. VIENNA, AUSTRIA, OCT. 25, 1825

d. VIENNA, JUNE 3, 1899

JOHANN STRAUSS, JR., the Waltz King, was the incarnation of nineteenth century Vienna. His waltzes completely captured the spirit of that light hearted city, for whose court balls he composed *The Beautiful Blue Danube*, *Vienna Woods*, *Artist's Life*, *One Lives but Once*, and hundreds of others. When his band performed one of them, the dashing leader faced his audience, playing the violin with a flourish that emphasized the ravishing melodies and infectious rhythm of a music which set everyone to tapping and swaying.

From his father, who strongly opposed his following in the paternal footsteps, he inherited the title and talent of waltz king, along with a professional jealousy that led to bitter dissension between them. He inherited also a band which, united with his own, became one of the best in Europe, "worth walking to Vienna to hear." Under his baton, it toured Germany, Austria and Poland, gave summer concerts at St. Petersburg, and played for the court balls in Vienna.

His fame extended to America; he conducted fourteen monster concerts for the American Jubilee in Boston in 1872, and four in New York. Audiences stood on chairs cheering in their enthusiasm, but they could not induce him to remain longer away from his Vienna. All over the world people whirled to his waltzes; he completely revolutionized the dancing habits of a whole generation.

His charming operetta *Die Fledermaus* (*The Bat*) is dance music in dramatic terms, elegant, spirited and tuneful, the best of his fifteen operettas, with *Zigeunerbaron* (*Gypsy Baron*) a close second. Twice married, both times to singers, the debonair and dashing Johann lived to be seventy-four years young. His waltzes, fresh with eternal youth, will probably live forever.

Stephen Collins Foster

(fŏs′tẽr)

b. LAWRENCEVILLE, PA., JULY 4, 1826 *d.* NEW YORK, JAN. 13, 1864

IF STEPHEN FOSTER WAS A QUEER DUCK in the middle-class Foster poultry yard, he was an extraordinarily lovable one. When he was six, his mother wrote that "there still remains something perfectly original about him," which meant that he liked to moon around by himself, play the flute, and scribble music. She allowed him to have flute and piano lessons, but he never was given the thorough grounding that as a composer he should have had.

In his twentieth year, he went to be a bookkeeper for his brother Dunning in Cincinnati, but the tunes in his head interfered with addition and subtraction, until *Old Uncle Ned* and *Oh, Susannah* convinced the family that his talent might be worth something in dollars and cents, and he was permitted to return home.

For the next few years he lived pleasantly on the top floor of his mother's house, and twice a week tried his songs with his friends, the Stephen Foster Quartet. In 1850, he married Jane Mac-

Dowell, who had mingled her soprano with his tenor at these meetings, and who inspired many of his best songs. A few years later he moved to New York in quest of a new market for his wares. He never had been happy away from Pittsburgh, and although the move resulted in permanent separation from his wife and child, he returned home to his mother.

There he worked industriously. Everybody loved the handsome dreamer, and moreover, he found a ready market for his songs. He wrote many for the Christy minstrels, then in their hey-day. So close was he to this troupe that Christy's name appeared on the title page of *Old Folks at Home* as the composer. The probably intentional error was corrected after *Old Folks at Home* had become the most popular song in the country, had been translated into all languages, and had brought large royalties to its rightful composer.

When his mother died in 1860, he could not bear the old home without her. He drifted, rudderless, to a dismal hall bedroom in New York, and, desperately lonely, took to drink. He would write a song in the morning, sell it in the afternoon, and drink up the money in the evening. His end came suddenly. He had been laid up with a fever, got out of bed and fell against the old-fashioned washstand, smashing the pitcher and basin. He was badly cut and lay, bleeding and unconscious, for some time before the chamber-maid found him. He died a few days later in the charity ward of Bellevue Hospital, in his wallet no money, but a scrap of paper scribbled with the line, "Dear friends and gentle hearts."

For an explanation of his unique position as the creator of a one-man American folk song, we must look to his era, which he typified. To the sentimentality of hoop skirt and honeysuckle he catered in *Jeanie with the Light Brown Hair*, and *Come Where my Love Lies Dreaming*. The pathos of the Negro he dramatized in *Old Folks at Home*, *Old Black Joe* and *My Old Kentucky Home*. Minstrels were provided with the doo-doo-dah of *Camptown Races* and with other tunes. After the Civil War began, *Willie, We Have Missed You* and *Massa's in de Cold, Cold Ground* caused all heartstrings to vibrate. In his thirty-eight years he wrote over two hundred songs which expressed a predominant mood of the times, and possessed much of the spontaneity and singability of true folksong.

Anton Gregorovitch Rubinstein

(rōō′bĭn-stīn)

b. WECHWOTINEZ, RUSSIA, NOV. 28, 1829

d. ST. PETERSBURG, RUSSIA, NOV. 20, 1894

THIS RUSSIAN COMPOSER AND PIANIST divided his time between Germany and Russia with such impartiality that both countries take a proprietary interest in him. His writing is in the idiom of Mendelssohn and the German Romantic school. Fluent, melodious and technically sound, it is marred by faults arising from his failure to criticize and edit. Although he wrote a great deal besides the *Melodie in F*, that hackneyed little piece has come to spell Rubinstein in every language.

As a pupil of his mother and of Alexander Villoing, he first played the piano in public when he was ten, his "fingers as light as feathers and yet as strong as a man's." On the ensuing tour he met Liszt, whom he admired but did not imitate. He concentrated on interpretation rather than technical display, and reduced his audience to tears which they could not wipe away because their hands were being used for applause.

He had two years of study in Berlin, from 1844

to 1846. Passport difficulties in returning to Russia resulted in the confiscation of the trunk containing all his manuscripts. They were later sold as waste paper, but, nothing daunted, he made a fresh start. Many of his compositions were published in Germany. He toured as a pianist everywhere, including America, where he was applauded to the echo.

He became court pianist and concert director at the Czar's court and founded the St. Petersburg Conservatory, which he directed until it was firmly established. He who as a baby had escaped in a covered wagon from an anti-Semitic decree of a Czar, now found himself ennobled, given a life pension, and loaded with honors by a descendant of that same Czar.

Though he has one hundred and nineteen opus numbers to his credit, including popular piano pieces, songs, chamber music, dramatic works, and a symphony, he is most lovingly remembered as one of the greatest pianists the world has ever known.

◇◇◇◇◇◇◇◇◇◇◇◇◇◇◇◇◇◇◇◇◇◇◇◇◇◇◇◇◇◇◇◇◇◇◇

Johannes Brahms

(brämz)

b. HAMBURG, GERMANY, MAY 7, 1833 *d.* VIENNA, AUSTRIA, APRIL 3, 1897

THE LAST OF THE THREE B'S—Bach, Beethoven and Brahms—was likened by his friend Robert Schumann to a young eagle. A plump eagle in later life, he did in fact soar to lofty heights. He wrote every kind of music but opera, and proved himself master of them all. His models were classic, so too his spirit and the forms he selected, yet his compositions were described as being like a gypsy woman dancing in a tight corset, "latent heat beneath a formal exterior."

His general education and preparation for his career were surprisingly thorough considering that the home of his childhood was in the slums of Hamburg, and that he was obliged to play the piano for a living from the time he was thirteen.

When he was twenty, the gypsy in him responded to the invitation of Eduard Reményi, a Hungarian violinist, to go on tour as his accompanist. The two visited the violinist Joachim, who sent Brahms with letters of introduction to Liszt in Weimar and Schumann in Düsseldorf. Schumann's glowing praise of Brahms' music in the *Neue Zeitschrift*, and Clara's immediate liking brought him two of the best friends he was ever to have. Though Schumann fell fatally ill five months later, their friendship ripened so fast that Brahms was the friend to whom Clara turned during the tragic months that followed.

After Schumann's death, the young man took Clara's place as teacher at the court of Lippe-Detmold, where for three or four years he lived pleasantly, free to compose, to ramble in the Teutoburger forest, and to acquire from books the encyclopedic knowledge for which he was noted. When, at twenty-nine, he resigned his post, he took to Vienna a number of new works.

He never married, probably because he could not bear to relinquish his freedom. He was openly impatient of ties of any kind. While conducting the Singakademie, he wrote some of his best choral works, but he resigned after a year. The same thing occurred with the Gesellschaft der Musikfreunde (Society of the Friends of Music), which he conducted until the desire for freedom again overpowered him. He was at his best when he could work at a leisurely pace in his little room in Vienna, and could take his recreation in the suburbs, in long walking trips, and in the companionship of his friends, who called themselves the Brahmins.

The first complete performance of his *German Requiem*, in 1868, made him famous throughout

Europe. His *First Symphony*, over which he toiled for ten years, he did not release until he was over forty. By the radicals it was accounted too conservative, by the conservatives too radical. As time has passed, the rich sonorities of his four symphonies and chamber music, the beauty of his two hundred and thirty songs, his choral works and instrumental pieces, have established him among the mighty in music, "Lord Keeper of the seal of classic heritage, in whom all threads united once more before they were lost in chaos."

◇◇◇◇◇◇◇◇◇◇◇◇◇◇◇◇◇◇◇◇◇◇◇◇◇◇◇◇◇◇

Alexander Porfyrievitch Borodin

(bŏ′-rŏ-dĭn′)

b. ST. PETERSBURG, RUSSIA, NOV. 12, 1833

d. ST. PETERSBURG, FEB. 28, 1887

BORODIN WAS THE YOUNGEST of "the Five" who pledged themselves to provide Russian music for the Russians. With Balakirev, Cui, Rimsky-Korsakoff and Moussorgsky, he worked devotedly to that end, though he was a busy doctor and scientist, writer of books and treatises on medicine, organizer of a Medical School for Women in St. Petersburg, and lecturer at the St. Petersburg

Medical Academy. Except for a visit to Liszt in Weimar in 1877, and a few concert trips, he remained all his life in Russia.

In 1863 he married a concert pianist, who, with his teacher Balakirev, inspired him to become more than an amateur in music. Liszt regarded this M.D., who was the illegitimate son of a Georgian prince, as one of the most gifted orchestral composers of the nineteenth century. The symphonic poem, *In Steppes of Central Asia;* the opera *Prince Igor*, with its splendid savage ballet of *Polovetzian Dances;* two symphonies; songs and chamber music are no small achievement for a man of divided work. His compositions display the sanity and clarity which may be expected from a scientist, beguiling melodies, powerful orchestration, and the strong national feeling of a musician who is Russian through and through.

Camille Saint-Saëns

(săn′säns′)

b. PARIS, OCT. 9, 1835 *d.* ALGIERS, DEC. 16, 1921

FROM HIS SIXTH TO HIS EIGHTY-SIXTH YEAR, Saint-Saëns wrote music "as an apple tree produces apples," blocked by no striving for emotional depth or originality. The enormous body of works in every form which resulted contains but a few that have held their appeal. The opera, *Samson and Delilah*, the symphonic poems *Rouet d'Omphale* (*The Spinning-Wheel of Omphale*) and *Danse Macabre* (*Dance of Death*), the *Carneval des Animaux* (*Carnival of Animals*), the *Third Symphony*, and possibly one or two of the piano concertos are played wherever the suavity and facile melody of this "French Mendelssohn" are admired.

His memoirs show him a highly cultured, witty gentleman, who had the precise intelligence and the powers of enjoyment of the French intellectual. He made his first concert appearance when he was about six, and after his studies at the Conservatoire, became a first class piano and organ virtuoso. He had a thorough command of form and a knowledge of musical craftsmanship in all its branches, but he never was awarded the Prix de

Rome. He was adjudged too immature on his first attempt, and already too successful a composer on his second. After the Franco-Prussian war, he founded, with Bussine, the Société Nationale de la Musique in Paris, which exercised a profound influence on the developing instrumental school of César Franck and his pupils. Gounod and Lalo stood with him in encouraging rising young composers. For the Société he wrote symphonic poems, modeled upon those of his friend and admirer, Liszt. The Opéra produced a number of his dramatic works, but rejected *Samson and Delilah,* in spite of the aria *Mon coeur s'ouvre a ta voix* (*My heart at thy sweet voice*)! To Liszt in Weimar fell the privilege of engineering and conducting the première. Not till fifteen years later was *Samson and Delilah* produced in Paris, where it became one of the most popular operas in the repertoire.

Saint-Saëns visited the United States in 1906, and again in 1915, and gave an organ recital in San Francisco when he was eighty. He traveled widely, especially in South Africa and Algeria, and described the latter in his suite, *Algérienne.* While visiting there in 1921, when he was eighty-six, he fell ill, and died. Philip Hale wrote of him: "Organist, pianist, caricaturist, dabbler in science, enamored of mathematics and astronomy, amateur comedian, critic, traveler, archaeologist —he was a restless man."

Max Bruch

(brŏŏk)

b. COLOGNE, GERMANY, JAN. 6, 1838

d. FRIEDENAU, GERMANY, OCT. 2, 1920

MAX BRUCH IS WELL-KNOWN to concert violinists for his *Violin concerto in G minor*, the imperative opening chords of which invite them to a grand technical and emotional display. He wrote seventy pieces between his ninth and his fourteenth year, climaxing that feat by winning the Mozart scholarship in Frankfurt. He became a well-known teacher, and was recognized as an excellent conductor, though inclined to carry his pedagogy onto the podium. After Sarasate had given a brilliant performance of the *G minor concerto* in London, Bruch was asked to conduct the London Philharmonic. But his drill-master methods so annoyed the men in the orchestra, that there was openly expressed relief when he resigned. Nevertheless, Berlioz and Rossini applauded him in Paris, in Leipzig Moscheles, Hauptmann and Ferdinand David were his staunch supporters, and he was invited to conduct in many cities.

In 1881 he was married to a singer, and two

years later went on a tour to America. Upon his return he settled in Germany, where honors and decorations were bestowed upon him. The last ten years of his life he spent quietly in retirement at Friedenau, near Berlin, and died there.

Odysseus, Das Feuerkreuz, Schön Ellen and other choral works were his best drawing card in Germany, while outside his native land his instrumental works won more friends. Their flowing Rhenish melodies and substantial harmonies, typically German, were romantically appealing. Though a lesser talent than Mendelssohn, Schumann or Brahms, he has been compared in style with all three.

◇◇◇◇◇◇◇◇◇◇◇◇◇◇◇◇◇◇◇◇◇◇◇◇◇◇◇◇◇◇◇◇

Alexandre César Leopold Georges Bizet

(bē′zĕ′)

b. PARIS, FRANCE, OCT. 25, 1838 *d.* BOUGIVAL, NEAR PARIS, JUNE 3, 1875

JUST A FEW MONTHS BEFORE Bizet's death, the alluring heroine of his one great opera, *Carmen*, made her initial bow to the French public. Into their hearts she was to nestle, never to be dislodged, taking with her the composer who immortalized her in music.

From his ninth to his twentieth year, Bizet worked diligently at the Paris Conservatoire, where he studied the piano with Marmontel and composition with Halévy. At twenty, he won the Prix de Rome, and composed several operas and symphonic works that didn't quite come off. The lyric *Djamileh*, a one-act opera, was mildly successful, but the charming music to Daudet's *L'Arlésienne* was coldly received, though today it is extremely popular as an orchestral suite.

The sensitive Bizet is said to have left the première of *Carmen* before the end, practically in tears because of the unresponsiveness of the audience. His death occurred on the day of its twenty-third performance. It had still not become a sellout. The philosopher Nietzche had not at that time owned up to having seen it twenty times and liked it better at each performance, nor had the public as yet turned to the frank enjoyment of its dramatic realism. Bizet did not live to hear it described as the perfect opera, nor to know that Puccini, Leoncavallo and Mascagni thought highly enough of it to imitate it. He died convinced that he had failed.

◇◇◇◇◇◇◇◇◇◇◇◇◇◇◇◇◇◇◇◇◇◇◇◇◇◇◇◇◇◇◇◇◇

Modest Petrovitch Moussorgsky

(mōō-sôrg′skê)

b. KOREVO, RUSSIA, MARCH 21, 1835 *d.* ST. PETERSBURG, MARCH 28, 1881

THE OPERA *Boris Godounoff* is the answer to the question, "Why is Moussorgsky the greatest of 'the Five' in Russia?" This is a realistic music drama, conceived and executed with fierce and powerful emotion. Moussorgsky was concerned with the problems of the People, both masses and classes. He prettified neither music, action nor characterization, but presented his Russians as they were, and in so doing became their spokesman in music, the founder of a school of musical realism in Russia.

He was born of a family of land owners, and educated at the School for Cadets. After graduation, he became an officer in the Prebroiansky Regiment, where drinking his comrades under the table was not the least of his military responsibilities. He had learned as a boy to play the piano, and when he met Dargomizhsky, the disciple of Glinka, and the rest of "the Five," he was drawn irresistibly to music. Balakirev, least renowned of the group as a composer, taught them the technique of composition, and was the power behind their musical thrones. Moussorgsky took from him what he required, but shied off from too much instruction, instinctively clinging to the crude power and originality he recognized as his own truth.

He resigned his army commission in 1857 to devote himself to music, and accepted a government clerkship at a pittance, which left him time to compose. Rimsky-Korsakoff, with whom he lived for a few years, edited and polished some of his compositions, notably *Boris*. Only when later published in their original form did they reveal the genius of their composer. After Rimsky-Korsakoff was married, Moussorgsky lived alone, and went rapidly to the bad. The huge bearded man drank too much, took drugs, and suffered from epileptic fits. He shuffled around all day in a sloppy dressing-gown, and his friends left him to himself.

When *Boris* was produced, in 1868, the public loved it, but Cesar Cui gave it such an unfavorable review that Moussorgsky denounced him as a "soulless traitor." Yet *Boris* was destined to live, while Cui's elegant little pieces are forgotten. Moussorgsky wrote hearty peasant melodies, delicate, tender lyrics and deeply philosophical song-soliloquies; the realistic piano suite, *In a Picture Gallery;* and many other characteristic works.

He died alone, a charity patient at the St. Nicholas Military Hospital. Not until after his death was his true stature revealed.

◇◇◇◇◇◇◇◇◇◇◇◇◇◇◇◇◇◇◇◇◇◇◇◇◇◇◇◇◇◇

Peter Ilitch Tchaikowsky

(chī-kŏf′-skē)

b. VOTKINSK, RUSSIA, MAY 7, 1840 *d.* MOSCOW, RUSSIA, NOV. 6, 1893

WERE TCHAIKOWSKY TO HEAR THE THEME of his *B flat piano concerto* used in commercial jazz as it is today, he would probably feel the distortion of its mood and rhythm to be a desecration.

Possibly he took himself so seriously because he

Peter Ilitch Tchaikowsky

was the first wholly professional composer in Russia. "The Five," with the exception of Rimsky-Korsakoff, were amateurs, all of whom earned their livelihood outside of music. They despised Tchaikowsky, who tolerated but disapproved of their somewhat limited interpretation of the Russian spirit. He was over twenty-one, an amateur pianist, boredly working as a law clerk, when the desire seized him to make music his profession. He resolved to study harmony, and enrolled at the St. Petersburg Conservatory, but wisely retained his clerkship until he was certain of his calling. His teacher, Anton Rubinstein, prepared him so thoroughly that after graduation he was made Professor of Harmony at Moscow in the new conservatory established by Anton's brother Nikolai. During those years, he met Turgenev and Tolstoi, Liszt, Saint-Saëns and Wagner. He composed the *Romeo and Juliet Overture* while recovering from a youthful passion for an opera singer. An entire opera was commissioned at that psychological moment, but it was never completed. The overture is much admired, however, especially the yearning Juliet theme. Other works,—the *Tempest* Overture, a tone-poem *Francesca da Rimini*, and the piano concerto, brought him into the limelight.

When he was thirty-four occurred a tragedy which was largely responsible for the melancholy of his later years. A young woman, Antonia Milukova, fancied herself in love with him, and proposed marriage. He gallantly accepted, though he hardly knew her. It took only three months to send him from her side, suffering from a high fever which was the forerunner of a severe nervous breakdown. He fled to Switzerland, where he remained for a year.

Then he returned to his post in Moscow. He had meanwhile met by mail Frau von Meck, the "beloved friend" who supported and corresponded with him for years on condition that they should never meet, and he was therefore able to write without one eye upon the almighty ruble. He had started his *Fourth Symphony* before his marriage; he set to work to finish it. His operas, *Eugen Onegin* and *Pique Dame* (*The Queen of Spades*), the *Violin Concerto*, the *Manfred Symphony*, the *Fifth Symphony* and *Nutcracker Ballet* followed.

In addition to teaching, he conducted in Moscow, St. Petersburg and Europe. In 1891 he visited New York to conduct a concert of his own works at the opening of Carnegie Hall. But he did not enjoy his visit. His correspondence with Mme. von Meck had ceased, and he was lonely and homesick. He returned to Russia in the depths of despondency, and in that mood he composed his *Sixth Symphony*. When it was finished, he was as elated as he had previously been depressed; nevertheless he accepted as suitable the subtitle *Pathétique* suggested by his brother Modest. Its Finale, Adagio Lamentoso, seems, says Philip Hale, "to set the seal of finality on all human hopes." Certainly, it marks him as the most expressive Romantic composer of Russia.

Upon his return to Moscow from Klin, where he had been working on the *Pathétique*, a cholera epidemic was raging. With reckless disregard of consequences, Tchaikowsky drank unboiled water and died within a few hours.

◇◇◇◇◇◇◇◇◇◇◇◇◇◇◇◇◇◇◇◇◇◇◇◇◇◇◇◇◇◇◇

Antonin Dvořák

(dvôr′zhäk)

b. NELAHOZEVES, BOHEMIA, SEPT. 8, 1841 *d.* PRAGUE, MAY 1, 1904

THE FOLKSONGS to which his jolly young father tinkled zither accompaniments while the villagers danced on the green were more important to Anton Dvořák than the three R's he learned from the village schoolmaster, and Anton in turn played these folksongs on the violin before going on to the serious study of music. He prevailed on his parents to let him attend the organ school at Prague, where he submitted to an ordeal of hunger while studying, since his only income came from occasional engagements in a small band.

The date of his graduation, 1860, was an important one. An imperial decree had lifted the

Austrian yoke from the neck of Bohemia and Smetana had just returned to Prague from Gothenburg, aflame with ambition to create a national school of music. Dvořák at once enlisted his talent under Smetana's banner. A job in the theater orchestra supported him. Then he caught Wagner measles, and wrote an opera, *Alfred* and a comic opera, *King and Collier*, which were nothing more than bad Wagner. But he erased the memory of these disasters with a cantata, *Hymnus*, and a rousing patriotic hymn, *The Heirs of the White Mountain.* He resigned his theater job for that of organist, which left him more time for composition. In 1875, the Austrian Ministry of Culture, urged by Brahms, voted him an annuity in recognition of his *Moravian Duets*.

Several years before this he had married. The death of his small daughter inspired him to compose the *Piano Trio in G Minor* and a *Stabat Mater*. A few months later, the folksong-like *Moravian Duets*, the *Slavonic Rhapsodies* and *Slavonic Dances* became immensely popular in Germany, as well as in Bohemia, and Dvořák found himself famous overnight. Liszt and Brahms sang his praises, publishers competed for his works.

An invitation from England to conduct his *Stabat Mater* in London proved a doubtful blessing. It brought him a number of commissions for oratorios, but he did not do himself justice in the ponderous works he dutifully delivered; his

Slavonic Dances, *Songs my Mother Taught Me*, and *New World Symphony* are worth a ton of oratorios.

The *New World Symphony* was written during the time that Dvořák was director of the National Conservatory in New York, from 1892 to 1895. On his travels he discovered Spillville, Iowa, a village of transplanted Bohemians, and went there to write his symphony and allay his homesickness. Many themes of the symphony resemble the spirituals sung for Dvořák by his negro pupil, Harry Burleigh; this caused Americans to accept the symphony as truly their own.

When he set sail for home in 1895, it was with a long sigh of relief. His estate in Southern Bohemia meant more to him than Niagara Falls, Longfellow, Negro songs, or his pupils in America, fond as he was of them all. He became director of the Prague Conservatory, during his last years acquired a fine collection of honorary degrees and gold medals, and was the first musician to be honored with a seat in the Austrian Upper House. Life was sweet when he died suddenly of apoplexy, at sixty-three. The simple directness of his peasant dialect in music, the beauty of sound and perfection of form of his best works, place him beside Smetana.

Jules Massenet

(mä′s-nĕ′)

b. MONTAUD, FRANCE, MAY 12, 1842 *d.* ÉGREVILLE, NEAR PARIS, AUG. 13, 1912

MASSENET'S OPERAS shared the opera vogue of nineteenth century France with Wagner's, their direct opposite. His twenty-five were of the Meyerbeer-Offenbach type,—that is, light and popular rather than "grand." Some of them helped to insure the success of Oscar Hammerstein's opera experiment in New York. When Mary Garden created there the roles of *Manon*, *Thaïs*, and *Le Jongleur de Notre Dame*, (*The Juggler of Notre Dame*) the composer shared in her dazzling triumph. The *Meditation* from *Thaïs* lives on in arrangements and transcriptions that amateurs can play. *Le Cid*, *Sapho*, and *Herodiade* also became extremely popular, the *Aragonaise* from *Le Cid* and "Il est doux, il est bon" from Herodiade being regulars on the Massenet "hit parade." *Manon* is a typical Massenet opera; to have heard it is to have heard them all. Its superficial appeal is strong, thanks to its extremely singable melodies, but its contribution to the development of grand opera is negligible.

Jules Massenet

Massenet wrote operas with one eye on the prima donna who was to sing them, a habit not discouraged by his wife, who knew that prima donnas were his bread and butter, and encouraged him to send them operas rather than pearl necklaces. He studied under Ambroise Thomas at the Conservatoire, and traveled his full three years as a Prix de Rome winner, making the acquaintance of the ubiquitous Liszt while in Rome. He returned to Paris in time to shoulder a gun during the siege of 1870 in the Franco-Prussian War, and then he settled down to teaching counterpoint at the Conservatoire, writing operas, and enjoying the footlight existence of the opera composer. His personal charm, and the vogue of the particular kind of operas he wrote at the particular time he wrote them brought him wide popularity. When he died at his villa, Égreville, near Paris, there were many besides the prima donnas bereft of their Massenet who mourned his loss.

◇◇◇◇◇◇◇◇◇◇◇◇◇◇◇◇◇◇◇◇◇◇◇◇◇◇◇◇◇◇◇

Sir Arthur Sullivan

(sŭl′lĭ-văn)

b LONDON, ENGLAND, MAY 13, 1842 *d.* THERE, NOV. 22, 1900

SULLIVAN was the English Offenbach, his satirical yet solid operettas the delight of his generation and ours. Though he resented their being preferred to his more serious works, nevertheless when he was made Doctor of Music at Cambridge and Oxford, and knighted by Queen Victoria, he was being honored for his operettas, not for the anthems and oratorios he laboriously produced to please her.

His father was a band master, so the handsome, curly-headed boy played with band instruments from the time he was old enough to blow. He had become thoroughly familiar with them when the Rev. Thomas Helmore, Master of the Children at the Chapel Royal, took over his education and made a choirboy of him. Instruction at the Royal Academy of Music in London followed, then a thorough course at the Leipzig Conservatory. He returned to London with his incidental music to Shakespeare's *The Tempest*, and began to earn his bread and butter as a church organist and teacher. One pleasant interruption to his routine was a trip to Vienna in 1867. He assisted Sir George Grove, the English musicologist, in bringing to light a lot of unknown Schubert compositions, including the *Rosamunde Overture*, and thereafter felt a special kinship with Schubert.

As a composer he allowed no grass to grow under his feet. His output is large. *Onward Christian Soldiers*, *The Lost Chord*, and *Orpheus with his Lute* are not bad songs. But it is the operettas, —the *Mikado*, *Pirates of Penzance*, *Pinafore*, *Iolanthe*, and the rest,—which fascinate the ear and delight the mind. Their semi-operatic melodies glove-fitted to the witty libretti of W. S. Gilbert, their sly topical hits, and their operatic orchestral accompaniments were irresistible. Sullivan used to slip into a gallery seat at the Savoy, in top hat and opera cloak, and conduct with his cane for baton the incredible patter-songs which always brought down the house. Each new operetta was an event, not to be missed by anybody from Queen Victoria on down.

Gilbert and Sullivan were perfect collaborators. During the series which ran from *Box and Cox* in 1867 to the *Gondoliers* in 1890, Gilbert bore tactfully with the temperamental tantrums during which Sullivan would swear that inspiration was gone forever, that he could not and would not write another note. It was after such a lapse that he produced *The Mikado*, musically one of the finest. The separation of the operatic Damon and Pythias was the result of a silly quarrel as to whether they could afford a new carpet for the Savoy Theatre. Silly or not, they wrote no more together, and very little separately. Ten years after their divorce, Sullivan died, and was buried with great ceremony in Westminster Abbey.

◇◇◇◇◇◇◇◇◇◇◇◇◇◇◇◇◇◇◇◇◇◇◇◇◇◇◇◇◇◇◇

Edvard Hagerup Grieg

(grēg)

b. BERGEN, NORWAY, JUNE 15, 1843 *d.* BERGEN, SEPT. 4, 1907

BORN INTO A MUSICAL HOME, permitted to study without hindrance, happily married, successful in his twenties, his deepest grief the loss of his only daughter in her babyhood; such in brief was the life of Edvard Grieg. It would have been all sunshine, had his delicate constitution not cast a shadow upon its happiest moments. A breakdown from overwork, complicated by pleurisy while he was a student at the Leipzig Conservatory, left him with but one lung, and an accident to one of his hands hampered him as pianist and conductor. Nevertheless he lived to be sixty-four, to become a very successful performer, and to write much music, including the famous *Peer Gynt Suite*, the brilliant *Piano Concerto*, and many charming songs and instrumental works.

He did more to establish a Norwegian national style than any of his countrymen. A family friend, the Norwegian violinist Ole Bull, steered him into professional music; Moscheles at Leipzig taught him to play the piano exquisitely; Nils Gade, of Copenhagen, corrected his exercises, and Richard Nordraak, another composer, helped him to found in Christiania the Euterpe Society, whose members vowed to further the development of Norwegian music. When he visited Rome in 1870, Liszt played his piano concerto at sight from the manuscript, and advised him: "Keep steadily on; I tell you, you have the capability, and do not let them intimidate you." His wife Nina Hagerup sang his songs enchantingly, especially one called *I Love You*, which he dedicated to her. With her, he concertized throughout Europe, bringing a cool breath from the Norwegian fjords to its stuffy concert halls. His music is lyric and refined, and makes liberal use of native folktunes. To more robust composers he left opera and symphony.

He received a pension from the Norwegian government, and in addition numerous honors and degrees from every country. Cambridge made him a Doctor of Music at the same time as it so honored Tchaikowsky, Saint-Saëns and Bruch. When he died in his sleep, as peacefully as he had lived, he was mourned as the dean of Norwegian composers. The marble urn containing his ashes was placed on the grounds of his villa Troldhaugen, among the hills and fjords.

◇◇◇◇◇◇◇◇◇◇◇◇◇◇◇◇◇◇◇◇◇◇◇◇◇◇◇◇◇◇◇◇

Nikolai Rimsky-Korsakoff

(rĭm′skē-kôr′sȧ-kôf)

b. ST. PETERSBURG, RUSSIA, MARCH 18, 1844 *d.* THERE, JUNE 21, 1908

THE ARISTOCRAT Rimsky-Korsakoff, who was the youngest and wealthiest of the Russian "Five," enjoyed many advantages denied the others. Like them, he followed another profession, the navy, and was merely a musical amateur on the violin and cello, until his friendship with the "Five" opened his ears to the music of his own country. He listened enraptured to the operas of Glinka, and compared his compatriot favorably with Mendelssohn, Beethoven, Weber, Meyerbeer and Donizetti. There were crying deficiencies in his musical education, and he set about correcting them, the more expeditiously since he was not obliged to remain in the navy for the sake of the pay-check.

In 1871 he was made professor of composition at the University of St. Petersburg, where by his own confession he bluffed consummately while learning his job. When he became an inspector of marine bands, he grew to know wind instruments so well that brasses and woodwinds later featured prominently in his orchestral scores. His wife, a concert pianist, was as ardent a minister as he of the gospel of national music.

He outgrew the school of Balakireff and became the leader of a new group consisting of his own pupils. Then the obliging Belaiev not only founded a publishing house to print, but a symphony orchestra to play their works. Korsakoff conducted the orchestra for many years, and also became a professor of composition at the St. Petersburg Conservatory. Orchestration was his passion,—his scoring is phosphorescent, sensuous, scintillating. The symphonic suites—*Antar*, *Russian Easter* and *Scheherazade*,—and the operas based on Russian legends,—*The Maid of Pskov*, *The Snow Maiden*, *Mlada and Sadko*,—have the quality of picture-books, illustrated in the style of Glinka, Liszt and Balakireff. He was recognized as an exceptionally gifted editor also, though his efforts to polish the writings of his friend Moussorgsky almost wrecked them.

During the revolution in 1905, Rimsky-Korsakoff was dismissed from the Conservatory for a time. He had written a letter in favor of severing the Conservatory from the Imperial Russian Musical Society, and had also advocated less police supervision of students. The authorities were enraged that the aristocratic Rimsky-Korsakoff should take such a revolutionary stand. For two months they forbade the performance of any of his works. They even refused to permit his opera, *Le Coq d'Or* (*The Golden Cockerel*) to be shown, though they reinstated him in his professorship. The opera, a satire on the stupidity of rulers and their advisors, too timely to be seemly, was not produced until 1910, two years after the composer had died.

◇◇◇◇◇◇◇◇◇◇◇◇◇◇◇◇◇◇◇◇◇◇◇◇◇◇◇◇◇◇

Gabriel Urbain Fauré

(fô′rā′)

b. PAMIERS, FRANCE, MAY 12, 1845 *d.* PARIS, NOV. 4, 1924

BEST KNOWN FOR HIS SONGS, Gabriel Fauré has exerted an unobtrusive but powerful influence on the music of his own country. *Clair de Lune* (*Moonlight*), *Les Roses d'Ispahan* (*Roses of Ispahan*) and *La bonne Chanson* (*The Good Song*) are titles chosen at random from over a hundred. Not only does the music of these songs fulfil the poetic promise of the titles, but the songs themselves are models of economy, melody and harmonic inventiveness. Chamber music works of classic elegance, church music, and graceful instrumental pieces support the assertion of Louis Laloy, the French critic, that "with him, the renaissance of French music began."

Like César Franck, he was a gentle, kindly, hardworking organist and teacher. The story of his life, after the completion of his musical training under Saint-Saëns at the Niedermeyer School of Religious Music in Paris, is a list of posts as organist in various churches. For the fifteen years from 1905 to 1920, he was the director of the French Conservatoire, where he had previously been a professor of composition. Among the pupils through whom his influence upon French music made itself felt were Georges Enesco, Nadia Boulanger, Maurice Ravel and Florent Schmitt. Fauré was made a member of the Académie, a Commander of the Légion d'Honneur, and, a year before his death, president of the Paris Section of the International Society of Contemporary Music. Paul Dukas wrote that Fauré's music is proof that an original mind can avail itself of traditional musical forms, and without doing them violence, use them to convey contemporary ideas.

Paul Marie Vincent Théodore D'Indy

(dăn′dē′)

b. PARIS, MARCH 27, 1851 *d.* THERE, DEC. 3, 1931

WHEN CÉSAR FRANCK DIED, his pupil Vincent D'Indy became his musical heir. In his youth, D'Indy roamed alone the forests of Ardèche surrounding the family estate, and developed the mysticism which endeared him and Franck to each other. At nineteen, he served in the army during the Franco-Prussian War. Almost his first act when he returned to civilian life was to visit Franck and tremblingly show him a string quartet. On the strength of the kindly criticism it received, he enrolled as a pupil and became Franck's most devoted disciple.

An erudite scholar, D'Indy published, besides his music, critical essays, biographies of Beethoven and Franck, and a *Cours de Contrepoint* (*Counterpoint Course*), a valuable textbook. The works which are most often played are the *Istar Variations*, *Jours d'été à la Montagne* (*Summer Days on a Mountain*), and *Symphonie sur un chant montagnard français* (*Symphony on a French Mountain Song*). Though he wrote chamber music and operas, his orchestral compositions are more successful. He often employed Franck's idiom, and also piled on effects in the stormy style of Berlioz and Wagner.

In the summer of 1873, he visited Liszt in Weimar, met Brahms in Vienna, and so placed his finger firmly on the pulse of European music, from which he never afterward lifted it. He conducted orchestras in many European cities, and was instrumental in founding in Paris the Schola Cantorum, where masterpieces of Monteverdi, Rameau, Gluck and Bach were revived at his initiative. He was a founder and director of the Société Nationale de la Musique (National Society of Music) which educated young French composers and helped them to a production of their works. As an officer of the Légion d'Honneur, and inspector of musical instruction in Paris, he was a power in education. He died at eighty, a musician who believed that "the creative flame finds its nourishment only in Love, and in a fervent enthusiasm for beauty, truth and the pure ideal."

◇◇◇◇◇◇◇◇◇◇◇◇◇◇◇◇◇◇◇◇◇◇◇◇◇◇◇◇◇◇◇◇

Engelbert Humperdinck

(hŏŏm′pĕr-dĭngk)

b. SIEGBURG, GERMANY, SEPT. 1, 1854

d. NEUSTRELITZ, GERMANY, SEPT. 27, 1921

WHILE HE WAS STILL A STUDENT at Cologne Conservatory, young Humperdinck won the Frankfort Mozart prize; in Berlin he carried off the Mendelssohn, and later the Meyerbeer prize. Enabled thus to study further, he went first to Naples, where he met Wagner and accompanied him to Bayreuth to help prepare the production of *Parsifal* in 1882. He traveled then in Italy, France and Spain, and taught in Barcelona for two years before returning to Germany. In 1893, his opera *Hänsel und Gretel* transformed a music teacher who composed a little into a famous composer. *Hänsel und Gretel* was given in Weimar, London and New York in rapid succession, and was as popular with grownup children as with the younger ones at whom it was directed.

There are those who know only the touching Children's Prayer which was for several years the signature of a well-known radio program; there are others who have been familiar with every note of the entire opera since their childhood. It is the accepted first opera for future opera fans, who are drawn to its delightful melody and humor, and the simplicity with which the time-worn fairytale is revealed in music. Admiration of its masterly scoring and subtle musical characterization is reserved for more sophisticated listeners.

Königskinder, in 1896, *Dornröschen*, in 1902, and other operas did not exert the special charm of *Hänsel und Gretel*, which was to Humperdinck a form of life insurance that assured him of immortality.

◇◇◇◇◇◇◇◇◇◇◇◇◇◇◇◇◇◇◇◇◇◇◇◇◇◇◇◇◇◇◇◇◇◇◇◇◇

John Philip Sousa

(sōō′-sa)

b. WASHINGTON, D. C., NOV. 6, 1854

d. READING, PA., MAR. 6, 1932

JOHN PHILIP SOUSA, band-master and composer of marches that stirred the world, earned his title of March King by life-long service. His father, a Spanish musician of whom Sousa said that "he knew everything except how to make a living," was a member of the U. S. Marine Band, and John learned to manipulate every instrument that blows before he took up the serious study of piano, violin, harmony and instrumentation. Until he was twenty-six, he served an apprenticeship in theater orchestras in and near Washington. Then he was appointed conductor of the U. S. Marine Band. It became his guinea-pig, which he vivisected in the interest of music. When he resigned, after twelve years, he had made it more than a band worth listening to. He had learned by experience how to draw beautiful sound instead of blare and blast from a brass band. When he organized his own band, he cut down on brass and percussion instruments and increased the woodwinds, he added a harp, and he instructed his men that playing "not good but awful loud" would get them nowhere musically. By concentrating on musical finesse, he built up the famous Sousa band, an organization able to perform programs as varied as any symphony orchestra's. With it, he toured the world. In immaculate white suit, his black goatee going up and down as his baton rose and fell, he became a familiar figure everywhere. His chest gleamed with decorations bestowed by monarchs with no appetite for highbrow music, who responded enthusiastically to Sousa's programs. Their Majesties enjoyed his marches—*Semper Fidelis, Stars and Stripes Forever, Hands Across the Sea, The Washington Post, King Cotton.* They beat time to *Smoky Mokes* and other ragtime. Sometimes he slipped in a bit from one of his dozen or so light operas—*El Capitan, The Smugglers, The American Maid,*—or a song or suite of his own. He had over two hundred Sousa compositions to choose from. In his book on band instruments, and his autobiography, *Marching Along,* he gives the world the benefit of his rich musical experience. In it he also tells us that he enjoyed trapshooting, riding, long walks, and most of all, friendships. Five presidents and any number of Pullman porters were among those who mourned him when he died after a banquet in his honor. His marches served the U. S. forces in the Spanish American war and in the First World War, and are again sending young men to their grim duty. Heroism to the beat of a Sousa March is in the best American tradition.

◇◇◇◇◇◇◇◇◇◇◇◇◇◇◇◇◇◇◇◇◇◇◇◇◇◇◇◇◇◇

Ernest Chausson

(sho-sôn′)

b. PARIS, FRANCE, JAN. 21, 1855

d. LIMAY, FRANCE, JUNE 10, 1899

ERNEST CHAUSSON died in mid-career, leaving many things unsaid. But his *Poème* is a "must" for violin artists, and his exquisite songs and passionate chamber music are islands of beauty on concert programs.

He was a sensitive, introspective young man, much inclined to melancholy. It was natural, then, that when he came to write music, he should make it an outlet for emotions for which he had no words. The simplicity, refinement and purity that he developed while a student of César Franck, moderated without destroying the spontaneity of his utterance. His *Poème* is so intensely expressive that it is like a cry of pain.

After his student days at the Conservatoire, he devoted all his time to composition. For ten years he served as secretary of the Société Nationale de la Musique, and was one of its most active promoters. To the young composers who drifted in and out of his office, he preached Franck's ideal of pure music, which he also practiced. When he was killed in a collision while bicycling, France lost one of the most gifted and promising of the Franck disciples.

◇◇◇◇◇◇◇◇◇◇◇◇◇◇◇◇◇◇◇◇◇◇◇◇◇◇◇◇◇◇◇

Sir Edward Elgar

(ĕl′gĕr)

b. BROADHEAD, ENGLAND, JUNE 2, 1857 — *d.* WORCESTER, FEB. 23, 1934

SOMEONE ONCE STATED that Elgar, typical English gentleman that he was, wrote "the sort of music that gives the composer the degree of Mus. Doc. from an English university." And it is true that Elgar, post-Victorian England's pride and joy, though decorated repeatedly on home territory, and officially honored abroad, never took very well with audiences outside of his own country.

The son of an organist, he learned in his youth to play the organ and other instruments, picking up much of his knowledge by himself. He succeeded his father as a church organist in Worcester, and became a member or leader of various bands. His life as a composer started in earnest with his marriage in 1889. Lady Elgar was so truly his best pal and severest critic, that her death in 1920 silenced him as completely as her presence beside him had made him eloquent.

His is a real success story. His first recognition was due to the *Enigma Variations*, a brilliant piece for orchestra in which each variation is a portrait of one of his friends. Guessing which friends were portrayed became an immensely popular game with audiences, who enjoyed the combination of music with mental exercise. Later, on the strength of a *Coronation Ode* for King Edward in 1902, he became *Sir* Edward. He wrote six military marches, *Pomp and Circumstance*, one of which, sung as "Land of Hope and Glory," has become as popular in England as "God save the King," and carried his name all over the world. When his first symphony appeared in 1908, it received ninety performances within the year. *The Dream of Gerontius*, an oratorio, was esteemed by the English at the Birmingham Festival as excellent Elgar, and provoked words of praise from the German composer Richard Strauss. The Elgar *Violin Concerto*, Introduced by Kreisler, created a sensation. An Elgar festival in England marked his seventy-fifth birthday. On tours of Europe and the United States as guest conductor, he was everywhere fêted and honored. And so, when he died, and was buried beside Lady Elgar in

Malvern, England mourned the most successful English composer of the nineteenth century.

◇◇◇◇◇◇◇◇◇◇◇◇◇◇◇◇◇◇◇◇◇◇◇◇◇◇◇◇◇◇◇◇◇◇

Giacomo Puccini

(pōōt-chē'nē)

b. LUCCA, ITALY, DEC. 23, 1858

d. BRUSSELS, BELGIUM, NOV. 29, 1924

TO SPEAK THE NAME OF PUCCINI is to recall with a glow of pleasure his most widely sung operas,—*Manon Lescaut*, *La Bohème*, *Madame Butterfly* and *La Tosca*,—and perhaps, after a moment, *The Girl of the Golden West*, *Gianni Schicchi* and *Turandot*. This is the sort of music which makes of every audience one big happy family of music-lovers. It is not written for those few who are in the know. It has no self-conscious pretensions to grandeur. It is ardent and spontaneous, its tuneful songs and skillful orchestration smoothly joined to the drama with a sense of theater not surpassed even by Verdi.

Puccini once said, "Just think of it, if I hadn't hit on music, I should never have been able to do anything in the world!" Since there were musicians in his family, his becoming one was no miracle, but he was twenty-two before a grant from Queen Margherita of Italy and some other assistance paid his way through the Milan Conservatory. His teacher, Ponchielli, persuaded him when he was graduated to submit his first opera, *Le Villi*, in a competition. It did not win the hoped-for prize, but it induced the publisher Ricordi to take a chance and commission the young composer's next opera. *Edgar* took him five years to write and then it was a failure. With *Manon Lescaut*, however, Puccini made a tremendous success. It was the first of a flock of operatic geese that laid golden eggs for their master. Had he not suffered from librettist trouble and lost much precious time looking for suitable libretti and people to write them, his flock might have been bigger. When he found two congenial men to work with him, he composed *La Bohème*, which Toscanini conducted at its première in Turin. Its exceptional charm has placed it, along with Gounod's *Faust* and Bizet's *Carmen*, in the repertory of every opera company with any regard for the wishes of its patrons.

Puccini was a sportsman who loved hunting, fishing and motoring on his enormous estate. Among his friends he had a great reputation for wit, but in large companies he was silent. When he came to New York to superintend the production of *The Girl of the Golden West* he found American hospitality rather overwhelming, but it did not turn his head, any more than did wealth and success which he enjoyed in whole-hearted Italian fashion. Mussolini made him a member of the Italian Senate, and when he died, gave him as big a state funeral as though he had been a politician. More politic than Toscanini and other anti-Fascist Italians, he must have been.

◇◇◇◇◇◇◇◇◇◇◇◇◇◇◇◇◇◇◇◇◇◇◇◇◇◇◇◇◇◇

Ruggiero Leoncavallo

(lā'ôn-kä-väl'lô)

b. NAPLES, ITALY, MARCH 8, 1858

d. MONTECATINI, ITALY, AUG. 9, 1919

LEONCAVALLO'S TWO-ACT OPERA, *I Pagliacci* (*The Clowns*) usually forms one part of a bill of which *Cavalleria Rusticana* is the other. Both represent the only significant contributions of their respective composers. As Bellini and Donizetti were to Rossini, so were Leoncavallo and Mascagni to Puccini. The difference was one of degree, not kind, in the lyric-dramatic-emotional-Italian form of entertainment they provided. At their best, these composers were very very good, but they were at their best only once.

Leoncavallo had a bad time after his graduation from the Naples Conservatory. The impresario who had flatteringly contracted to produce his first opera, *Chatterton*, took French leave with all his funds. Stranded and penniless, the composer was reduced to playing the piano in cafés. He traveled wherever the job led into France, England, Germany, Holland, even Egypt. When he returned to Italy, the publisher Ricordi gave him a contract for an opera, but still his hard luck persisted. Publication was delayed on one pretext or another long after the music of *I Medici* was completed. So he took his next opera, *I Pagliacci*, to a rival publisher, Sonzogno. It was produced at once, and was immediately successful. *The Prologue*, the aria *Vesti la giubba*, and other arias caught on rapidly. The composer was solvent at last. He wrote his own libretti, and thus escaped one trouble, but he had plenty of others. He accused Puccini of plagiarism when Puccini's *La Bohème* was playing to crowded houses while Leoncavallo's version of the same story was being given the cold shoulder. Puccini disregarded the accusation, and left the decision to posterity. Leoncavallo's is forgotten, as are the very names of his other operas. His reputation rests on *I Pagliacci* alone.

Victor Herbert

(hûr′bĕrt)

b. DUBLIN, IRELAND, FEB. 1, 1859

d. NEW YORK, U. S. A., MAY 26, 1924

VICTOR HERBERT'S OPERETTAS are enjoying a second lease on life, thanks to the screen and radio, which are introducing them to a whole new generation. Of the genial cellist and bandmaster it was said that he could write music to any words, even to a telephone directory if put to it, and he nearly proved the truth of this extravagant statement by the ease with which he set texts that were good, bad and indifferent. He was twenty-seven years old when he came to this country, bringing with him his wife, his cello, and a sound German musical training. All three were turned to account when he became first cellist at the Metropolitan Opera, and his wife was engaged there as a singer. A number of such posts kept the pot boiling for some years before he felt free to devote himself to composition. As bandmaster of the Twenty-second Regiment of the National Guard, conductor of the Pittsburgh Symphony Orchestra, and soloist at many concerts, he led a busy life.

When he settled in New York to compose in good earnest, he had a wouldbe soundproof apartment built to serve as a studio. His efforts to shut out the noises of the city proved fruitless, save as they provoked goodnatured spoofing from the newspapers, but fortunately he was not deterred from composition. He wrote one operetta after another. *Naughty Marietta*, *It Happened in Nordland*, *Babes in Toyland*, *Mlle. Modiste*,—there are forty titles, some of which are familiar to practically everyone. Jazz apparently did not appeal to him, for there is no trace of it in his work, but his music is so tuneful that jazz is not missed. Gay and singable, soundly conceived and written, it makes friends everywhere. Two grand operas, *Natoma* and *Madeleine*, and other serious works caused the operettas to shine the brighter by contrast.

Gustav Mahler

(mä′lẽr)

b. KALISCHT, BOHEMIA,
JULY 7, 1860

d. VIENNA, AUSTRIA,
MAY 18, 1911

GUSTAV MAHLER'S AMBITIONS were monumental. His industry was equally so, but though in the eyes of the world he became a successful composer and conductor, he was never satisfied with the results of his efforts.

He was the son of a struggling Jewish tradesman who stretched the budget to give him an excellent education. At four, the boy displayed musical talent when he played by ear on the accordion the soldiers' marches he heard issuing from the nearby garrison of Iglau. By the time he entered the conservatory of Vienna in 1875, he was already a fine pianist, and a strange person, who walked in his sleep and went into sleep-like trances during his waking hours. His admiration for his teacher, Bruckner, and for Wagner, and the offer of a cash prize induced him to attempt an opera, *Das Klagende Lied* (*The Song of Woe*). It failed, and he turned to conducting as a means of livelihood.

Though he wanted above all to write music, he

became one of the world's finest opera conductors, and was promoted ever higher, until he reached the summit of a conductor's ambition, the directorship of the Imperial Opera in Vienna. To do so, he became a Catholic, and sincerely so, his Second Symphony being an expression of the Resurrection. He applied his perfectionist ideas to the opera in Vienna, and virtually revolutionized modern opera production. This achievement did not save him. Jealous rivals intrigued against him, until they succeeded in depriving him of his post, and what was worse, of his health and his poise. The heart trouble from which he suffered was greatly aggravated by this misfortune.

Despite his ill-health, he accepted an offer to conduct at the Metropolitan Opera in New York. He wanted to earn enough to live in comfort with his wife and child. Later he reorganized and conducted the New York Philharmonic Orchestra. He worked like a dog, and was treated like one by the public and critics, who failed to understand what the supersensitive, misanthropic little man was driving at. During a concert, in 1910, he collapsed on the platform. He was taken back to Vienna to die.

He wrote beautiful songs, notably his *Kindertotenlieder* (*Funeral Songs for a Child*), but he is best known for his symphonies. Ten symphonies, characterized by a restlessness expressive of his spiritual turmoil, and by a startling prodigality of instruments, came from his pen, or rather from his tortured soul. He was a master especially in the use of the horn, and other brasses and wood-winds. His symphonies are very long. Some have six movements instead of four, several make use of a solo singer and chorus. Like their composer, they cannot be loved except by the few who are willing to make the effort required to know them well.

◇◇◇◇◇◇◇◇◇◇◇◇◇◇◇◇◇◇◇◇◇◇◇◇◇◇◇◇◇◇

Hugo Wolf

(vôlf)

b. WINDISCHGRÄTZ, LOWER STYRIA, MARCH 13, 1860 *d.* VIENNA, AUSTRIA, FEB. 22, 1903

HUGO WOLF is the "temperamental" composer celebrated in fiction. When in the grip of an uncontrollable force, he had to write music or go mad. When that force left him for months at a time, he was struck dumb, and could only write despairingly: "I have given up all idea of composing. Pray for my poor soul."

His early years were a bitter struggle against ill-health and poverty, and a fiery temper and impatient spirit did little to bring him friends.

When he was fifteen he met Wagner, and fell completely under that hypnotic spell. A few years later, he went to Salzburg to take a position in the orchestra there, carrying in his modest bundle as his most prized possession a plaster bust of his idol.

Although he attended the Conservatory of Vienna, he was too impatient to complete the course. He preferred to pursue his musical education in his own way. On the park benches of the Prater, or in the library, he pored over the scores of the great masters. He got a bare living from odd jobs none of which he was able to hold for long. At different times he taught, wrote musical criticism, and played in an orchestra. The best of his songs were written between his twenty-eighth and thirty-third year. Gradually they became known, and brought him friends and a little money, but not before he had endured all the miseries of extreme poverty.

Fortunately, he could always take refuge from a niggardly world in poetry. To Wolf, the poem was the thing, music the means of enhancing it. He would read aloud chosen verses, over and over, until their inner music sang in his soul; then he would do his best to set down that music, making an agonized effort to catch and transfix its subtle beauty. He would lock himself up for days at a time, to emerge red-eyed, unshaven, and ravenously hungry, with a sheaf of songs under his arm. Moericke, Eichendorff, Goethe, Paul

Heyse, and Gottfried Keller were the poets he turned to. The piano accompaniments were an important part of every song; rich piano harmonies dominated without drowning the voice which declaimed the poem. In fact, he called one large volume *Songs for Voice and Piano*, instead of *Songs with Piano Accompaniment.* He wrote one complete and one unfinished opera and some other works, but his genius was unquestionably for song. His two hundred and seventy-five Lieder represent the high point of modern song writing, and place him in the worthy company of Schubert, Schumann, Franz and Brahms.

To the outside world he died at thirty-seven, when he became violently insane. He was placed in a sanitarium, from which he was discharged as cured, only to be confined again after a few months of freedom. Five miserable years passed before death brought peace to his uneasy spirit.

◇◇◇◇◇◇◇◇◇◇◇◇◇◇◇◇◇◇◇◇◇◇◇◇◇◇◇◇◇◇◇◇◇◇◇

Isaac Manuel Francisco Albéniz

(äl′bâ-nēth′)

b. CAMPODON, SPAIN, MAY 29, 1860 *d.* CAMBO-LES-BAINS, FRANCE, MAY 18, 1909

UNTIL HE STARTED to study music seriously, Albéniz strongly resembled Peck's bad boy. Every once in a while, he ran away from home, and had to be rescued from some childish escapade. His father took the troublesome six-year-old, who was a pianist, as well as a problem child, to apply for admission to the French Conservatoire. The judges were in the act of praising his performance, when the boy whirled around on the piano stool, drew a hard ball from his pocket, and threw it full force at a mirror in the room. The crash which destroyed the mirror also shattered his hopes of admission. He stowed away on a boat to South America, and vagabonded about, playing the piano in cafés, until his twelfth year. Then his father wrote him to come home. He entered the Madrid Conservatory. Later, a pension from his king paid his way through the Brussels Conservatory, and later still he took his exuberant talent to Liszt.

In 1880 he toured America in joint recitals

with Anton Rubinstein, and thereafter gave many successful piano concerts himself,—not in cafés this time. Between 1880 and 1892 he wrote about two hundred and fifty piano pieces for his own nimble fingers, including the swinging *Seguidillas* and the *Tango in D*. A short period of teaching on his return to Madrid convinced him that his was not the pedagogue's temperament. During a stay in London he composed *Pepita Jimenez*, his most successful stage work. Then, in 1893, he settled permanently in Paris. His wife, his three children, and his good friend and neighbor the Spanish pianist Arbos brought him such supreme contentment that he became enormously stout. With D'Indy, Dukas and Fauré, he followed the trend of music in France, and accepted the impressionism of Debussy with enthusiasm.

Although he composed a few operas, his piano music is his most lasting contribution. The suite *Iberia*, which consists of twelve pieces whose harmonies and rhythms vividly reproduce the charm of each of the Spanish provinces, is intensely national. *Catalonia*, *La Vega* and *Navarra* are loved for the syncopating castanets, the twang of the guitar and the shake of the tambourine that convey the folk flavor. He built upon the researches of his predecessors Barbieri and Pedrell; while Granados, De Falla and other Spanish composers who followed built upon his.

When Albéniz died, he was only forty-nine. His output was not large, yet his place in the twentieth century upswing of Spanish music is an important one, particularly in relation to the composers of his own country.

◇◇◇◇◇◇◇◇◇◇◇◇◇◇◇◇◇◇◇◇◇◇◇◇◇◇◇◇◇◇◇◇◇

Charles Martin Loeffler

(lĕf′lẽr)

b. MÜLHAUSEN, ALSACE-LORRAINE, JAN. 30, 1861

d. MEDFIELD, MASS., MAY 19, 1935

CHARLES LOEFFLER'S PARENTS were Alsatian, but his education was of mixed blood. When the family moved first to Russia, then to Hungary, their little Charles kept his ears wide open to music, especially the songs of the gypsies. Then he went to Berlin to study the violin with Joachim, and he wound up in Paris, which suited him best of all. He became a violinist in the Pasdeloup orchestra, and developed a permanent affection for the music of César Franck, Fauré, D'Indy and Debussy. The French poets Maeterlinck, Baudelaire, Verlaine and Mallarmé also became dear to him. At the same time, he turned back the clock several centuries, and studied Gregorian chant and plainsong.

In 1881, the blond, bearded giant came to New

York, and shortly thereafter became second concert master of the newly formed Symphony Orchestra in Boston. Through the years, several of his orchestral works were performed by his colleagues, and he was encouraged to devote himself entirely to composition. So he retired in 1905 to his farm in Medfield, Massachusetts, where he spent the rest of his life as a composer and farmer, and came to be known as the Sage of Medfield.

Loeffler wrote American music with a French accent. His most successful work, the *Pagan Poem*, was first performed several years after his retirement. It is a fantasy, a "rich and rare orchestral dress which covers a well shaped and vigorous body." There are other works in other moods,—a tender choral setting of the psalm *By the Waters of Babylon*, the orchestral *La Mort de Tintagiles* (*The Death of Tintagiles*), chamber music and songs. *The Hora Mystica* for orchestra and chorus, and the *Canticle to the Sun* contain themes taken from the plainsong the composer studied long and lovingly.

Loeffler is a significant figure in the twentieth century music of America. He touched dissonance, but was undefiled. He touched jazz with chuckling approbation, and late in his career wrote a jazz piece for the band of his friend, Leo Reisman. He could do this, he could go to Harlem for jazz inspiration. But then he would return to his firelit study in Medfield to meditate on poetry and mysticism, and to write French impressionistic music.

◇◇◇◇◇◇◇◇◇◇◇◇◇◇◇◇◇◇◇◇◇◇◇◇◇◇◇◇◇◇

Edward A. MacDowell

(măk-dou'-ĕl)

b. NEW YORK, DEC. 18, 1861 *d.* PETERBOROUGH, NEW HAMPSHIRE, JAN. 23, 1908

THE COMBINATION of Celtic ancestry, European training, and American environment plus an extremely gentle and receptive nature produced in Edward MacDowell a performer and composer of more than usual gifts. He started the study of the piano with a pupil of the fiery Venezuelan virtuoso, Teresa Carreño, and had a few lessons with Carreño herself when she visited New York. At fifteen, he won in competition a place at the Paris Conservatoire where, torn between equal talents for painting and music, he decided with difficulty to stick to the latter. From Paris, he went on to Wiesbaden, Stuttgart, and finally Frankfurt, where his studies in composition with Joachim Raff fired his ambition to become a composer. On the train rides back and forth from the lessons he gave to young suburban pianists, he prepared many works for the exacting Raff. One of his pupils—who complained at being assigned to so young and inexperienced a master—was Marion Nevins, whom he fell in love with and married.

The young couple spent three happy years in a vine-clad house in Wiesbaden before they returned to make their home in Boston. Although MacDowell was so shy he shrank from public appearances, he was too good a pianist to keep his fingers still, and too handsome besides, with his fresh coloring, deep blue eyes, and thick wavy brown hair. He performed his first and second piano concertos, and introduced the four sonatas which are considered among his finest works,—the *Tragica*, *Eroica*, *Norse*, and *Keltic*. Many of his piano pieces have descriptive titles, such as *The Eagle*, *Fireside Tales* and *Woodland Sketches*. Some, written for his students, are amateurs' delight, while others, like the *Twelve Virtuoso Studies*, are brilliantly difficult.

In writing songs, he sometimes selected poems he loved, sometimes wrote poems himself. Of his forty well-known songs, *Menie*, *Thy Beaming Eyes*, *The Robin Sings in the Apple Tree*, *The Swan Bent Low to the Lily*, and *The Sea* are among the best. The smoothly flowing melody for the voice is a genuine solo, the piano accompaniment is subservient and secondary. His piano works rank highest, his songs next, and his few orchestral works last. The *Indian Suite*, in which he employed as themes authentic Indian songs, is a fine example of his orchestral writing.

When MacDowell was invited to head the newly-created department of music at Columbia University in 1896, his eye lit up at the prospect of bestowing the gift of beauty on a new generation. But the crowded classroom was not like his own quiet study, and the bell which rang for the end of the class often interrupted him in the midst of an exquisite thought. Besides, dry matters of organization, intrigues and disagreements within the faculty disturbed him. He was a babe in the Columbia woods. When his resignation was finally forced, in 1904, his health was seriously impaired. An injury a few months later, when a cab struck him, brought on a complete mental collapse.

The last two years of his life he spent reading fairy-tales upside down or staring into space in his log cabin in Peterborough, New Hampshire. It was a tragic end for the composer who represents the high point of the romantic school in America.

Frederick Delius

(dē′lĭ-us)

b. BRADFORD, ENGLAND, JAN. 29, 1862

d. GREZ-SUR-LOING, FRANCE, JUNE 10, 1934

THE GERMAN-BORN PARENTS of Frederick Delius were so set upon his becoming a business man that neither of them ever would listen to one of his compositions, even after he became famous. Misled by the young man's professed desire to raise oranges in Florida, they staked him to an orange grove in Jacksonville. Once there, his first act was to buy a piano. Then, oblivious of whether his oranges ripened or not, he worked daily at music, with a local organist, Thomas Ward, as teacher. When his father next heard from him, after a lapse of time, he had deserted the oranges, and had gone to teach music in Jacksonville. He was retrieved and, since there was no way out, was sent to the Leipzig Conservatory. In 1897 he married a painter, Jelka Roszen, and made his home in a villa near Fontainebleau.

When the Germans invaded France in 1914, he took refuge in England, where his countrymen were just beginning to become aware that there was an Englishman named Delius who wrote music. His works were played and respected in Germany, but they remained almost unknown in France, his home for forty-five years, and were not recognized in England until the latter part of his life.

Delius became paralyzed, blind and helpless ten years before he died; still, he dictated music to his wife and his secretary until the very end. In 1929, he visited London, and attended in a wheelchair six concerts of his works conducted by his devoted admirer, Sir Thomas Beecham. It was his last visit to his native land.

Delius was the first English impressionist, as Debussy was the first in France. To compare them is not to place his inspiration on a par with the matchless Debussy's. His place in music has not been fully agreed upon, but he is undoubtedly one of the better English composers. *Sea-drift*, based on Walt Whitman's poem, the symphonic poem *Appalachia*, and the opera *Koanga* are reminiscent of his stay in the United States. *Brigg Fair*, *Summer Night on the River*, *On Hearing the First Cuckoo in Spring*, *In a Summer Garden*, and *North Country Sketches*, are English in the folksong, countryside sense. They are pictorial, and at the same time subjective in that they convey the composer's impressions of the scenes they describe. This combination is characteristic of Delius, and is coming to be better understood as his works become better known.

Claude Achille Debussy

(dĕ-bü-sē′)

b. ST. GERMAIN-EN-LAYE, FRANCE, AUG. 22, 1862 *d.* PARIS, MARCH 26, 1918

CLAUDE ACHILLE DEBUSSY, "musicien français," as he signed himself, was described by others as "un original—très exceptionnel, très curieux, très solitaire" (an original, very exceptional, very strange, very solitary). His poet friends Mallarmé and Verlaine; the women he loved—Gaby of the green eyes, Rosalie Texier, who became his wife, and Emma Bardac, to marry whom he divorced Rosalie—and his work, filled his life. The greatest of these was his work.

Destined for the navy by his father, he succeeded in switching to the Conservatoire. There he spent eleven years alternating between hot and cold, the chill disapproval of his unorthodox writings expressed by the authorities balanced by the satisfaction of winning prizes in spite of it. He studied improvisation with César Franck, and learned to play the piano with a "glancing touch" that had an unearthly beauty. He visited Russia, and found the music of Borodin, Rimsky-Korsakoff, and Moussorgsky a heathy antidote to

Wagner's. Then, when his cantata, *L'Enfant Prodigue* (*The Prodigal Son*), won the Prix de Rome, he went abroad. In Rome he met Verdi, Liszt and Leoncavallo, but became too desperately homesick to remain the allotted term. After his return he left Paris as seldom as possible. He composed at night, issuing forth for his constitutional during the afternoon, a striking figure, black-bearded, carrying a walking stick to ward off his pet hates,—crying children, ugly people and cats.

During the twenty years of artistic maturity after 1890 appeared most of the works which made him famous:—his one string quartet, a marvel of firm structure overlaid with shimmering sound; big orchestral works, *L'Aprèsmidi d'un Faun* (*The Afternoon of a Faun*), *Nocturnes*, and *La Mer* (*The Sea*); exquisite songs; and for the piano the *Children's Corner Suite* written for his little daughter Chou-Chou, the *First Book of Preludes*, and a great many others. His one opera, *Pelléas et Mélisande*, on which he worked for ten years, perfected an alliance of text, action and music such as no previous composer had achieved, though many had striven for it. *Pelléas* is unique, a silvery opera whose whispering understatement is a defiance of Wagnerian thunder.

During his last decade, he composed less, though the quality remained high. When the First World War broke, he was fifty-two, and already weakened by the cancer which eventually killed him. Deeply affected by the events of the War, he lingered for four painful years, and died while Paris was undergoing a heavy bombardment.

Debussy is the first great master of twentieth century music. He crusaded all his life for what he called French music—that is, music in the style of Rameau and Couperin, not of Weber and Wagner. He made original use of the whole tone scale introduced to him by the Russians, and of harmonies which his sensitive ear adjudged beautiful though contrary to rule. His plastic rhythmic patterns, and his disregard of conventional structure, are now admitted to be proper means to the end he had in view. He tried to convey in music the *impressions* excited by scenes and events, not the events themselves, and his music therefore is known as impressionistic. It has put a stamp on all French composers of the twentieth century, and on many from other lands.

Pietro Mascagni

(mäs-kän′yē)

b. LEGHORN, ITALY, DEC. 7, 1863 *d.* ITALY, AUG. 2, 1945

PIETRO MASCAGNI, composer of the operatic best seller, *Cavalleria Rusticana*, (*Rustic Chivalry*), hit the bull's eye just once, never again. But that once, he hit squarely in the center. *Cavalleria* won the prize in a competition sponsored by the Italian publisher, Sonzogno, in 1890. It became an international nine days' wonder, and the wonder continued long past the allotted nine days, even to the present.

Mascagni's early musical education was financed by his uncle in defiance of his father, who considered the law more dignified and lucrative. After the uncle's death, however, his father permitted Pietro to attend the Conservatory of Milan. He deserted formal study to become conductor of a traveling opera company, then married, and went to teach piano at the Municipal School of Music in Cerignola. When *Cavalleria Rusticana* made him famous overnight, he promptly gave up his obscure little job. He became director of the conservatory at Pesaro, and took long leaves of absence for extended tours, until a too-long visit to

America in 1903 cost him that job. But he composed fifteen more or less successful operas, of which *Iris* is the best known, while *L'Amico Fritz* and *Nerone* attracted mild attention. One and all lack *Cavalleria's* "brutal strength and insidious charm . . . and the blood-red spontaneity that has given it a mighty impetus," and made it a model one-act opera, an outstanding example of Italian verismo, or realism. He died at eighty-two.

◇◇◇◇◇◇◇◇◇◇◇◇◇◇◇◇◇◇◇◇◇◇◇◇◇◇◇◇◇◇◇

Richard Strauss

(shtrous)

b. MUNICH, GERMANY, JUNE 11, 1864 *d.* GARMISCH, SEPT. 8, 1949

AN INFLEXIBLE CLASSICIST in his youth, Richard Strauss at twenty went all overboard for romantic music, and took Liszt, Berlioz and Wagner for his models. He became the last of the German romanticists à la Liszt, and the first of the German realists in his own right.

A *Schneiderpolka* for the piano, composed when he was six, was one of the first indications of a powerful and precocious talent. His father, first horn player at the Munich court opera, gave him an excellent general and musical education, with stern insistence on the classic. When young Strauss became assistant conductor to Hans von Bülow in Meiningen, he met Alexander Ritter, the champion of romanticism. Ritter persuaded him that the two quartets, cello sonata, and symphony he had written to date were old hat. With a symphonic fantasy, *Aus Italien* (*From Italy*) in 1887, he made his transition to the tone poems for which he became famous.

Don Juan, *Macbeth*, and *Tod und Verklärung* (*Death and Transfiguration*) appeared in rapid succession. They are like Liszt's symphonic poems, greatly enlarged, and they employ the augmented orchestra and complicated harmonic structure foreshadowed by Berlioz. To these complex borrowings Strauss applied his prodigious virtuosity, and worked toward a musical language whose meaning would be open to all. He wrote musical motifs to characterize different people and episodes, and furthermore supplied a written program, which explained in words the broad humor, irony and satire, or the hysteria, rage and perversity depicted in his music. Realism was what he was after.

He won success without a struggle. He guest-conducted widely, and composed incessantly. In 1894 he married Pauline de Ahna, who was the prima donna in his first opera, *Guntram*. He turned out successively the tone poems *Till Eulenspiegel*, *Also Sprach Zarathustra* (*Thus Spake Zarathustra*), *Don Quixote*, *Ein Heldenleben* (*A Hero's Life*),

Sinfonia Domestica (*Domestic Symphony*) and *Alpensymphonie* (*Symphony of the Alps*). The bleating sheep and creaking windmills of *Don Quixote*, the crying baby and smashing china of the *Domestic Symphony* and other such pieces of photographic realism brought the critics down on the "triviality," "vulgarity" and "sensationalism" of these works, while healthy dissonances added little to their popularity. Today these works are accepted and applauded, and are even considered a little oldfashioned.

Strauss wrote over a hundred art songs, including the always satisfying *Allerseelen* (*All Souls' Day*), *Zueignung* (*Dedication*), *Ruhe meine Seele* (*Rest, my spirit*) and *Traum durch die Dämmerung* (*Dream at Twilight*). He turned his attention to opera, inspired by a visit to Bayreuth in 1891. After *Guntram* he wrote *Feuersnot*, *Salome*, *Elektra*, and *Rosenkavalier*. *Salome* and *Elektra* are somewhat grim but musically impressive; the light *Rosenkavalier* is the high point of his opera achievements. Since 1911 there has been a steady decline in the quality of his output.

When Stefan Zweig, who wrote the libretto for *The Silent Woman*, was banished from Nazi Germany, Strauss selected Joseph Gregor, a librettist presumably endorsed by the government, and produced two or three dull, stale and unprofitable operas. He has been criticized for his willingness to adapt himself to the new order in Germany. It does not seem in character that, at his comfortable villa in Garmisch, the greatest realist in Germany should have turned his back on that grimmest of realities, the Second World War. But so it appears. Though he composed until the day of his death, Sept. 8, 1949, he touched no heights, plumbed no depths, during those bitter last years.

◇◇◇◇◇◇◇◇◇◇◇◇◇◇◇◇◇◇◇◇◇◇◇◇◇◇◇◇◇◇◇◇

Jan Sibelius

(sĭ-bā′lĭ-o͝os)

b. TAVASTEHUS, FINLAND, DEC. 8, 1865

"HE WRITES MUSIC first of all to free himself of what is in his heart and brain and must out," writes Philip Hale of Sibelius. That makes him Finland's most personal, as well as most national composer. Like youth and age are the early symphonic poems *En Saga* and *Finlandia*, and the brooding, introspective symphonies of his later years. He emphasized national feeling in the early works by using melodies which resemble Finnish folksong, and subjects taken from the legends of the Fnnish epic, the *Kalevala*. In the symphonies, he is personal in something of the sense that Beethoven was,—that is, concerned with the philosophic solution of universal problems.

In his youth, he roamed the rugged woods near his home, with his violin under his arm, playing as the spirit moved him. He also improvised excellently at the piano. Yet, up to his second year at Helsingfors University, he expected to study law. When he decided to become a composer, there was no opposition from his family, who probably expected some such development. He transferred to Helsingfors Conservatory, and later went to Berlin. Upon his return to Finland, his name as the composer of *En Saga* was already known, and he experienced little difficulty in having his works published and performed. He composed songs, pieces for solo violin and piano, and a fine string quartet, *Voces Intimae*. These are more conventional than the orchestral works, of which the symphonic poem *Tapiola* and the four later symphonies are considered best. He wrote the *Fifth*, and planned the *Sixth* and *Seventh* Symphonies, when he returned from a visit to the United States in 1914 to find his country on the brink of revolution. A bombardment actually was going on within earshot of his study while he sat absorbed in his deliberate, careful labors. It was several years before these works were completed and published.

Sibelius has conducted at Scandinavian festivals in all the major cities of Europe. Outside of his own country, he is most popular in England and America. A pension from the government, which enabled him to devote himself to composition early in his career, was substantially increased on his sixtieth birthday. He lived quietly with his wife and daughters at his villa, Jarvenpää, near Helsingfors, until the Russian war of 1940, when he was spirited away to safety. Idolized by his countrymen, he is an "erudite, primitive, national modern," if not the Finnish Beethoven he aspires to be. He has that special kind of enlarged mysticism which is expressed in Fascism and which makes Wagner, also, a Nazi favorite.

◇◇◇◇◇◇◇◇◇◇◇◇◇◇◇◇◇◇◇◇◇◇◇◇◇◇◇◇◇◇

Paul Abraham Dukas

(dü'kä')

b. PARIS, FRANCE, OCT. 1, 1865 *d.* THERE, MAY 17, 1935

LONG BEFORE WALT DISNEY picturized Dukas' symphonic poem, *L'Apprenti Sorcier* (*The Sorcerer's Apprentice*), it was loved for itself alone. Dukas wrote this delightful music for a chuckling ballad by Goethe concerning a sorcerer's apprentice who plays at magic in his master's absence, orders the broom to carry water from the well, and, forgetting the formula for making it desist, is almost drowned in the ensuing flood. The animated rhythms, brilliant orchestration, and malicious satire of the music brought unstinted recognition of Dukas when it had its first performance in 1897.

He was not a one-piece composer, but his published output is small for a man of his industrious habits and long life. The fact is, that a short time before his death, having tried his works in the fire of self-criticism and found them wanting, he destroyed a large number of unpublished manuscripts. Judging from his opera, *Ariane et Barbe Bleue* (*Ariadne and Bluebeard*) (which bears comparison with Debussy's *Pelléas*), his poem-ballet *La Péri*, and several others noteworthy for mastery of orchestration, classic polish and refinement of style, he may have been over hasty in his decision.

Dukas was a highly cultured man. Not content with seven years at the Conservatoire (1882–1889), which culminated in his winning a second Prix de Rome, he sought more study, and found it, surprisingly, while doing military service. He detested the routine drill so heartily that he escaped whenever he could to study scores, which for him held all the fascination of a thrilling mystery story. When he left military service, he composed *Polyeucte*, a brilliant overture, which was followed with a *Symphony in C major*, and a year later with the inimitable *Apprenti Sorcier*. A masterly *Sonata*, and *Variations Prelude and Finale on a Theme by Rameau* are piano works which survived his self-imposed Burning of the Books. He also wrote penetrating musical criticism for leading French periodicals.

He taught at the Conservatoire from 1909 until

his death, and also at the École de Musique, where he influenced in the direction of classic simplicity and refinement the musical thought of a whole generation.

◇◇◇◇◇◇◇◇◇◇◇◇◇◇◇◇◇◇◇◇◇◇◇◇◇◇◇◇◇◇◇◇◇◇◇◇◇◇

Enrique Granados y Campina

(grä-ná′-dōs)

b. LÉRIDA, SPAIN, JULY 29, 1867 — *d.* AT SEA, MARCH 24, 1916

GRANADOS IS FAMED as the man who opened the ears of Europe to modern Spanish music, both to his own and to that of other composers. He became a successful pianist, thanks to the teaching of Pujol and Pedrell in Spain. When he went to Paris, ill-health prevented his regular attendance at the Conservatoire, but he studied privately with De Beriot. He toured widely with such artists as Thibaud, Manèn and Casals, playing Spanish music, especially his own, and composing as he went. Although he was a Catalan, he seemed to have a sense for the dialect of every Spanish province, and to be able to fix in music the individuality of each. His first opera, *Maria del Carmèn*, was produced in 1898. A couple of years later, he founded the Society of Classical Concerts in Barcelona, and also founded and directed his own piano school the Academía Granados.

His four books of Spanish Dances, the symphonic poem *Dante*, his chamber music and piano works are distinguished for graceful stateliness, melody and a pre-Debussy style better suited than a more modern idiom to the traditional rhythms of Spain. It was in the two books of *Goyescas*, piano pictures suggested by the paintings of Goya, that he achieved his maximum of elegance and poetic charm. They are said to have created modern Spanish piano music. He converted them into an opera, *Goyescas*, which was to have been given at the Opéra in Paris in 1914. Because of the First World War, the performance was canceled, and not until 1916 was it produced at the Metropolitan in New York. The composer and his wife left their six children in Spain to witness the triumph of *Goyescas* in New York. Granados wrote a new *Intermezzo* to the opera for the occasion.

But the war followed his opera even across the seas. The composer embarked for home on the English boat Sussex, which was torpedoed by a German submarine. Both Granados and his wife were drowned.

Alexander Scriabin

(skryâ-bĭn′)

b. MOSCOW, JAN. 6, 1872 *d.* MOSCOW, APRIL 27, 1915

ALEXANDER SCRIABIN was a mystic impressionist, who used music as medieval flagellants used the lash, to whip himself into a religious ecstasy. He was a law unto himself when he translated his ecstasy into music, especially in the matter of harmony. He wrote many pieces without a fixed tonality. He crowded as many notes as possible into a single chord. One of his favorite chords is built in fourths, instead of the accustomed thirds. It is made up of C, F sharp, B flat, E, A, D. Try it on your piano. He called it the mystic chord, and employed it often enough to make it peculiarly his own.

Always a dreamer, passionately fond of music, he developed with little interference from the aunt and grandmother who brought him up. When they sent him to military academy, he devoted more thought to music than to military tactics. Finally he was permitted to transfer to the Moscow Conservatory. The rigid teaching of Taneieff and Arensky in composition was at variance with his own ideas, and he left without his diplima, though he won a gold medal for piano. Fortunately, Belaieff, Rimsky-Korsakoff's publisher, staked him to a concert tour and an annuity contingent on compositions published. He was an exceptionally sensitive pianist, and interpreted his own works perfectly.

He and his wife Vera Ivanovna, whom he married in 1897, gave many All-Scriabin two-piano recitals. Then, after a few years of teaching at the Conservatory, he set out on a long tour alone. A separation from his wife in 1905 turned him toward a new love, Tatiana von Schloezer, though Vera continued loyally to play his works in public. In 1910 he met Koussevitzky, then head of the Russian Music Publication Society. That befriender of young composers not only contracted for the publication of Scriabin's compositions, but performed many of them with his own orchestra. Scriabin visited the United States in 1907. When he imported Tatiana after his arrival, he created a terrific scandal. Many concerts were canceled, and his reputation suffered severely.

All-Scriabin recitals of piano pieces are given in an atmosphere of hushed devotion by his disciples. They have ten *Sonatas*, many *Preludes*, the *Piano Concerto*, and numerous impressionistic shorter pieces to choose from. Rachmaninoff has played many of them.

Scriabin's *Poème d'Extase* (*Poem of Ecstasy*), for orchestra, is most often performed, for despite repetitiousness that prolongs the ecstasy to the point of collapse, it has marked originality and freedom in many passages. *Prometheus* calls for a full orchestra, a color organ, and perfume,—a blending of three senses and of all senses for those who bring chocolates and wear soft furs to the concert hall. Scriabin was planning an epic work, *The Mystery*, in which he would embody his entire metaphysical philosophy. He had written as a prelude a cantata, *L'Acte Préalable* (*The Initial Act*), when all his metaphysical problems were resolved by death.

◇◇◇◇◇◇◇◇◇◇◇◇◇◇◇◇◇◇◇◇◇◇◇◇◇◇◇◇◇◇◇◇◇◇◇◇

Ralph Vaughan-Williams

(vôn wĭll′yămz)

b. DOWN AMPNEY, ENGLAND, OCT. 12, 1872

RALPH VAUGHAN-WILLIAMS LOVES "the lilt of the chorus at the music hall . . . children dancing to a barrel organ, the rousing fervor of a Salvation Army hymn, St. Paul's and a great choir singing in one of its festivals . . . the Welshmen striking up one of their own hymns . . . the cries of street pedlars, the factory girls singing their sentimental songs." He considers all this as truly folk art as its conventional country counterpart, and he ought to know, for he is, among other things, a folksong specialist.

He studied music at the Royal Academy in London, took his degree of Doctor of Music at Cambridge, and did supplementary work with Bruch in Berlin and Ravel in Paris. As he was under no necessity to earn a living, he was free to pursue his profession at a leisurely pace. He joined the English Folksong Society in 1904 and utilized some results of his researches in *Three Norfolk Rhapsodies* and other works for orchestra. The choral pieces, *Toward the Unknown Region*, and *A Sea Symphony*, were produced at English choral festivals. *A London Symphony*, now well known in this country through repeated performances, was given its first hearing in 1914, in England. The War put a stop to further performances at that time, and although Vaughan-Williams was forty-two, he served with combat troops until demobilization. Then, in 1918, *A London Symphony* was heard again, and a couple of years later it was presented at the first annual congress of the British Music Society, who pronounced it the most significant work composed by an Englishman. In his postwar writings, the use of old Tudor madrigals and church music, of Purcell tunes and old-time counterpoint strengthens the national quality.

He teaches at the Royal College of Music, and is president of the English Folksong Society. But he holds himself as free as possible from administrative entanglements, so that he can live quietly with his family in Dorking, and continue to compose. A big, genial Englishman, complete with pipe, walking stick and baggy clothes, he is an exponent of his expressed conviction that "if the roots of your art are firmly planted in your own soil, and that soil has anything to give you, you may still gain the whole world and not lose your own souls."

◇◇

Sergei Vassilievitch Rachmaninoff

(räk-mä′nĕ-nôf)

b. NOVGOROD, RUSSIA, APRIL 1, 1873 — *d.* NEW YORK, MAR. 28, 1943

THIS ARISTOCRATIC RUSSIAN was born on a large estate in Czarist Russia, but he lives today in democratic America. He is known here both as a piano virtuoso and a composer, for he made concert tours in America before ever he thought of making it his home.

During his years at the Moscow Conservatory he preferred the study of composition with Tanaieff to piano classes with Zvereff. When he was graduated, his opera *Aleko* won a gold medal, but the hopes thus raised were rudely dashed by the failure of his *First Piano Concerto* and *First Symphony*. For a time he went sour on music. Like one who has been disappointed in love, he plunged into dissipation. But he soon tired of so superficial a substitute for work. He sought help from a Doctor Dahl, who practiced auto-suggestion on him until he was himself again. The *Second Concerto* which marked his return to normal living and the beginning of his success, he dedicated to the doctor.

He was made manager and director of the Grand Theater of Moscow, and became one of the most celebrated musicians in that city. Tchaikowsky was his idol. They stood together in opposing the extreme nationalist school of Moussorgsky and his group, and Rachmaninoff turned his home into a sort of club for conservative composers. But he grew weary of his duties in Moscow, and took his wife and two daughters to Dresden. In a few months he had written the successful symphonic poem, *The Isle of the Dead*, the *Second Symphony* and the *First Piano Sonata*. American audiences knew him for the *C sharp minor Prelude*, which he had composed at twenty and had grown thoroughly sick of. He now wrote his *Third Piano Concerto* especially for a tour of America in 1909. It was a successful tour, and he received flattering offers to remain in America, but he refused them and returned to Moscow. Scriabin's death in 1915 moved him to vow romantically over the open grave to tour the large cities playing nothing but Scriabin.

The Revolution drove him from his homeland in 1918, never to return. His sympathies were uncompromisingly aristocratic; there was no place for him in Soviet Russia. From then on until the Second World War, he divided his time between Europe and America, touring constantly. From then until his death, on March 28, 1943, he made his home in New York, where he lived in dreams of the past, and wrote lyric sonorous pieces which have an old-fashioned charm, and which, perhaps, provide a valuable link between the romantic tradition of the past and the hard reality of the present.

◇◇◇◇◇◇◇◇◇◇◇◇◇◇◇◇◇◇◇◇◇◇◇◇◇◇◇◇◇◇◇◇◇◇◇◇◇

Arnold Schönberg

(shûn′-bĕrk)

b. VIENNA, SEPT. 13, 1874

"ADVENTUROUS, DARING, TIRELESS, INDOMITABLE" are the adjectives used to describe—not the Lone Ranger—but the mild-mannered, soft-spoken Arnold Schönberg. And all because, though performances of his music have been greeted with hisses and jeers enough to bring out the riot squad, he has dauntlessly fought to create a new form of music. "I am the slave of an internal power," he says quietly. It is a power that compels him to compose mathematically. He uses chords in fourths instead of thirds, themes with such wide spaces between one note and the next that they do not sound like tunes at all. He bases his writing on a twelve-tone system instead of the conventional scale. Form is as much a fetish with him as content has been with others. Audiences hearing his music for the first time ask, "Who's loony now?" But Schönberg is far from loony. His knowledge is enormous, his industry unwearying and his originality challenging.

He is practically self-taught. For schoolmates with whom he played the violin he composed little pieces. Then at sixteen he decided to become a musician; he went to Zemlinsky in Vienna, and from him learned the technique of composition. Mahler, whom he met at about the same time, encouraged him to stick to his artistic guns. He needed some such boost when his works were performed. So hostile were the demonstrations that in 1920 he founded in Berlin the Society for Private Musical Performances. The unappreciative public was barred from its doors.

But that same year, at the Mahler festival in Amsterdam, some of his works attracted more tolerant attention, and his fortunes began to mend. Zemlinsky's sister, whom he had married in 1900, died shortly before her husband's triumph when, on his fiftieth birthday, a celebration was given him at the Vienna Town Hall. That recognition procured him an invitation to teach in Berlin, and he remained at the Prussian Academy of Arts there until 1933, when he was dismissed from his position because music by a Jew was classed as Degenerate Art. He had long since renounced the religion of his fathers, but at this affront, he defiantly reaffirmed his faith.

He took refuge in America with his second wife, and is at present teaching in California. His pupils Alban Berg, Anton von Webern, and Egon Wellesz, have been eloquent interpreters of his ideas, many of which are expounded in his book, *Die Harmonielehre* (*The Teaching of Harmony*). In time these ideas may become as clear to the many as they are to the few who have studied them closely. Meanwhile, their novelty continues to attract the speculative interest and respect of specialists.

Charles Ives

(īvz)

b. DANBURY, CONN. OCT. 20, 1874

CHARLES IVES grew up in and with Danbury, Connecticut, which was a small town when he was a small boy, and became a modern city during his maturity. In the intervals of labors as leader of the town band, Ives Senior taught his son a great deal about music. If the boy later decided to invent his own musical alphabet, it was not because of ignorance of the established one. He studied also with Harry Rowe Shelley and with Dudley Buck, and topped off his training with a course under Horatio Parker at Yale.

Ives became a successful business man, active as a partner in a large insurance firm from 1906 until his retirement in 1930. At the same time, he attended every musical event in Danbury. He played the organ in the church, attended the performances of the town band, never missed selections rendered by local talent. When he began to write songs and piano works descriptive of the town, he included the wheeze of the harmonium, the squeaky and out-of-tune violin efforts, and the off-key singing, all of which, like the faults of one who is near and dear, he loved the more for their imperfections. To read an Ives score is a labor of love. Notes are dotted all over the page, and complex unfamiliar chords are strung along without being separated into measures. Ives often uses a strongly accented off-beat that resembles jazz though it isn't.

His second sonata for the piano, *Concord, Massachusetts, 1840–1860*, is in four movements entitled respectively *Emerson*, *Hawthorne*, *the Alcotts* and *Thoreau*. It expresses in twentieth century Ives terms the spirit of mid-century Concord. Paul Rosenfeld wrote of the *Finale* "It seemed music as beautiful, at the very least, as any composed by an American." And in a lengthy article, entitled *A Lonely American Composer*, Olin Downes not only praised this sonata, but recalled the "kick" in Ives' Symphony for Orchestra and Piano, performed in New York in 1927,—"music . . . characterized by a vitality, humor, pathos, and audacity which took the audience by storm." Ives, he said, is "a dreamer, yes. A weakling, no. An amazingly effective person, as his career, and above all, his complex scores show. . . . And, we understand, as American as Samuel Clemens."

Maurice Ravel

(rȧ'vĕl')

b. CIBOURE, FRANCE, MARCH 7, 1875 — *d.* PARIS, DEC. 28, 1937

RAVEL was born in a seacoast town close to the Pyrenees Mountains, and when the family moved to Paris shortly after his birth, some of the Basque folksongs of the region moved with them. The Basque influence is plainly to be seen in much of Ravel's writing, especially the comic opera *L'Heure Espagnol* and the *Rhapsodie Espagnole* for orchestra.

When the boy was twelve, his father placed him in the Conservatoire. He had not been a child wonder nor displayed any indecent enthusiasm for music; nevertheless he made rapid progress under such teachers as Gedalge, de Bériot and Fauré. His radical leanings toward harmonic combinations not in the textbooks kept him from winning the first Prix de Rome, though the judges could not withold the second prize. He tried again and again, until his elimination from the preliminaries at his third attempt roused such indignation that Dubois, the director of the Conservtoire, was forced to resign. By this time, the young composer had written the glittering *Jeux d'Eau* (*The Fountain*), and the *Pavane pour une Infante Defunte* (*Pavane for a dead Infanta*), both for piano, as well as a number of songs with orchestra. He had won his musical spurs without question,—or so one would think. But he was presented with even a single spur until several years later. Then works for piano such as *Miroirs* and *Gaspard de la Nuit*, for orchestra such as *Ma Mère L'Oye* (*Mother Goose Suite*), described as "lace-work with exquisite thoughts" and *Le Tombeau de Couperin* (*The Tomb of Couperin*) brought him recognition. Diaghileff commissioned a ballet, *Daphnis et Chloe*, which was performed in 1912. This gorgeously orchestrated piece displays Ravel's poetic imagination at its height. It is highly effective music, even without dancers.

The composer patriotically interrupted his career to drive an ambulance during the First World War. He went in, a high spirited, adventurous young man. He came back, after a few months, his hair streaked with grey, his outlook sobered, and his nerves in such a state that he was obliged to take a rest-cure.

After he resumed work, a ballet for Ida Rubinstein, *Bolero*, brought him world renown. Toscanini's remarkable performance introduced it to a wide public, and soon the *Bolero* throbbed everywhere. It was heard in concert halls, on radio programs, gramophone records, even juke boxes, and Ravel became the most popular composer in France. He was constantly compared with Debussy, but the resemblance is too superficial to be taken seriously. Both were impressionists, but each went his own way.

Like Debussy, Ravel remained in France as much, and traveled as little as possible. He was a bachelor, which was just as well, since his passion for collecting curios and cats would probably have driven a wife insane. In 1932 an automobile accident precipitated a nervous breakdown from which he never recovered. His thoughts were lucid, but his memory was gone, and so, too, was his creative power. He remained quietly in his villa at Montfort L'Amaury, near Paris, and died in 1937.

John Alden Carpenter

(kär′pĕn-tẽr)

b. PARK RIDGE, ILLINOIS, FEB. 28, 1876

CARPENTER ACKNOWLEDGES descent from the John Alden who, while wooing Priscilla for Miles Standish, provoked the famous retort, "Why don't you speak for yourself, John?" This John speaks poetically in music. Thanks to a musical mother, and a thorough course at Harvard University, he acquired a fairly fluent musical vocabulary; nevertheless he entered the family firm after graduation, and devoted his attention to mill, railway and boat supplies, taking time out to study composition with Edward Elgar in London, and with Bernard Ziehn in Chicago.

His songs in the romantic idiom, to Tagore's *Gitanjali*, and to Chinese poems, represent a side of his art which he realized more fully in a large tone-poem based on Walt Whitman's *Sea-Drift*. On the other hand, the diverting symphonic suite, *Adventures in a Perambulator* presents with considerable humor the impressions of an infant in its go-cart, whose resentment at the policeman's attentions to the nursemaid vies with his gurgling enjoyment of his nursingbottle and of the passing organ grinder. Of the same school are *Krazy Kat*, a jazz ballet describing the adventures of that comic-strip acrobat, and *Skyscrapers*, written for Diaghilev, the great Russian ballet impresario, in 1924. "Not for jest or satire is jazz used here," wrote Olin Downes, "but as a very serious idiom with which to express the enervating life we lead in the modern city."

Carpenter occupies an honored position among the older groups of living American composers, his humor, poetic insight and skilful craftsmanship a healthy influence on the younger men of today.

Manuel de Falla

(dā fäl′yä)

b. CADIZ, SPAIN, NOV. 23, 1876

d. ARGENTINA, NOV. 14, 1946

WHEN SPAIN WAS TORN by revolution in 1936, the friends of De Falla were deeply concerned over rumors that, as a Loyalist, he was in an insane asylum, his mind unhinged by the sufferings of his people, or that he had been shot by a firing squad, or had committed suicide. Another report had it that he was living in Granada as usual, and that as the foremost composer in fascist Spain, he had accepted from Franco the presidency of the Institute of Spain. The truth is that he escaped from his unhappy country, and is now living in South America, near Buenos Aires. His health is poor, and he is not composing at present.

De Falla knew that he wanted to be a composer when he returned from the first symphony concert he ever attended. He was seventeen at the time. He studied at the Madrid Conservatory, and made some tentative experiments in writing the *zarzuela*, the native type of comic opera. *La Vida Breve* (*Life is Short*) was awarded a prize by the Academy of Fine Arts, and shortly thereafter De Falla won a first prize in a contest open to all Spanish pianists. A couple of years later he went gaily off to Paris, resolved to make the most of a seven-day excursion ticket. He remained in Paris a year for each day of the ticket, poor as a church mouse, but rich in the friendship of such men as Debussy, Dukas, and Charpentier, especially Debussy, whose interest in Andalusian music matched his own.

When, in 1914, the World War dislocated the Paris he loved, he returned home. He made a thorough tour of Andalusia, gathering folksong as he went. Pedrell, the highest authority on Spanish folklore, had been his teacher, and he had absorbed Pedrell's enthusiasm. He collected a great deal of thematic material before he settled down to cultivate the three S's—Solitude, Silence and Seclusion—which he considered essential for artistic creation. In his home in Granada at the foot of the snow-capped Sierra Nevadas, only the sound of tumbling waterfalls and perhaps an occasional church bell disturbed the silence. He lived alone, a bachelor and ascetic. Long walks over the hills, and occasional visits from close friends were his sole diversions. Two ballets *El Amor Brujo* (*Love the Sorcerer*) and *El Sombrero de Tres Picos* (*The Three-Cornered Hat*), and a piece for piano and orchestra, *Noches en Los Jardines de España* (*Nights in the Gardens of Spain*) were composed in Granada. They are by turns intimate, passionate, tragic, sorrowful, and gay, with all the wildness of Spanish gypsy music. De Falla is fortunate, too, in the expression of gentle emotions, as witness his *Concerto for the Harpsichord*, which he wrote for Mme. Wanda Landowska, and dedicated to her after she had visited him in Granada. His music is typically Spanish, yet carries a general appeal. The "dry flower" of the guitar keeps it moving, the song of the people keeps it living.

The last years of De Falla were most unhappy. He fled from Fascist Spain to Argentina, where he tried to forget politics in work. He was only partially successful, however, for he died, broken-hearted, before he was able to complete the orchestration of his magnum opus, the oratorio *Atlántida*.

◇◇◇◇◇◇◇◇◇◇◇◇◇◇◇◇◇◇◇◇◇◇◇◇◇◇◇◇◇◇◇◇◇◇◇

Ernest Bloch

(blŏk)

b. GENEVA, SWITZERLAND, JULY 24, 1880

THOUGH THIS GIFTED COMPOSER'S PARENTS were not musicians, they encouraged him to study the violin. Lessons with Jacques Dalcroze of Geneva, with the great violinist Ysaye in Brussels, and with Knorr in Germany fanned the creative fire in him; nevertheless Bloch as a young man was to be found traveling in Switzerland and Germany trying to sell Swiss cuckoo-clocks. But his mind was not on cuckoo clocks, and while still in his twenties, he had some works performed. When his opera *Macbeth* was produced at the Opéra Comique in Paris, in 1910, Romain Rolland and other critics wrote stoutly in praise of it, yet it was eighteen years before it was played again.

Bloch saw his great opportunity when Maud Allan, the English dancer, engaged him as her orchestra leader on a dance tour of America, in 1916. She left him stranded when the company went broke in Ohio, but he worked his way to New York. There he took a hall bedroom and awaited developments. Within two years, the Flonzaley Quartet performed his *String Quartet*, the Boston

Symphony his *Trois Poèmes Juifs*, the New York Friends of Music under Bodanzky put on an all-Bloch program and the Philadelphia Orchestra followed suit. Then his *Suite for Viola and Piano* won the Coolidge prize at the Berkshire Festival of 1919, in spite of the judgment passed upon its quarter-tones by a volunteer critic, "I really don't call that being *friendly* to music." Years of teaching for a livelihood ensued—at the Mannes School in New York, the Cleveland Institute of Music, the San Francisco Conservatory—until he was able to devote himself to composition without starving.

A vegetarian to please his wife, Bloch occasionally swallows a surreptitious beefsteak, and it may be the flavor of these that imparts to his music its red-blooded quality. Particularly is this noticeable in the pieces in which he strives to express "the venerable emotion of the Jewish race, that slumbers deep down in our soul." The world-famous *Schelomo, a Hebrew Rhapsody* for cello and orchestra, the *Israel Symphony* for voices and orchestra, and *Nigun*, a violin piece taken from his *Baal Schem Suite*, all of which were produced during his middle period, are Jewish music. He did not, however, confine himself to racial utterances. Between *America*, an epic attempt to compress into a symphony three hundred years of American History, and *Avodath Hakodesh*, the Jewish Sacred Service which he wrote in 1932, intervene a magnificent *Concerto Grosso* and *Four Episodes* for chamber orchestra, a piano sonata, and chamber music works. Bloch's passionate expression of human aspirations and frustrations has made many friends; the individuality of his harmonic idiom has puzzled some listeners. But his music is increasingly recognized in America, where its rolling-stone composer has at last come to rest.

◇◇◇◇◇◇◇◇◇◇◇◇◇◇◇◇◇◇◇◇◇◇◇◇◇◇◇◇◇◇◇◇◇◇

Béla Bartók

(bā'lȧ bär-tŭk')

b. NAGYSZENTMIKOS, HUNGARY, MARCH 25, 1881 — *d.* NEW YORK, SEPT. 26, 1945

THE MUSIC of Bartók has a powerful personality, a crisp strength strangely at variance with the outward appearance of the little composer who, like a sensitive plant, curls up and draws into himself at the lightest touch. The riotous rhythms, aggressive percussion, and dissonance of Bartók are pushing many composers toward the new trends which were inaugurated by Schönberg and Stravinsky.

He built his art upon folkmusic, which he began to hear and collect while very young. When he was eight years old, his father died, and he traveled about Hungary with his mother, a teacher who went from school to school. When the family settled in Pressburg, he plunged head over ears into musical studies, and into rapt attendance at operas and concerts. Afterward he entered the Royal Hungarian Music Academy in Budapest; Dohnányi, his composition teacher, and Kodály, his fellow student there are, with him, the outstanding composers of Hungary today.

After he had completed his studies, he started, with Kodály's assistance, to look for folk material other than the hackneyed gypsy tunes known to all. He learned to differentiate among Magyar, Slovak and Rumanian, and made a scientific study of the characteristics of each. Eventually, he had over six thousand examples, many of which he published in a volume, *Hungarian Folk Music*, and in small collections. He was recognized as a research musicologist before he was known as a composer, though a *Violin Sonata*, *Piano Quintet*, *Suite for orchestra*, and some other works had appeared. Educated in his own country, and using its native material, he wrote characteristic Hungarian music in his own idiom.

He became professor of the piano at the Budapest Conservatory, and with Kodály founded a New Hungarian Musical Society. By this time he was known in Europe, but his first success in Hungary was a stage work, *The Woodcut Prince*. He was unfortunate in his choice of a libretto for this, and for two others, *Duke Bluebeard's Castle* and *The Miraculous Mandarin*. But after his *Second String*

Quartet was performed in 1918, Hungary was proud of him. Many of his chamber music and piano compositions were played at the annual festivals of the International Society for Contemporary Music, of which he was an honorary life member. With his young and pretty wife, the white-haired composer made recital tours, and played many of his own compositions for one or for two pianos. Mr. and Mrs. Bartók took refuge in America from the New Order, and lived in Riverdale, New York, until the composer's death there, in 1945.

◇◇◇◇◇◇◇◇◇◇◇◇◇◇◇◇◇◇◇◇◇◇◇◇◇◇◇◇◇◇

Georges Enesco

(ĕ-nĕs′-cō)

b. DOROHOIU, RUMANIA, AUG. 19, 1881

FEW COMPOSERS living today command as much affection and respect as the Rumanian Georges Enesco. "Ask Enesco, he knows," say his colleagues. His musical memory compares with Toscanini's; he rarely refers to a score when conducting. Though he made his reputation as a concert violinist, he is in fact a one-man chamber music group, equally proficient on the viola, cello and piano. As a composer he is an outstanding national figure. His simplicity, lively intelligence, and sparkling wit have won him friends in the Rumanian court (where he was court violinist to Queen Carmen Sylva), and among the peasants of his home village, Cordaremi,—with men of high and low degree.

He walked away with all the first prizes in violin-playing at the Conservatory of Vienna and at the Paris Conservatoire. Immediately, he started gathering laurels on the concert stage, where his individual style of playing,—the enormously longdrawn bow, wide vibrato, and profound emotion, moved audiences deeply.

As a composer, he was successful at an early age. His *Poema Romana* was conducted by Colonne in Paris when Enesco was only sixteen, and a year later his *Fantaisie Pastorale* was played. He was nineteen when he composed the *Rumanian Rhapsodies* for orchestra, which contain the gypsy essence of Rumania, and which he has conducted with orchestras all over the world. His *Symphonie Concertante* caused him to be singled out as "the most modern of contemporary composers." He has founded a National Prize for works by young Rumanian composers, and has given generously to all kinds of national enterprises. He teaches a picked group,—Yehudi Menuhin is his prize violin pupil.

He married, when he was over fifty, the woman he had loved devotedly for twenty years. His home is in Paris; his opera, *Oedipe*, was triumphantly produced there in 1936. Since the fall of France, Enesco has been sunk in melancholy, his muse refusing to sing for the conquerors of his native and adopted countries.

◇◇◇◇◇◇◇◇◇◇◇◇◇◇◇◇◇◇◇◇◇◇◇◇◇◇◇◇◇◇◇◇◇◇◇◇

Igor Fedorovitch Stravinsky

(strȧ-vĭn′-skē)

b. ORANIENBAUM, RUSSIA, JUNE 17, 1882

THERE ARE TWO COMPOSERS in one Stravinsky, and those who like one are apt to dislike the other. There is the one who created a new idiom, employing folkmusic in ways so novel that his name was barked at every musical side show as "Stravinsky, the sensational." Then there is the Stravinsky born of the First World War and the Russian Revolution, who writes for an orchestra of few instruments, rations color and sloughs off modernism, and exchanges it for an eighteenth century directness in which there is only an occasional reminder of the other Stravinsky.

Educated in music but intended for the law. Stravinsky escaped to music by way of Rimsky-Korsakoff, who was sufficiently impressed with the nineteen-year-old's amateur talent to urge that he develop it professionally. He never got as far as the Conservatory, but he studied assiduously with Rimsky-Korsakoff, who was by turns pleased and annoyed with his protégé's original exercises. At twenty-four, Stravinsky married and became a composer, all in one decision. But when his teacher died, a couple of months later, he went all to pieces for a time. A fortunate meeting with Diaghileff charged his creative batteries anew. *The Firebird*, in 1910, was the first of an amazing series of ballets—*Petrouchka*, *Le Sacre du Printemps* (*Rites of Spring*), *Le Chant du Rossignol* (*Song of the Nightingale*) and others. These were Stravinsky's most sensational works; they set a new high in ballet music.

A change of style is foreshadowed in *L'Histoire d'un Soldat* (*The Story of a Soldier*), *Pulcinella*, and *Mavra*. He scaled down *L'Histoire d'un Soldat* to a narrator and seven instruments. Then, in the *Octet* for wind instruments, he abandoned the free style which had signified his escape from the concentration camp of German romanticism and assumed instead the classic detachment of the eighteenth century. The *Concerto* for piano and wind instruments, the opera-oratorio *Oedipus Rex*, the ballet *Apollon Musagète* (*Apollo, Leader of the Muses*), and the choral *Symphony of the Psalms*, followed the austere course of his choice.

His compositions have been popular in the United States, where he visited for the first time in 1925. His home was in St. Cloud, near Paris; he became a French citizen, and his wife and four children are more French than Russian. The Second World War drove him again to the United States, where he has found the friends and admirers without whom no place is home to Stravinsky.

◇◇◇◇◇◇◇◇◇◇◇◇◇◇◇◇◇◇◇◇◇◇◇◇◇◇◇◇◇◇◇◇◇

Karol Szymanowsky

(chĭ-măn-ŭv′skē)

b. TYMOSZKOWA, UKRAINE, SEPT. 21, 1883 — *d.* LAUSANNE, SWITZERLAND, MARCH 28, 1937

LIKE HIS COMPATRIOT CHOPIN, Szymanowski devoted his life to the cause of Polish music. Like him, too, he enjoyed a happy childhood on his parents' estate, though in boyhood he suffered an accident to his leg which kept him from attending high school for several years. He was obliged thereafter to use a cane, but the physical handicap did not retard his musical development. While a student at Warsaw Conservatory, he formed an organization called Young Poland in Music. When later he returned and made his home in Warsaw, after the Russian government had confiscated the family estates in the Ukraine, it was natural that the young composers should again look to him for leadership.

He was made director of the Warsaw State Conservatory and resigned that position only when the appearance of symptoms of tuberculosis obliged him to go to Switzerland.

In the meantime, he had composed a number of works. He went through a spell of German romantic music, then turned to the French impressionists, and finally developed a personal Polish language which derives from Chopin, but is peculiarly his own. The violin pieces *Fontaines d'Arethuse* (*Fountains of Arethusa*), *Notturno e Tarantella* (*Nocturne and Tarantelle*), the *First Violin Concerto* and others, he wrote for his friend Paul Kochanski, whose death in 1933 almost broke Szymanowsky's heart. For another friend, Artur Rubinstein, he composed piano works, including *Nine Preludes*, *Four Studies*, études, and mazurkas. The *Stabat Mater*, performed in 1928, was his first conspicuous success. The ballet *Harnasie*, composed that year, was a rousing nationalistic work which took its themes from the songs of the brigands of the Tatra Mountains.

Attendance at a performance of this ballet sealed the composer's death warrant. He had worked too hard at composing, and had moreover played the piano part of his *Symphonie Concertante* in public when he was far too weak for the effort. He had been resting in the south of France, and had made the trip to Paris especially for the performance of *Harnasie* at the Opéra. Afterward he collapsed. His doctors packed him off with his sister to the south of France, and later sent him to Lausanne. But his disease had progressed too far, and he died in the sanatorium there. His music marked the beginning of a Polish renascence which was cut short by the Nazi conquest and the resultant banning of Polish music.

◇◇◇◇◇◇◇◇◇◇◇◇◇◇◇◇◇◇◇◇◇◇◇◇◇◇◇◇◇◇◇◇

Hector Villa-Lobos

(vē′-yä lō′bŭsh)

b. RIO DE JANEIRO, MARCH 5, 1884

HECTOR VILLA-LOBOS, the foremost composer of Brazil, keeps his music untamed by preference. He was educated in Rio de Janeiro, and after his marriage at twenty-four to a Brazilian pianist, Lucilla Guimarâes, he toured his own country as a pianist. Wherever he went, he collected Brazilian folkmusic, and went so far as to cut his way into the jungle to capture the tribal tunes of its inhabitants.

He has spent much time in Paris since a visit in 1923, when a successful performance of his works there led to his appearance in Brussels, Barcelona and other cities as pianist and conductor. The International Society for Contemporary Music has given his works at several of its annual festivals. In Rio de Janeiro he founded and conducts his own orchestra, is Superintendent of Musical and Artistic Education, and the Big Man in Brazilian music. His book of folksongs, *Almo do Brasil*, brings together the raw materials from which he has already fashioned over one hundred and thirty compositions. "In his nature," says Irving Schwerke, "the quality of savage races and of exquisite civilized people meet." In his vehement, sensuous music, the quality of the savage predominates.

Jerome David Kern

(kûrn)

b. NEW YORK, JAN. 27, 1885 — *d.* BEVERLY HILLS, CAL., NOV. 11, 1945

THE MANTLE OF VICTOR HERBERT, Jacques Offenbach, and Arthur Sullivan is worn in America today by Jerome Kern, a modest man who is so little a self-advertiser that even those who most enjoy his music frequently fail to give him the credit for it.

Kern has turned the craftsmanship he developed in his studies with Paul Gallico, Alexander Lambert and Albert von Doenhoff, to making of the patchwork hodgepodge known as musical comedy, a unified entity. In a field where musicianship was not regarded as essential, he proved it could actually be a great advantage! The pay-off occurred when, as staff musician for a producer of English shows, he interpolated his own songs to liven up soggy British comedy. When he realized that the interpolations were more popular than all the rest of the show put together, he started out on his own. Seven operettas in one year, 1917, was his all-time high. *Very Good Eddie*, *Sally*, *Sunny*, *Have a Heart*, and *Show Boat* are some of his best. His influence on other composers of light opera has been consistently in the direction of more and better tunes, and an orchestral score that isn't ashamed to be heard. He moved to Beverly Hills, Cal., to write music for films. Like Old Man River in *Show Boat*, he "just kept rollin' along" until death caught up with him.

Serge Prokofieff

(prŭ-kŭf'yĕf)

b. EKATERINOSLAV, RUSSIA, APRIL 23, 1891

PROKOFIEFF is a Russian composer who had no ancestral estates and who has not fled from the Soviet régime, but has remained to become one of its prized assets. A massive cantata on the speeches of Lenin, Marx and other leaders, written for the twentieth anniversary of the October revolution, is one of his tributes to Soviet Russia. He writes with dynamic power and intense masculinity, in an idiom which varies according to the subject.

Since he was a noticeably talented child who composed at the age of five, there was never a question of his pursuing any career but music. Early instruction from Glière was followed by study at the St. Petersburg Conservatory,—in composition with Rimsky-Korsakoff and Liadoff, in piano with Essipova, in conducting with Tcherepnin. During his student years and afterward he composed an amazing variety of works. For example, at the very time he wrote his *Classical Symphony*, limpid as any by Mozart or Haydn, he produced a cantata, *Seven, They Are Seven,* which contains an astounding aggregation of dissonant chords and cross-rhythms in the modern manner. The naïveté of his charming musical fairy-tale of *Peter and the Wolf* contrasts mightily with the superb barbarism of his *Scythian Suite.*

During the First World War, he was exempted from military service, and so he could continue to compose while others fought. In 1921 he was married, and the following year he went to Chicago to witness the production of his witty opera, *The Love of Three Oranges.* Its overture is a favorite concert piece. He returned to take up his residence in Paris, where Diaghileff seized upon him and commissioned a ballet, then another and another: *Chout* (*Buffoon*), a grotesque humorous pantomime of two clowns; *Le Pas d'Acier* (*The Age of Steel*), a modernistic interpretation of the machine age, and *L'Enfant Prodigue* (*The Prodigal Son*). All were gorgeously produced in the Diaghileff manner; with the impresario's death in 1929, Prokofieff's ballet inspiration died also. During his stay in Paris, he wrote symphonies, piano concertos, and other works as well as ballets. His dramatic score for the film *Lieutenant Kije* is often played as an orchestral suite.

In 1934 he made his home in Moscow, where he remains save for concert tours in Europe and America. With his return to Moscow, he returned also to a simplicity in his style of writing foreshadowed in the *Classical Symphony.* To ruthless boldness and impish humor is added a lyricism which makes his works appear less fantastic, though still highly individual. Since the invasion of Russia, he has written marches and army songs, a symphonic suite *1941*, an opera *War and Peace* based on Tolstoi's novel, film music for *Lermontov* and *Ivan the Terrible* and other rousing pieces. "One would have guessed," says Aaron Copland, "that his musical style, so full of melodic invention and joie de vivre, would have been just what was needed in the Soviet Republics. And one would have guessed right."

◇◇◇◇◇◇◇◇◇◇◇◇◇◇◇◇◇◇◇◇◇◇◇◇◇◇◇◇◇◇

Darius Milhaud

(mē'yō')

b. AIX-EN-PROVENCE, SEPT. 4, 1892

IN THE PARIS of the First World War, a little group of composers who called themselves "Le Six" (The Six) enrolled under a banner lettered "Back to Simplicity." Around marble-topped café tables, they held long discussions, led by Erik Satie, a composer who believed that music needed to be jollied out of taking itself too seriously. He was somewhat older than The Six, who listened to him with respect, regarded his short, satiric pieces as works of genius, and did their best to follow his flippant example. Some of the results were downright silly, but by no means all. Since as a group they found a readier hearing and greater publicity than singly, they were content to be known as "Le Six,"—Darius Milhaud, Arthur Honegger, Georges Auric, François Poulenc, Germaine Tailleferre and Louis Durey. They dissolved their association because of a quarrel between Auric and Satie, but for a while they provided amusement and novelty for a post-war world badly in need of both. Poulenc, Honegger and Milhaud continue to play a part in the music of today.

Honegger, of Swiss parentage, was not long content with the tongue-in-cheek prescription of Satie. Flippant little pieces left him cold, though his music to the operetta *Le Roi Pausole* is very flippant and anything but cold. Opera and oratorio in the grand manner appealed to him much more. *Le Roi David*, an oratorio, and *Pacific 231*, a symphonic poem having a locomotive as hero, are his bestknown works. Poulenc attracted attention with his ballet, *Les Biches* (*The Darlings*), his clever piano pieces, and songs.

The acknowledged leader of the group is Darius Milhaud. Though, chameleon-like, he successively took on the colors of Debussy and French impressionism, Brazil and South American exoticism, of Stravinsky modernism, jazz syncopation and Satie-esque impishness, he nevertheless managed to retain a basic background color of his own. He is tremendously facile, and writes in every form, but no one work can be said to be characteristically Milhaud. He keeps audiences guessing.

His studies at the Paris Conservatoire were interrupted by the First World War, and he went for two of the war years as attaché to the French Legation in Rio de Janeiro. His *Saudades do Brasil* for the piano reflect the music he heard there and are deservedly popular. In Rio he met Paul Claudel, who became his librettist for a number of successful operas, such as *The Tidings Brought to Mary*, and *Christopher Columbus*. A setting for voice and orchestra of a florist's catalogue is among the startling works he continues to produce. He lectures, concertizes and teaches, and now makes his home in the United States, whose freedom appeals to a liberty-loving nature nurtured by the nontraditional "Six."

Paul Hindemith

(hĭn′dĕ-mĭt)

b. HANAU, GERMANY, NOV. 16, 1895

A PRACTICAL ARTIST is Paul Hindemith, who specializes in music made to order, saying, "A composer should write today only if he knows for what purpose he is writing." He coined the term *Gebrauchsmusik*, which can be variously translated as music for functional purposes, workaday, utilitarian. In his hands, *Gebrauchsmusik* ranges from a grand opera like *Mathis der Mahler* (*Matthew the Painter*), or a ballet like *Nobilissima Visione* (*The Vision of St. Francis*), to little teaching pieces, and music for children, for films, for a mechanical organ, for a harmonica. He writes jazz pieces, song suites and chamber music in any and every combination, an infinite variety with one thing in common—all are designed for immediate public performance.

He started as a practical musician, or at least, as a practicing one, at eleven, when he played the viola in cinemas, cafés and theaters. After a few years as concert master at the Frankfort Opera House, he organized with Licco Amar the Amar String Quartet, with which he toured as violinist until 1929. Much of his music was composed on trains, and introduced to the public by the quartet. The International Society for Contemporary Music performed, at the successive festivals of 1923, 4, and 5, his *Clarinet Quintet*, *String Trio*, and *Chamber Music No. 2* for piano and twelve solo instruments. He was appointed a teacher at the Berlin Hochschule in 1927.

By the time Hitler appeared, Hindemith had to his credit a large body of compositions, the recognized ability to play fourteen instruments, to conduct, and to teach, and a textbook he had written explaining his system of harmony, *Unterweisung in Tonsatz* (*Groundwork of Musical Composition*). All this, and his reputation, did not save him. In 1934, his works were banned. He was not banished from Germany, but, ever-practical, he preferred not to remain where he was gagged. For several years he has been in the United States, teaching and composing.

Streamline architecture and forthrightness are characteristic of Hindemith's music. At times, it is true, he is accused of dryness because of his preoccupation with form. And in some of his works, the lack of a central tonality is confusing. But his works have been a welcome antidote to German romanticism, the Old-Man-of-the-Sea persistently riding German music. His ideas are original and abundant,—his is unquestionably one of the finest creative minds that has appeared in the twentieth century.

◇◇◇◇◇◇◇◇◇◇◇◇◇◇◇◇◇◇◇◇◇◇◇◇◇◇◇◇◇◇◇◇◇◇◇◇

William Grant Still

(stĭl)

b. WOODVILLE, MISSISSIPPI, MAY 11, 1895

MANY NEGRO COMPOSERS have contributed to American music. Henry T. Burleigh, Nathaniel Dett, Rosamund Johnson, and William C. Handy are well-known names. One whose voice is being effectively lifted in serious music today is William Grant Still.

In his infancy he was crooned to sleep by his mother and grandmother with traditional slave songs and Christian hymns. As a small boy he amused himself making toy violins, an occupation that may have hastened his decision to become a composer instead of a doctor. He was trained at Oberlin College and the New England Conservatory; later he studied with the explosive Varèse in New York. At the start of his professional career, he became an arranger for jazz bands, and turned to serious composition as soon as the Harmon award and a Guggenheim fellowship made it financially possible. In his music all the elements of his varied background are mingled. He consciously uses a great deal of racial material, developing it in a modern idiom. Much of his output at present is for the theater, film or radio, and he lives with his wife and family close to the scene of action, in Hollywood.

The first Negro to write a significant symphony and conduct a major orchestra, he is extremely modest; in him racial pride goes hand in hand with intense personal humility. He dedicated his largest symphonic effort, which is regarded in Europe as a typically American work, "with humble thanks to God, the source of inspiration." Johann Sebastian Bach might have phrased that dedication. The *Afro-American Symphony* has four movements, entitled respectively *Longing*, *Sorrow*, *Humor* and *Aspiration*. They are introduced with verses by Paul Dunbar, the Negro poet, and over the finale, Still wrote, "Be proud, my Race, in mind and soul."

George Gershwin

(gûr′shwĭn)

b. BROOKLYN, N. Y., SEPT. 26, 1898   *d.* HOLLYWOOD, CAL., JULY 11, 1937

GERSHWIN AS A BOY was roller-skating champion of his block—a somewhat unconventional preparation for music. But at the first opportunity he took over a Brooklyn "professor" engaged to teach his brother Ira. George took Ira's lessons, on Ira's piano; Ira later got even by writing knockout lyrics to George's tunes. At sixteen, George found a job, with Remick in Tin Pan Alley, pounding out other people's song hits on the piano. He tried out little things of his own, too, until his song, *I Was So Young, You Were So Beautiful* brought him notice. He soon started writing musical comedies, with Ira scribbling words to his melodies. *Fascinatin' Rhythm*, *I Got Rhythm*, *Lady Be Good*, *The Man I Love* and *Clap Yo' Hands*, are some of the dozens of his popular hits.

The *Rhapsody in Blue*, which made him famous, he wrote in ten days. He clung to the manuscript up to rehearsal time, insisting almost tearfully that it wasn't good enough. Whiteman's terse comment after a first reading was "The damn fool, did he think he could improve it?" The *Rhapsody* leaped into fame, and remained the most popular work by any American. It was performed in concerts everywhere, and the gramophone and radio sowed it broadcast. George had made an honest woman of a social pariah; he had established an international reputation for symphonic jazz.

After that he started to take himself seriously. He went to Paris, and asked Stravinsky to teach him composition. Stravinsky inquired, "Monsieur, what was your income last year?" George admitted to about a hundred thousand dollars. "And you want to take lessons from me? Oh no, Monsieur, it is I who should take lessons from you." Stravinsky had the right idea. Gershwin was at his best before he knew all the rules. The *Jazz Piano Concerto*, commissioned in 1925 when he had been studying from books, never equaled in popularity the *Rhapsody in Blue*.

He continued to write the musical comedies which paid for his transition from a flat in Brooklyn to a penthouse in New York. The semi-operatic *American in Paris* paved the way for his last important work, the Negro opera *Porgy and Bess*. In this grand-folk-opera, Gershwin demonstrated the importance of Negro material not before considered suitable for grand opera, in much the same way as he had revealed jazz on the symphonic level in the *Rhapsody*. But he was taken ill too soon after *Porgy's* first successful season to realize that again he had led the way in a new direction. In July 1937, the news was flashed from Hollywood that he was dying of a brain tumor, and the end came a few days later.

◇◇◇◇◇◇◇◇◇◇◇◇◇◇◇◇◇◇◇◇◇◇◇◇◇◇◇◇◇◇

Roy Harris

(hăr′ĭs)

b. LINCOLN COUNTY, OKLAHOMA, FEB. 12, 1898

ROY HARRIS was born a farmer, and his Western twang and lean rangy body are typically American Farmer. Lawrence Gilman, music critic, wrote of him, "He could not have happened in any other part of the globe. He speaks our imaginative and spiritual language, springs from our soil, breathes our air, walks our plains and woods and hills."

Yet his musical idiom is not self-consciously national. He uses early Greek modes as freely as American folksong, and is not unduly partial to jazz. His works are virile, energetic, and well-made, with a tendency to be intellectual. They comprise a great deal of chamber music, three symphonies and other orchestral works, pieces for single instruments, and choral music, of which last his *Song for Occupations* is a striking example.

He was educated in the public schools of Southern California, where his family made their home. His early training in music was meagre, consisting of piano lessons from his mother, a bit of clarinet, some evening study by himself. As soon as he was strong enough, farming became his trade, a trade which left little time for other interests. But his enlistment as a private in the First World War changed all that. When he returned, at twenty, he knew that he craved music more than anything in the world. He took special courses at the University of California, won two Guggenheim fellowships, and studied for two crowded years in Paris with Nadia Boulanger. An accident to his spine compelled him to lie flat on his back for six months, but he composed a string quartet while staring at the ceiling, and made the discovery that he was able to compose away from the piano. Since then, when genius burns, he takes long walks with note-book and pencil in his knapsack, like Beethoven.

As fluent with words as with notes, he has taught and lectured widely. No festival of American music is complete without his presence, if not in the flesh, then as represented by his music, by a speech, or by well-written program notes. He has won several competitions, and in 1942 was awarded the prize of the Coolidge Foundation in

Washington, D. C., for his outstanding contribution to chamber music. His wife, Johanna, an accomplished pianist, performs his works. As teacher, writer, and composer, Roy Harris is a force to be reckoned with in American music today.

Carlos Chavez

(chä′vĕs)

b. OUTSIDE MEXICO CITY, JUNE 13, 1899

CHAVEZ' CHILDHOOD was a thorough preparation for his present role of musical interpreter of Mexico. He was the youngest of the six children of a Spanish father and Spanish-Indian mother, and took his first music lessons from his older brother Manuel, saving pesos which in the Chavez family were not plentiful. From his tenth to his twentieth year, revolution in Mexico interfered seriously with his study of music. At fifteen he was assigned to the dangerous task of taking the train to town several times a week for supplies. Once, when the military were hunting revolutionaries, a bullet came flying through the train window beside which he sat. It whistled within an inch of his head, and killed the man in the seat beside him. The iron which entered the head of his neighbor left its mark on the soul of the boy, giving him a hatred of cruelty and oppression which he always retained.

When Ponce, his teacher, talked to him about the Indian folk melodies he had heard in his childhood, he turned to them as a basis on which a national music might conceivably be developed. With that idea in his mind, he went to Berlin for further study, but shortly returned to the New World, where he felt freer to develop in his own way. He came to New York in 1923, a comparatively unknown young man, bringing with him a ballet, *The New Fire* (*El Fuego Nuevo*), commissioned by the Secretary of Education in Mexico. He brought also *Los Cuatros Soles* (*The Four Suns*), and part of *H.P.* He used his own collection of Indian instruments to illustrate the talks he gave in Spanish English on Mexican music.

He returned to Mexico after the production of *The New Fire* with renewed belief in himself. In 1928, he became director of the National Conservatory of Music, and founded the Orquesta Sinfonica di Mexico, which he has directed ever since that date. All his efforts were directed to bringing music, which had been the privilege of the few, within the reach of the many. He demonstrated the value of participation by the people in community choruses and folksong fiestas. *Llamadas*, a chorus he wrote for a large worker's group, was publicly given by workers with enormous success. This was a significant step in the democratization of music in Mexico.

For some years Chavez has made regular annual visits to this country. As guest conductor of major orchestras, he has been able to bring his own compositions to American audiences, especially *Antigona*, *H.P.*, and *Sinfonia India.* Intense vitality, violent contrasts of color and mood, and rhythmic onslaughts which are almost savage, characterize them. To Chavez the only good Indian is a live Indian, particularly those who are alive to music in an awakening Mexico.

Aaron Copland

(cōp′lănd)

b. BROOKLYN, N. Y., NOV. 14, 1900

WHEN AARON COPLAND left Brooklyn to be a composer, it was to Nadia Boulanger and the Fontainebleau School near Paris that he made his way. He had studied piano with Victor Wittgenstein and Clarence Adler, and theory with Rubin Goldmark—a good beginning in view of the fact that his home folks were unmusical. In Paris he heard the compositions of "the Six," of Hindemith, Prokofieff, Szymanowsky, Stravinsky, and Schönberg, and met most of them at the concerts of modern music put on by Koussevitzky. He returned to New York, shy, unknown, and with no visible means of support, except a few compositions for sale. But it was not long before the League of Composers had set a seal of approval upon two piano pieces, *The Cat and the Mouse* and *Passacaglia*. At Nadia Boulanger's urgent instigation, Walter Damrosch presented his *Symphony* for organ and orchestra, and Koussevitzky then suggested that the League commission a new work from the young man. A Guggenheim scholarship permitted him to live while executing the commission for *Music for the Theatre*, a suite for small orchestra. It was produced at a League concert, with Koussevitzky conducting. Then Copland played his jazzy *Piano Concerto* with the Boston Symphony Orchestra. He had arrived.

He considers radio and film legitimate outlets for his best efforts. While writing scores for *The City*, *Of Mice and Men*, and *Our Town*, he sat in projection booths for hours at a time watching while the film was run off again and again. As a result, his scores are profoundly expressive of the action, in contrast with the hastily written and unrelated product of those who regard film music as a job rather than an opportunity. In the ballet *Billy the Kid*, the music is fitted to the choreography with absolute dramatic precision. He has written prize-winning pieces for the radio, including the *Dance Symphony* and *Music for Radio*. He uses jazz and dissonance, and is rhythmically resourceful, the result being taut brilliant music with restraint and individuality. He is the outstanding modern American composer. He has been at various times director of the Copland-Sessions Concerts of Contemporary Music, of the International Society of Contemporary Music, of the festival of Contemporary Music in Saratoga, and of the League of Composers.

Laurels rest lightly upon Copland. With quiet impersonality he pleads the cause of contemporary music in the classroom and lecture hall, in print, and most of all in his own music. He is a consistent sponsor of causes involving social betterment, a spokesman for exploited groups. The whirling social and political currents of the twentieth century reflected in his music make it a valuable commentary on the world we live in.

Dmitri Shostakovich

(shŭsh′-tä′-kŭ-vĭtch)

b. PETROGRAD, RUSSIA, SEPT. 25, 1906

THE SPIRIT OF SOVIET RUSSIA lives in the music of Dmitri Shostakovich. His entire life has been spent in the city which was Petrograd, and became Leningrad in 1917. Dmitri, then eleven, signalized this event and the revolution with a *Hymn to Liberty* and a *Funeral March for the Victims of the Revolution*, written after seeing his dead and dying countrymen in the streets. He sees many more of them dying today while he serves as an auxiliary fireman defending his city against German aggression.

Student years at the Leningrad Conservatory were crowned with a *First Symphony*, "sufficiently modern to be interesting, and sufficiently academic to be agreeable." It was well received. The nineteen-year-old composer followed it with the *Second*, or *October* and the choral *Third*, or *Mayday*, symphonies. They added to his reputation, and success encouraged him to write an opera, *The Nose*, which was criticized as a piece of bourgeois decadence.

Nothing daunted, he wrote a second opera, *Lady Macbeth of Mzensk*, a remarkable work. It was introduced to America by Artur Rodzinski in Cleveland, and was successfully given at the Metropolitan Opera in New York in 1935, but in Leningrad Stalin walked out on it, and an unfavorable notice in *Pravda*, the official newspaper, precipitated a violent controversy as to its merits. *Lady Macbeth* continued to play in Russia despite the "unbuttoned" scenes which hostile critics pronounced vulgar. Shostakovich taught at the Lenin Conservatory, wrote piano pieces, chamber music and film music, and bided his time.

The V of his *Fifth Symphony* spelt Vindication for him. The symphony was played in Leningrad and Moscow, and glowingly reviewed, and has since been performed everywhere. In his latest symphony, the *Seventh*, which treats of the greatest war in history, Shostakovich expresses his passionate belief in a Soviet victory against Germany. In a triumphant finale the brasses blare a prophecy of "the victory of light over darkness, of humanity over barbarism."

The Unknown Composer

The shy, bespectacled young composer who crumbles cigarettes between his fingers as he talks is completely wrapped up in the political, social and economic ideology of the new Russia. He asserts that "Music cannot help having a political basis. . . . It may be tragic, but it must be strong. It is no longer an end in itself, but a vital weapon in the struggle." He uses that weapon so powerfully that his music is like the voice of Russia itself, a ringing mass cry that resounds throughout the world.

The Unknown Composer

Lives of great men all remind us we can make our lives sublime—or become famous, but this is difficult, especially if we are composers. It is one thing to produce great music, and another to have the music recognized. As their biographies have told us, many composers never knew how much they had contributed unless the information reached them in another world,—for they died leaving unpublished or unappreciated compositions which afterward became famous. And conversely, many who created a sensation in their own generation are hardly even names today.

It is a pity recognition comes so slowly that it often comes too late, yet in a way comforting because of the possibility that among the unknowns of today may be the Beethoven of tomorrow. As to where he will be found one man's guess is as good as another's. He may prove to be a professional composer who executes musical commissions for his daily bread, and already has something of a reputation. Or music may be an avocation to which he turns from the humdrum of earning a livelihood. In that case, his audience is limited to one—himself—and no matter how good his music may be, he gets no credit for writing it. Again, he may be a self-denying idealist, living frugally while composing richly. He is in all likelihood among us, striving, creating, and hoping that his works will be tolerantly listened to and intelligently judged. In the ranks of the composers of today, known, partly known, or ignored are those who, some time, will be recognized as the great men of this century.

Some Definitions

Académie française: one of five academies of the arts and sciences, which together form the Institut de France. The Académie française was founded in 1635, for the purification of the French language. Membership is limited, and by election only.

a cappella music: unaccompanied choral music, as sung in a chapel.

aria: a melody or song, usually found in opera or oratorio. (Italian *aria* = tune.)

art song: a song in which the music follows the line of the words without repetition of verse and chorus, as opposed to ballad or folksong.

atonal music: music in which all tones and chords are not related to a central keynote, or tonality, as opposed to polytonal music, in which several keynotes or tonalities are used simultaneously.

ballad: a simple narrative song, each stanza sung to the same melody, and having a chorus or refrain. Originally a dance tune. (Italian *ballare* = to dance.)

cantata: a vocal work with instrumental accompaniment, like an oratorio, only shorter.

case of viols: a set of oldfashioned stringed instruments, forerunners of the violin, viola and cello, popular in Elizabethan England.

chamber music: music written for performance in a room. (Italian, *camera* = room.)

chord: the simultaneous sounding of three or more tones of different pitch.

classical music: traditional term for music written before about 1830. It is generally more impersonal, abstract, and intellectual than so-called romantic music.

clavichord: a keyboard instrument, forerunner of the piano, in which the strings were struck, not plucked, to produce the tone.

clavier: a keyboard; another name for the clavichord. (German *klavier* = piano.)

coloratura: florid, decorative.

concerto: a composition for solo instrument with orchestra, usually in three movements.

concerto grosso: a composition for several soloists with full orchestra, written as a dialogue between soloists and orchestra. Popular in the 17th century.

Conservatoire française: a famous school of music in Paris, supported by the state, where talented students receive musical tuition free of charge.

consonance: a supposedly agreeable combination of closely related sounds.

counterpoint: see polyphony.

cyclical form: a form in which a certain motive or theme appears in several movements of a composition, somewhat altered but always recognizable.

Davidsbund: an imaginary society of artists with common interest in waging a war of the ideal against the prosaic in music. Conceived by Robert Schumann, and musically described in the "Davidsbündlertänze." (Dances of the League of David.)

dissonance: a supposedly disagreeable combination of remotely related elements.

étude: a piece of music written as a study.

fantasie: a composition of improvisational nature, which does not necessarily adhere to conventional forms.

folksong: song that springs spontaneously from the people.

fugue: a form of polyphonic writing in which one theme or subject is imitated by others, in strictly conventional intervals and successions, in the manner of a flight and pursuit. (Italian, *fuga* = flight.)

harmony: the science of combining tones.

harpsichord: a keyboard instrument, forerunner of the piano, its tone produced by quills plucking the strings.

impressionist music: music which describes the sentiments and emotions aroused by an object or an event rather than the object or event itself.

International Society for Contemporary Music: an international society to foster performances of the new music of all nations. Annual festivals are held, at which new works are performed.

interval: the distance or relationship between two tones, including them both.

kapellmeister: the leader of a chapel or choir; also, the leader of an orchestra.

Légion d'honneur: Legion of honor; a French honorary society, instituted by Napoleon in 1802 as a military and civil order of merit for men and women.

Lied: German art song (see Art song).

Leitmotif: a musical idea characterizing a person or episode, which recurs in the music whenever that person or episode is recalled. Much used in operas by Weber and Wagner, and in the program music of Richard Strauss.

madrigal: a secular song for two or more voices, unaccompanied.

mass: part of the Roman Catholic service, consisting of the Kyrie, Gloria, Credo, Sanctus, Benedictus, and Agnus Dei.

mazurka: a Polish dance in triple time.

melody: a series of tones which possess shape, pattern and coherence, and are logically organized as to pitch.

motet: a sacred madrigal, not liturgical.

motif, or motive: a short melodic phrase or pattern.

neo-classicism: new classicism which revives the spirit of the eighteenth century.

opera: a drama set to music.

opera grande, or grand opera: opera containing no spoken words.

opéra comique or operetta: opera containing some spoken words.

opus (op.): work. A composer's published works are numbered Op. I, II, etc. in the order of their publication.

pizzicato: plucking the string of a bowed instrument, instead of playing with the bow, to produce a tone.

plainsong: unaccompanied choral chant of the Roman Catholic church, also known as Gregorian chant; collected by Pope Gregory in 6th century A.D.

polonaise: a Polish dance in slow triple rhythm.

polyphony: counterpoint, or the harmonious combination of two or more voices, retaining their melodic individuality and independence.

prelude: an introduction.

Prix de Rome: a prize awarded annually by the Institut de France to a candidate selected by competition from the composition students of the Conservatoire. Winner receives a pension from the state for four successive years, part of which time he was required to spend in Rome until the Second World War. The Second Grand Prix de Rome is a gold medal.

program music: music with a descriptive title, motto, or foreword supplied by the composer.

recitative: declamatory singing with a few chords of accompaniment.

romantic music: traditional term for music written in the nineteenth century, which is more subjective and emotional than so-called classical music.

scherzo: a rapid playful piece.

Schola Cantorum: a French school originally intended to promote Gregorian and a cappella church music, later broadened into a full conservatory.

Société nationale de la Musique: a French society for the encouragement of instrumental composition, founded by Saint-Saëns and Bussine.

sonata: a three-movement piece for one or more instruments.

sonata form: the name of the form in which the first movement of sonatas, symphonies and concertos is traditionally cast.

symphony: a sonata for orchestra, usually in four movements.

symphonic poem: a large orchestral work in one continuous movement, usually with a program.

symphonie concertante: a symphony with solo passages for one or more instruments.

theme: a subject; an important melody in a composition.

theory: the science of composition.

toccata: a touch-piece written for keyboard instruments, rapid, showy, effective. (Ital. *toccata* = touched.)

tonality: the key in which a piece is written.

tremolo (violin): the rapid repetition of a single note, producing a shivering sound.

trio sonata or sonata a tre: a sonata for three instruments.

variations: a form in which a melody is stated, then repeated with changes and amplifications.

virginal: a small keyboard instrument, originally popular in Elizabethan England, played on the lap.

Appendix

THE WORKS OF ONE HUNDRED GREAT COMPOSERS

[These lists have been compiled from the "*International Encyclopedia of Music and Musicians*," edited by Oscar Thompson. They are as complete as limited space permits.]

ALBÉNIZ, ISAAC. Operas: *Henry Clifford; Pepita Jimenez.* Operettas: *Cuanto mas Viejo; Catalanes de Gracia; The Magic Opal; Poor Jonathan; San Antonia de la Florida.* Voice and Piano: *To Nellie* (Six songs); *Two Songs; Quatre Mélodies; Il en est de l'Amour.* Orchestra: *Catalonia* Rhapsody. Piano: *Chants d'Espagne; Six Spanish Dances; Espagne; Souvenirs; Rapsodia Cubana; Recuerdos de Viaje; Serenata Española; 1st Spanish Suite; 2nd Spanish Suite; España; Zambra Granadina; Yvonne en Visite* etc., *La Vega, Iberia,* (4 books); *Rapsodia Española.*

BACH, J. S. Organ Works: Preludes on the chorales, *Christ lag in Todesbanden* and *Erbarme dich mein, O Herre Gott;* Variations on the chorales *O Gott, du fromme Gott, Christ, der du bist der helle Tag*, and part of *Sei Gegrüsset, Jesu gütig; Passacaglia and Fugue* in C Minor; The *Toccatas* and most of the great *Preludes* and *Fugues;* Four transcriptions of Vivaldi Concertos; The *Orgelbüchlein;* Canonic variations on *Vom Himmel hoch da komm ich her;* Six "Schübler" *Chorale Preludes;* Clavier Works: Part III of the Clavierübung. *Sonata in D major; Prelude and Fugue in C minor; Toccata and Fugue in C major; Capriccio on the departure of his brother; Capriccio in honour of his Brother; Chromatic Fantasia and Fugue; English* and *French Suites; The Well-Tempered Clavier* Part I.; the *Inventions; Little Preludes and Symphonies;* the *Goldberg Variations;* the *Italian Concerto; Musikalisches Opfer; Art of the Fugue;* Six Partitas; Part II. of *Well-Tempered Clavier*. Orchestra: Six *Brandenburg Concertos; suites; violin concertos*. Music for Various Instruments: *Suites* or sonatas for violin, flute, cello and viola da gamba; sonata for flute, violin and clavier. Masses, Passions and Oratorios: *B Minor Mass, F Major, A Major, G Minor, G Major; St. John, St. Matthew, St. Mark Passions; Christmas, Easter*, and *Ascension Oratorios; Magnificat*. Church Cantatas, Secular Cantatas, and Motets: *Denn Du wirst meine Seele nicht in der Hölle lassen; Gott ist mein König; Gottes Zeit ist die allerbeste Zeit; Aus der Tiefe rufe ich; Der Herr denket an uns; Meine Seele rühmt und preist; Nach dir, Herr, verlanget mich; Uns ist ein Kind geboren; Gleich wie der Regen und Schnee; Ich hatte viel Bekümmernis; Ich weiss dass mein Erlöser lebt; Nun komm, der Heiden Heiland; Himmelskönig, sei Willkommen; Ach, ich sehe; Barmherziges Herze der ewigen Liebe;*

Bereitet die Wege; Der Himmel Lacht; Komm, du süsse Todesstunde; Nur jedem das Seine; Tritt auf die Glaubensbahn; Herz und Mund und Tod und Leben; Mein Gott, wie lang; Wachet, betet; Wer mich liebet; Was mir behagt; Wer sich selbst erhöhet; Durchlauchtster Leopold; Motets, and other Cantatas not specified.

BACH, CARL PHILIPP EMANUEL. Songs: Numerous Collections. Instrumental Compositions: *Prussian*, *Würtemburgian* Piano Sonatas; 210 solo clavier pieces; 52 concertos with orchestral accompaniment; sonatas for violin and piano; and many more. Also *Versuch über die wahre Art das Clavier zu spielen.* Masses, Passions, and Oratorios: 22 Passions; 2 Oratorios; many Cantatas.

BARTÓK, BÉLA. Operas: *Duke Bluebeard's Castle; The Wooden Prince; The Miraculous Mandarin.* Orchestra: *Scherzo; Kossuth Symphony; Burlesque; First Suite; Second Suite; Two Portraits; Two Pictures; Dance Suite.* Concertos: *Rhapsody* piano and orchestra; Two *Piano Concertos;* Two *Rhapsodies* for violin and orchestra. Chamber Music: *Piano Quartet, String Quartet, Violin Sonata, Piano Quintet, First String Quartet, Second String Quartet, First Sonata, Second Sonata.* Piano: *Sonata, Three Hungarian Folksongs, Rhapsody, Fourteen Bagatelles, Three Burlesques, Two Elegies, Two Rumanian Dances, Allegro Barbaro, Sonatina, Rumanian Christmas Songs, Out of Doors, Mikrokosmos. Fifteen Hungarian Peasant Songs, Four Dirges* (Nenien); and others. Voice: *Hungarian Folksongs* in various collections. Chorus: *The Village; Cantata Profana;* and others.

BEETHOVEN, LUDWIG VAN. Three Trios for piano, violin, and cello, E-Flat, G, C Minor; Three Sonatas for piano: F Minor, A, C; Trio in E-Flat for violin, viola and cello; Quintet in E-Flat for 2 violins, 2 violas, and cello; Two Sonatas for piano and cello; Sonata in D for piano, 4 hands; Sonata in E-Flat for piano; Serenade in D for violin, viola and cello; Three Trios for violin, viola and cello; Three Sonatas for piano; Trio in B-Flat for piano, clarinet and cello; Three Sonatas for piano and violin: D, A, E-Flat; Sonata *Pathétique* in C Minor for piano; Two Sonatas for piano: E, G; Concerto in C for piano and orchestra; Quintet for piano, oboe, clarinet, bassoon, French horn; Sonata for piano, French horn or cello; Six String Quartets: F, G, D, C Minor, A, B-Flat; Concerto in B-Flat for piano and orchestra; Septet in E-Flat for violin, viola, French horn, clarinet, bassoon, cello, and contra-bass; Symphony No. 1 in C; Sonata in B-Flat for piano; Sonata for piano, violin and viola; Sonata in F for piano and violin; Serenade for flute, violin and viola; Sonata in A-Flat for piano; No. 1 *Sonata quasi una Fantasia* in E-Flat for piano; No. 2 *Sonata quasi una Fantasia* ("Moonlight") in C Sharp Minor for piano; Sonata ("Pastoral") in D for piano; Quintet in C for 2 violins, 2 violas, and cello; Three Sonatas for piano and violin: A, C Minor and G; Three Sonatas for piano: G, D Minor, E-Flat; Song, *An die Hoffnung;* Seven Bagatelles for piano: E-Flat, C, F, A, C, D, A-Flat; Six Variations on an original theme for piano; Fifteen Variations on theme from *Prometheus* for piano; Symphony No. 2 in D; Concerto No. 3 in C Minor; Trio for piano, clarinet or violin, and viola; Two Preludes for piano or organ; Romance in G for violin and orchestra; Serenade in D for piano, flute or violin; Notturno in D for piano, viola; Ballet *The Creatures of Prometheus;* Fourteen Variations in E-Flat for piano, violin and cello; Three Grand Marches for piano, 4 hands; Song *Adelaide;* Sonata ("Kreutzer") for piano and violin; Six Songs for Soprano: *Bitten*, *Die Liebe des Nächsten*, *Vom Tode*, *Die Ehre Gottes*, *Gottes Macht*, *Busslied;* Two Easy Sonatas for piano: G Minor, G Major; Romance in F for violin and orchestra; Two Rondos for piano: C, G; Eight Songs: *Urians Reise*, *Feuerfarb*, *Das Liedchen v.d. Ruhe*, *Mailied*, *Molly's Abschied*, *Die Liebe*, *Marmotte*, *Das Blümchen Wunderhold;* Sonata in C ("Waldstein") for piano; Sonata in F for piano; Symphony No. 3 in E-Flat. ("Eroica"); Triple Concerto in C for piano, violin, cello and orchestra; Sonata in F Minor for piano "Appassionata"; Concerto No. 4 in G for piano and orchestra; Three Quartets: F, E Minor and C ("Rasoumowsky"); Symphony No. 4 in B-Flat; Concerto in D for violin and orchestra; Overture to *Coriolanus;* Arrangement of Op. 4 as trio for piano and strings; Arrangement of Op. 3 for piano and cello; Scena and Aria, *Ah, Perfido!* for soprano and orchestra; Twelve Variations in F on "Ein Mädchen" for piano and cello; Symphony No. 5 in C

Minor; Symphony No. 6 in F ("Pastoral"); Sonata in A for piano and cello; Two Trios, D, E-flat for piano, violin and cello; Sextet in E-Flat: 2 clarinets, 2 French horns, 2 bassoons; Opera, *Fidelio;* Concerto No. 5 in E-Flat for piano and orchestra ("Emperor"); String Quartet in E-Flat ("Harp"); Six Songs: *Kennst du das Land*, *Herz, mein Herz*, *Es war einmal*, *Mit Liebesblick*, *Einst Wohnten*, *Zwar schuf das Glück*, for soprano and piano; Six Variations in D for piano; Fantasie in G Minor for piano; Sonata in F-Sharp for piano; Sonatina in G for piano; Fantasia in C Minor for piano, orchestra and chorus; Sonata in E-Flat, *Les Adieux, l'absence, et le retour*, for piano; Four Ariettas and Duet for soprano and tenor with piano; Three songs: *Trocknet nicht*, *Was zieht mir*, *Kleine Blumen* for soprano and piano; Music to Goethe's *Egmont;* Oratorio: *Christus am Ölberge;* Mass in C; Trio for two oboes and English horn; Song, *Das Glück der Freundschaft;* Polonaise in C for piano; Sonata in E Minor for piano; *Wellington's Victory* for orchestra; Symphony No. 7 in A; Symphony No. 8 in F; Song, *An die Hoffnung;* String Quartet in F Minor, No. 11; Sonata in G for piano and violin; Trio in B-Flat for piano, violin and cello; Song Cycle: *An die ferne Geliebte;* Song, *Der Mann von Wort;* Duet, *Merkenstein;* Sonata in A for piano; Two Sonatas in C, D, for piano and cello; Octet in E-Flat for 2 oboes, 2 clarinets, 2 French horns, 2 bassoons; Quintet in C Minor for 2 violins, 2 violas and cello; Six very easy themes; Sonata in B-Flat ("Hammerklavier") for piano; Ten national themes with variations for piano, flute, or violin; Twenty-five Scotch Songs; Sonata in E for piano; Sonata in A-Flat for piano; Sonata in C Minor for piano; *Calm Sea and Prosperous Voyage* for four voices and orchestra; *The Ruins of Athens* for chorus and orchestra; March and Chorus from *The Ruins of Athens;* Overture in C, sometimes called *Namensfeier;* Terzetto, *Tremate* for soprano, tenor, bass; *King Stephen* Overture; Elegiac Song; Bagatelles for piano: G Minor, C, D, A, C Minor, G, G, C, C, A Minor, A, B-Flat, G; Thirty-three variations on Waltz by Diabelli; Variations on *Ich bin der Schneider Kakadu; Bundeslied* for soprano, alto, chorus and wind; Mass in D (*Missa Solemnis*)*;* Overture in C, *Consecration of the House;* Symphony No. 9 in D Minor ("Choral"); Bagatelles: G, G Minor, E-Flat, B Minor, G, E-Flat, E-Flat; String Quartet in E-Flat; Arietta, *The Kiss;* Rondo a capriccio in G for piano. ("Rage over a Lost Penny"); String Quartet in B-Flat, No. 13; String Quartet in C-Sharp Minor, No. 14; String Quartet in A Minor, No. 15; Great Fugue in B-Flat for string quartet; Great Fugue in B-Flat for piano, 4 hands; String Quartet in F, No. 16; *Der glorreiche Augenblick:* Cantata for vocal quartet, chorus, and orchestra; Fugue in D for 2 violins, 2 violas and cello; Overture, known as *Leonore No. 1.* Works to which Opus numbers have been added. For Orchestra or Orchestral Instruments: Twelve Minuets; Twelve Deutsche Tanze; Twelve Contretanze; *Minuet of Congratulation* in E-Flat; Triumphal March in C; Military March in D; Military March in F; Rondino in E-Flat; Three Duos for clarinet and bassoon; Allegro con Brio in C for violin and orchestra; *Musik zu einem Ritterballet.* For Piano, with and without Accompaniment: Sonatina and Adagio in C Minor for mandolin and cembalo; Rondo in B-Flat for piano and orchestra; Three Quartets, E-Flat, D, C; Trio in E-Flat for piano, violin and cello; Trio in B-Flat in one movement for piano, violin and viola; Rondo, Allegro, in G for piano and violin; Twelve Variations in F on *Se vuol ballare* for piano and violin; Twelve Variations in G on *See the Conquering Hero* for piano and violin; Seven Variations in E-Flat on *Bei Männern;* Variations in G on a theme by Count von Waldstein for piano 4 hands; Air with six variations in D on *Ich denke dein* for piano 4 hands; Three Sonatas for piano: E-Flat, F Minor, D; Sonata in C, called "Easy" for piano; Two Sonatinas for piano; Rondo, Allegretto in A for piano; Menuet in E-Flat for piano; Prelude in F Minor for piano; Six Menuets: C, G, E-Flat, B-Flat, D, C; Seven Ländler Dances, all in D; Six Ländler Dances, all in D except No. 4 in D Minor; *Andante favori* in F for piano; Six Allemandes for piano and violin; *Ziemlich lebhaft* in B-Flat for piano; Bagatelle, "Für Elise" in A Minor for piano; Andante maestoso in C for piano; Ten cadenzas to Beethoven's piano concertos; Nine Variations in C Minor on a March by Dressler for piano; Twenty-four Variations on Righini's air *Vieni;* Thirteen Variations in A on Dittersdorf's air *Es war einmal* for piano; Nine Variations in A on Paisiello's air *Quant é piu bello* for piano; Six Variations in G on Paisiello's duet *Nel cor più* for piano; Twelve Variations in C on minuet from Haibel's ballet *Le nozze disturbate* for piano; Twelve Variations in A on the Russian Dance from Paul Wranizky's *Waldmädchen;* Six Variations in F on a Swiss air for piano or harp; Eight Variations in C on Grètry's air *Une fièvre brulante* for piano; Ten Variations in B-Flat on Salieri's air, *La Stessa, La Stessima*, for piano; Seven Variations in F on Winter's quartet, *Kind, willst du* for piano; Eight Variations in F on Süssmayer's trio for piano; Six Variations in G on an original theme for piano; Seven Variations in C on *God Save the King* for piano; Five Variations in D on *Rule, Britannia* for piano; Thirty-two Variations in C Minor for piano; Eight Variations in B-Flat on *Ich hab' ein kleines Hüttchen nur* for piano; many songs and choruses.

BELLINI, VINCENZO. Operas: *Adelson e Salvina, Bianca e Fernando, Il Pirata, La Straniera, Zàira, I Capuletti ed i Montecchi, La Sonnambula, Norma, Il fù ed il sarà, Beatrice di Tenda, I Puritani.*

BERLIOZ, HECTOR. Stage Works: *Lèlio, ou Le Retour à la Vie; Benvenuto Cellini; Les Troyens; Béatrice et Bénédict.* Orchestra: *Waverley; Les Francs-Juges; Symphonie Fantastique; Le Roi Léar; La Corsaire; Rob Roy; Harold en Italie; Rêverie et Caprice; Symphonie Funèbre; Le Carnaval Romain;* etc. Works for Voice and Orchestra: *La Mort d'Orphée; Cléopatre; Huit Scènes de Faust; Roméo et Juliette; Hymne à la France; La Damnation de Faust; Herminie; Sardanapale; Le Cinq Mai; Sara la Baigneuse; Le chant des Chemins de Fer; Marche*

Funèbre; La Menace des Francs; L'Impériale. Works for Voice and Piano: *Neuf Mélodies Irlandaises; La Captive; Je Crois en Vous; Les Nuits d'Été; Premiers Transports; Feuillets d'Album; Page d'Album; Fleurs des Landes; L'Apothéose.* Religious Music; and Literary and Critical Works.

BIZET, GEORGES. Stage Works: *La Prêtresse; David; Clovis et Clothilde; Don Procopio; Le Docteur Miracle; Les Pêcheurs de Perles; La Jolie Fille de Perth; Djamileh; L'Arlésienne; Carmen.* Orchestra: *Vasco da Gama; Roma; Marche Funèbre; Petite Suite D'Orchestre; Patrie; Symphony.* Piano: *La Chasse Fantastique; Les Chants du Rhin; Trois Esquisses; Marine; Premier Nocturne; Jeux d'Enfants; Variations Chromatiques.* Voice: *Saint Jean de Pathmos; La Fuite; Chanson du Rouet; Le Golfe de Bahia; Les Nymphes des Bois; Le Retour; Revons; Feuilles d'Album;* and others.

BLOCH, ERNEST. Operas: *Macbeth; Jézabel.* Orchestra: Symphony in C-Sharp Minor; *Vivre et Aimer; Hiver-Printemps; Voice in the Wilderness* for orchestra with cello; *Trois Poèmes juifs; Schelomo; Israel* Symphony; *La Montagne* Symphony; *America* Symphony; *Symphonie orientale;* and others. Chamber Music: String Quartet in B Minor; Viola and piano Suite; violin sonata; piano quintet; *Three Landscapes* for quartet. Voice and Orchestra: Four *Historiettes au crépuscule;* Four *Poèmes d'automne;* settings of three Psalms.

BOCCHERINI, LUIGI. Opera: *La Clementina.* Orchestral Works: 20 Symphonies; 1 Suite for full orchestra; 4 cello concertos. Chamber Music: 102 string quartets; 33 sonatas; 6 duets; 60 trios; 154 quintets; 16 sextets; 2 octets; etc. Voice and Orchestra: 14 Concert Airs and Duets; Christmas Cantata; *Stabat Mater;* Motets for Christmas time; and other works totalling 467.

BORODIN, ALEXANDER. Operas: *Prince Igor; The Bogatyrs;* Fourth Act of the composite opera, *Mlada.* Orchestra: Symphony No. 1 in E-Flat Major; Symphony No. 2 in B Minor; Symphony No. 3 in A Minor; *In the Steppes of Central Asia; Scherzo.* Chamber Music: String Quartet No. 1 in A Major; String Quartet No. 2 in D Major; *Serenata alla Spagnola; Scherzo* for string quartet. Songs: *The Sleeping Beauty; The Song of the Dark Forest; The Discord; Queen of the Sea; My song is fierce and bitter; The Sea; Of my tears are born; Of distant shores; A Song of Arabia; Pride; With others and with us; The Magic Garden; Serenade of Four Swains to a Lady.* Piano: Petite Suite; Polka, Requiem, Dead March and Mazurka.

BRAHMS, JOHANNES. Orchestra: Serenade D Major; Serenade A Major; Variations on a Theme by Haydn; Symphony No. 1, C Minor; Symphony No. 2, D Major; *Academic Festival Overture; Tragic Overture;* Symphony No. 3, F Major; Symphony No. 4, E Minor; Hungarian Dances. Choral: *Ave Maria; Funeral Hymn; Marienlieder; 13th Psalm; A German Requiem; Rinaldo; Rhapsodie; Triumphlied; Nanie; Gesang der Parzen; Schicksalslied; Zigeunerlieder;* Motets, Canons, and many more. Chamber Music: 3

String Quartets C Minor, A Minor, B-Flat Major; Quintet, clarinet and strings, B Minor; 3 piano Quartets G Minor, C Minor, A Major; piano Quintet F Minor; Horn Trio E-Flat Major; Sonata No. 3 for piano and violin, D Minor; 2 String Sextets B-Flat, G; 2 string quintets F Major, G Major; and others. Concertos: 2 Piano Concertos D Minor, B-Flat Major; Violin Concerto D Major; Double concerto, A Minor for violin, cello, orchestra. Piano Solos: Sonata No. 1 C Major; *Sonata* No. 2, F-Sharp Minor; *Sonata* No. 3, F Minor; *Variations* on a theme by Schumann; *Variations and Fugue* on a Theme by Handel; *Rhapsodies; Fantasien;* 4 *Ballads; Variations* on a Theme by Paganini; and many more. Songs: *Liebestreu* (better known as *O versenk); Vergebliches Ständchen; Vier ernste Gesänge; Die Nonne und der Ritter; Mondnacht; Sapphische Ode;* and many others, over 300 in all. Miscellaneous: Piano duets; organ works; arrangements.

BRUCH, MAX. Operas: *Scherz, List und Rache; Hermione.* Chorus and Orchestra: *Schön Ellen; Odysseus; Arminius; Das Lied von der Glocke; Das Feuerkreuz; Rorate Coeli; Lied vom Deutschen Kaiser; Gruss an die heilige Nacht;* and others. Instrumental: Violin Concerto in G Minor; *Scottish Fantasy* for Violin; *Kol Nidrei* for cello and orchestra; *Konzertstück; Romance in A minor; Serenade; In Memoriam;* and others. Symphonies: No. 1, E-Flat; No. 2, F Minor; and No. 3, E Major. Chamber Music: 2 string quartets, C Minor and E; Trio C Minor. For Piano, op. 2, 11, 12, 14.

BRUCKNER, ANTON. Orchestra: Overture in G Minor; Symphony in F Minor; Symphony in D Minor; Symphony No. 1 in C Minor; Symphony No. 2 in C Minor; Symphony No. 3 in D Minor; Symphony No. 4 in E-Flat Major; Symphony No. 5 in B-Flat Major; Symphony No. 6 in A Major; Symphony No. 7 in E Major; Symphony No. 8 in C Minor; Symphony No. 9 in D Minor. Choral: *Requiem*, D Minor; *Missa Solemnis*, B-Flat; *Germanenzug;* First Mass, D Minor; Second Mass, E Minor; Third Mass, F Minor; *Abendzauber; Te Deum;* 150th Psalm; *Helgoland*. Chamber Music: String Quintet.

BYRD, WILLIAM. Sacred: Latin Church Music: Masses; Motets—*Cantiones Quae ab Argumento Sacrae Vocantur; Cantiones Sacrae* Books No. 1 and 2; *Gradualia* Books 1 and 2. English Church Music: Preces, Psalms and Litany; Services; Anthems; Sacred Songs. Secular: Madrigals: *Psalmes, Sonets & Songs; Songs of sundrie natures; A Printed Broadside;* 31 songs; *Canons; Rounds;* and others. Instrumental Music: Chamber Music for strings; 120 pieces of Keyboard Music in various collections.

CARPENTER, JOHN ALDEN. Ballets: *Birthday of the Infanta; Krazy-Kat; Skyscrapers.* Orchestra: *Adventures in a Perambulator; Concertino; Skyscrapers; Sea Drift; Danza; Concerto; Symphony.* Chamber Orchestra: *Water Colors; Gitanjali; When I Bring You Colored Toys; On the Day When Death Will Knock at Thy Door; The Sleep That Flits on Baby's Eyes; I am like a Remnant of a Cloud in Autumn; On the Seashore of Endless*

Worlds; Light, my Light. Chorus: *Song of Faith.* Chamber Music: *Sonata; String Quartet; Piano Quintet.* Piano: *Polonaise Americaine.*

CHAUSSON, ERNEST. Stage Works: *Jeanne d'Arc; Les Caprices de Marianne; Hélène; Le Roi Arthus;* and others. Choral: *Hymne Védique; Deux Duos; Chant Nuptial; Chant Funèbre; Ballata.* Orchestral Works: *Viviane;* Symphony in B-Flat; *Poème* for violin and orchestra; *Soir de Fête.* Chamber Music: Trio; *Concert* for piano, violin, and string quartet; piano quartet; string quartet. Voice and Piano: *Sept Mélodies; Le Colibri; La Caravane; Chansons de Miarka; Serres Chaudes; Chansons de Shakespeare; Pour un Arbre de Noel; Deux Poèmes*, etc. Voice and orchestra: *Poème d'amour et de la mer; Chanson Perpetuelle.* Religious Music: Motets etc.

CHAVEZ, CARLOS. Orchestra: *Sinfonia India; Sinfonia de Antigona;* Ballets *H.P.*, and *The New Fire.* Chamber Music: *Sonatina* for piano; *Sonatina* for violin and piano; *Sonatina* for piano and cello; Piano Sonata; *Energia; Unidad;* and others. Choral Music: *Llamadas* and others.

CHERUBINI, MARIA. For the Stage: Fifteen Italian and fourteen French operas; one Ballet; seventeen Cantatas; "occasional" vocal works with orchestra. Church Music: Eleven solemn masses; two Requiems; many detached *Kyries, Glorias*, etc.; 8-voice *Credo* with organ; *Oratorio;* motets, hymns, graduals; *Magnificat; Miserere; Te Deum;* four *Litanies;* two *Lamentations;* 20 antiphones. Instrumental: One symphony; one overture; eleven marches; eleven dances, etc.; one string quintet; six string quartets; one Sonata for two organs; six Sonatas for piano; one grand Fantasia; one Minuet; one Chaconne; and other music for the piano. Miscellaneous: Many single airs, romances, nocturnes, duets, etc.; fourteen choruses, four sets of solfeggi. Book, *Cours de Contrepoint et de la Fugue.*

CHOPIN, FRÉDÉRIC. Piano Works: Rondo in C Minor; Variations on *La ci darem la mano;* Introduction and Polonaise, piano and cello; Sonata in C Minor; Rondo alla Mazurka; Four Mazurkas—F-Sharp Minor, C-Sharp Minor, E Major, E-Flat Minor; Five Mazurkas; Trio for piano, violin and cello; Three Nocturnes, B-Flat Minor, E-Flat Major, B Major; Twelve Studies; Concerto in E Minor; Variations on *Je vends des scapulaires* of Hérold; Grande Fantasie on Polish Airs, with orchestra; *Krakowiak*, Rondo with orchestral accompaniment; Three Nocturnes; Rondo in E-Flat Major; Four Mazurkas, B-Flat Major, E Minor, A-Flat Major, A Minor; Waltz in E-Flat Major; Boléro; Scherzo in B Minor; Concerto in F Minor, piano & orchestra; Andante spianato and Grande Polonaise brillante; Ballade in G Minor; Four Mazurkas, G Minor, C Major, A-Flat Major, B Minor; Twelve Studies; Two Polonaises, C-Sharp Minor, E-Flat Minor; Two Nocturnes, C-Sharp Minor, D-Flat Major; Twenty-four Preludes; Impromptu in A-Flat Major; Four Mazurkas, C Minor, B Minor, D-Flat Major, C-Sharp Minor; Scherzo in B-Flat Minor; Two Nocturnes, B Major, A-Flat Major; Four Mazurkas, G-Sharp Minor, D Major, C Major, B Minor; Three Waltzes, A-Flat Major, A Minor, F Major; Sonata in B-Flat Minor; Impromptu in F-Sharp Major; Two Nocturnes, G Minor, G Major; Ballade in F Major; Scherzo in C Sharp Minor; Two Polonaises, A Major, C Minor; Four Mazurkas, C-Sharp Minor, E Minor, B Major, A-Flat Major; Waltz in A-Flat Major; Tarantelle; Polonaise in F-Sharp Minor; Prelude in C-Sharp Minor; Allegro de Concert; Ballade in A-Flat Major; Two Nocturnes, C Minor, F-Sharp Minor; Fantaisie in F Minor; Three Mazurkas, G Major, A-Flat Major, C-Sharp Minor; Impromptu in G-Flat Major; Ballade in F Minor; Polonaise in A-Flat Major; Scherzo in E Major; Two Nocturnes, F Minor, E-Flat Major; Three Mazurkas, B Major, C Major, C Minor; Berceuse; Sonata in B Minor; Three Mazurkas, A Minor, A-Flat Major, F-Sharp Minor; Barcarolle; Polonaise-Fantaisie in A-Flat Major; Two Nocturnes, B Major, E Major; Three Mazurkas, B Major, F Minor, C-Sharp Minor; Three Waltzes, D-Flat Major, C-Sharp Minor, A-Flat Major; Sonata in G Minor, piano and cello; and others.

COPLAND, AARON. For the Theatre: *Grohg; Hear Ye, Hear Ye!; The Second Hurricane.* Orchestra: *Cortège Macabre;* Symphony for Organ and Orchestra; First Symphony; *A Dance Symphony;* Concerto for Piano and Orchestra; *Symphonic Ode;* Short Symphony; *Statements; El Salón Mexico; Three Cabaret Dances; Music for Radio.* Chamber Orchestra: *Music for the*

Theatre; Two Pieces for String Orchestra; *Prelude* from First Symphony. Chorus: *The House on the Hill; An Immorality; What Do We Plant?* Chamber Music: *As It Fell upon a Day;* Two Pieces; *Vitebsk;* Sextet. For Piano: *Variations; The Young Pioneers*, and others. Film: *The City; Of Mice and Men; Our Town;* and others. Ballets: *Billy the Kid; Rodeo;* and others.

CORELLI, ARCANGELO. Instrumental: Suonate a tre (12); Suonate da camera a tre (12); Suonate a tre (12); Suonate da camera a tre (12); Suonate a violino e violine o cembalo (12); Concerti grossi con duoi violini e violoncello de concertino obligati.

COUPERIN, FRANÇOIS. Harpsichord: *Pièces de Clavecin*, 4 Books. Also *Régle pour l'accompagnement* and *L'Art de toucher le Clavecin.* Chamber Music: Four *Concerts Royaux; Les Gouts-Réunis ou Nouveaux Concerts; Les Nations; Concert instrumental sous le titre d'Apothéose composé à la Mémoire Immortelle de l'incomparable Monsieur de Lully;* Pieces for Viols, with figured bass; unpublished Sonatas; etc. Organ: *Pièces d'Orgue.* Songs: *Qu'on ne me dise plus que c'est la seule absence; Doux liens de mon coeur; Épitaphe d'un paresseux; Quel bruit soudain vient troubler nos retraites?; La femme entre deux draps; A moy! Tout est perdu!; La Pastorelle; Les Solitaires; Musette; Brunete; Vaudeville; Les Pellerines.* Religious Vocal Music: *Laudate Pueri Dominum;* Motets; *Elévations; Leçons de Ténèbres.*

DEBUSSY, CLAUDE. Stage Works: Operas: *Pelléas et Mélisande; Rodrigue et Chimene*, (unfin.);

Ballets: *Jeux, Khamma, La Boîte aux joujoux, Le martyre de Saint Sebastien.* Orchestra: *Printemps; Prélude à l'Après-midi d'un faune; Nocturnes; La Mer; King Lear; Images; Fantaisie; Rapsodie; Danse sacrée; Danse Profane.* Chamber Music: *Premier quatuor; Première rapsodie; Petite pièce; Syrinx; Sonatas; Trio* in G; *Chansons de Bilitis.* Piano: *Danse bohémienne; Deux arabesques; Rêverie; Ballade; Valse romantique; Nocturne; Suite Bergamasque; Mazurka; Pour le Piano; Estampes; Masques; Images* (2 series); *Children's Corner; Hommage À Haydn; La plus que lente; Douze Préludes* (2 books); *Douze Études* (2 books); *Berceuse héroique pour rendre hommage a S.M. le Roi Albert de Belgique et à ses soldats; D'un Cohier d'esquisses; L'Île joyeuse;* and others. Songs: *Nuit d'étoiles; Beau soir; Fleur des blés; Mandoline; La Belle au bois dormant; Voici que le printemps; Paysage sentimental; Zéphyr; Rondeau; Pantomime; Clair de lune; Pierrot; Apparition; Cinq poèmes de Baudelaire; Ariettes oubliées; Deux Romances; Les Angelus; Dans le jardin; Trois Mélodies; Fêtes galantes* (2 series); *Proses lyriques; Chansons de Bilitis; Trois chansons de France; Le Promenoir des deux amants; Trois Ballades de Villon; Noel des enfants qui n'ont plus de maisons; Chanson espagnole; Berceuse; Les Roses;* and others. Cantatas and Choral Works: *Printemps; Invocation; L'Enfant prodigue; La Demoiselle élue; Trois chansons de Charles d'Orléans; Ode à la France; Daniel;* and others. Literary Works: *Monsieur Croche antidilettante*, etc.

DELIUS, FREDERICK. Stage Works: *Irmelin; The Magic Fountain; Koanga; A Village Romeo and*

Juliet; Margot la Rouge; Fennimore and Gerda; Norwegian Suite; Hassan. Orchestra: *Florida; Hiawatha; Paa Vidderne; Marche Caprice; Rhapsodic Variations; Petite Suite d'orchestre; Sur les Cîmes; Over the Hills and Far Away; The Dance Goes On; Paris; Life's Dance; Brigg Fair; In a Summer Garden; A Dance Rhapsody; Summer Night on the River; On Hearing the First Cuckoo in Spring; North Country Sketches; Eventyr.* Chamber Music: 2 *String Quartets; Sonatas* for Violin and Piano; *Sonata* for Cello and Piano; *Romance* for Cello and Piano; *Romance* for Violin and Piano. Concertos: *Concerto* for Piano and Orchestra; *Concerto* for violin and cello with orchestra; *Concerto* for violin and orchestra; *Concerto* for cello and orchestra; *Pastorale* for violin and orchestra; *Legendes*, for piano and orchestra; *Legend* for violin and orchestra. Chorus: *Appalachia; Sea Drift; A Mass of Life; Songs of Sunset; On Craig Dhu; Midsummer Song; Wanderer's Song; Arabesk; A Song of the High Hills; Requiem; To Be Sung of a Summer Night on the Water; A Song Before Sunrise; A Poem of Life and Love.* Songs with Orchestra: *Sakuntala;* Seven Danish Songs; *Eyle; Nachtlieb Zarathustras; Cynara.* Songs with Piano: *Zwei braune Augen;* Songs from the Norwegian; Three English Songs; *Black Roses; It Was a Lover and His Lass; Avant que tu ne t'en ailles;* and others. Instrumental: Two *Pianoforte Pieces;* A *Dance* for the Harpsichord.

DONIZETTI, GAETANO. Operas: *Enrico di Borgogna; Il Falegname di Livonia; Le nozze in villa; Zoraïde di Granata; La Zingara; La Lettera anonima; Chiara e Serafina; Il fortunato inganno; Aristea; Alfredo il grande; Una Follia; L'ajo nel imbarazzo; Emelia di Liverpool; Alahor in Granata; Il castello degli invalidi; Elvida; Olivo e Pasquale; El Borgomestro de Saardam; Le convenienzi teatrali; Otto mese in due ore; Elisabetta a Kenilworth; La Regina di Golconda; Gianni di Calais; Il Giovedi grasso; L'esule di Roma; Il Paris; Il castello di Kenilworth; Il diluvio universale; I pazzi per progetto; Francesca di Foix; Isnelda di Lambertazzi; La Romanziera; Anna Bolena; Fausta; Ugo Conte di Parigi; L'Elisir d'Amore; Sancia di Castiglia; Il Nuovo Pourceaugnac; Il furioso; Parisina; Torquato Tasso; Lucrezia Borgia; Rosamonda d'Inghilterra; Maria Stuarda; Gemma di Vergy; Marino Faliero; Lucia di Lammermoor; Belisario; Il campanello di notte; Betly; Roberto Devereaux; Pia de Tolemei; Maria di Rudenz; Poliuto; Gianni di Parigi; Gabriella di Vergy; La Fille du Regiment; La Favorita; Adelasia; Maria Padilla; Linda di Chamounix; Maria di Rohan; Don Pasquale; Don Sebastian; Catarina Cornaro; Rita, ou le mari battu; Il Duca d'Alba.* Also two masses, other church music, cantatas, songs, 12 string quartets, orchestral works, and piano pieces.

DUKAS, PAUL. Stage Works: *Ariane et Barbe-Bleue*, opera; *La Péri*, ballet. Orchestra: *Polyeucte*, overture; *L'Apprenti Sorcier*, scherzo; *La Péri*, symphonic suite. Piano: Sonata in E-Flat Minor; *Variations, Interlude et Finale* on a theme of Rameau; *Prélude Élégiaque; La Plainte au Loin du Faune.* Voice and Piano: *Sonnet de Ronsard*. Horn and Piano: *Villanelle.*

DVOŘÁK, ANTON. Operas: *King and Collier; The Pig-headed Ones; Vanda; The Peasant a Rogue; Dimitrij; The Jacobin; The Devil and Kate; Rusalka; Armida.* Orchestra: 9 Symphonies, in D; D Minor; F; G; E Minor; E-Flat; D Minor; C Minor; B-Flat. Symphonic Poems: *The Watersprite; The Midday Witch; The Golden Spinning Wheel; The Wood Dove; Heroic Song.* Overtures: Dramatic Overture to *Alfred; My Home; Hussite* Overture; *Amid Nature; Carnaval; Othello; Serenade* in E for Strings; *Suite* in D; *Notturno* in B for Strings; *Serenade* in D Minor; *Festival March; Scherzo Capriccioso; Polonaise* in E-Flat; *Suite in D* (Czech); *Slavonic Rhapsodies in* D, G Minor, A-Flat; *Slavonic Dances* (2 series); and others. Solo Works with Orchestra: *Romance*, violin and orchestra; *Piano Concerto* in G Minor; *Mazurka*, violin and orchestra; *Violin Concerto* in A Minor; *Rondo*, cello and orchestra; *Forest Calm*, cello and orchestra; *Cello Concerto* in B Minor. Chamber Music: 9 String Quartets; 3 String Quintets; 1 String Sextet; 4 Trios; 1 Quartet, piano and strings; 1 Quintet, piano and strings; and others. Choral Music: *Stabat Mater; The Specter's Bride; St. Ludmila;* Psalm 149; Mass in D; Requiem; *The American Flag;* Te Deum; *Hymn of the Czech Peasants;* Three Slovak Folksongs; *Amid Nature; Festival Song; Song of the Czech;* and others. Songs: *Cypress Trees; The Orphan;* Songs based on Serbian folk poetry: *Evening Songs;* Modern Greek Songs; Gypsy Songs; Love Songs; Biblical Songs; *Slumber Song; Fresh from the Hearth; Songs in Folk Style;*

and others. Also vocal duets: *Sacred* Duets; *Moravian* Duets; *Strains from Moravia; Soldier's Farewell; There on our Roof*. Instrumental: Piano: *Silhouettes;* Dumka and Furiant; Minuets; Scotch Dances; Polka and Galop; Waltzes; Mazurkas; *Poetic Tone Pictures; Humoresque; Eclogues; Album Leaves;. Impromptu* in D Minor. Also duets. Violin: *Ballad; Sonata* in F Major; *Romantic Places; Sonatina; Humoresque; Capriccio.* Cello: *Rondo; Concerto* in A Major; *Polonaise* in A Minor.

ELGAR, SIR EDWARD. Orchestra: Symphonies No. 1, A-Flat; No. 2, E-Flat; No. 3 unfin. Overtures: *Froissart; Cockaigne; In the South.* Also *The Wand of Youth;* Two Romances; *Sevillana; Sursum Corda; Serenade* for string orchestra; *Enigma Variations; Pomp and Circumstance; Dream Children;* Elegy; Coronation March; *Falstaff; Sospiri; Polonia; The Starlight Express; Nursery Suite;* 2 *Concertos*, for violin in B Minor; for cello in E Minor. Choral Works: Cantatas: *The Black Knight; King Olaf; The Banner of St. George; Caractacus.* Oratorios: *The Light of Life; The Dream of Gerontius; The Apostles, The Kingdom.* Miscellaneous Works: Songs; Part Songs; Violin pieces; Chamber Music; etc.

ENESCO, GEORGES. Opera: *Oedipus.* Orchestra: *Poéma Româna; Symphonie Concertante; Suite* in C Major; *Rumanian Rhapsodies; Symphony* No. 1 in E-Flat Major; *Symphony* No. 2 in A Major; *Suite* No. 3 in A Major. Chamber Music: *Intermezzos* for wind instruments;

Dixtuor in D Major for wind instruments; *Octet* in C Major for strings; string *Quartet* in D Major. Instrumental: Piano: *Suite in Ancient Style* in G Minor; *Suite* No. 2 in D Major; *Pièces Impromptus;* Sonata in F Minor; *Variations* on an original theme. Violin: *Sonata* in D Major; *Sonata* No. 2 in F Minor; *Sonata* No. 3 in A Minor *In the Popular Rumanian Style.* Songs and miscellaneous works.

FALLA, MANUEL DE. For the Theatre: *La Vida Breve; El Amor Brujo; El Sombrero de Tres Picos; Fuego Fatuo; El Retablo de Maese Pedro.* Chamber Music: *Psyché,* for mezzo-soprano, flute, harp, oboe, clarinet, violin and cello; *Concerto* for harpsichord, flute, oboe, clarinet, violin, and cello. Instrumental: Piano: *Aragonesa; Cubana; Montañesa; Andaluza; Fantasia Boetica;* Andante; *Pour le Tombeau de Paul Dukas.* Guitar: *Homenaje; Pour le Tombeau de Debussy.* Songs: Trois Mélodies; Seven Spanish Popular Songs. Miscellaneous: Transcriptions and arrangements.

FAURÉ, GABRIEL. Stage Works: *Prométhée; Pénélope;* incidental music to *Caligula; Shylock; Le Voile du Bonheur.* Orchestra: Concerto for violin and orchestra; Ballade for piano and orchestra; Suite d'Orchestre; Romance for violin and orchestra; Pavane; Allegro Symphonique; suite *Pelléas et Mélisande;* Fantaisie for piano and orchestra; suite *Masques et Bergamasques.* Chamber Music: 2 Sonatas for piano and violin; 2 Piano Quartets; Berceuse for violin and piano; *Élégie* for cello and piano;

Petite Pièce for cello and piano; Romance for cello and piano; Andante for violin and piano; *Papillon* for cello and piano; *Sicilienne* for cello and piano; *Fantaisie* for flute and piano; 2 Quintets for piano and strings; Sérénade for cello and piano; 2 Sonatas for piano and cello. Miscellaneous Vocal Works: *Puisqu'ici-bas; Cantique de Jean Racine; Les Djinns; Le Ruisseau; La Naissance de Vénus; Madrigal; Pleurs d'Or.* Religious Music: *O Salutaris; Messe de Requiem; Ecce fidelis Servus; Tantum Ergo*, solo and 4-part chorus; *Ave Verum; Salve Regina; Ave Maria; Tantum Ergo*, for soprano or tenor & mixed chorus; *Tu es Petrus; Messe Basse.* Piano: *Trois Romances sans Paroles;* 5 Impromptus; 13 Barcarolles; 4 Valse-Caprices; 13 Nocturnes; and others. Voice and Piano: *Le Papillon et la Fleur; Mai; Dans les Ruines d'une Abbaye; Les Matelots; Seule!; Sérénade Tuscane; Chanson de Pêcheur; Lydia; Chant d'Automne; Rêve d'Amour; L'Absent; Aubade; Tristesse; Sylvie; Après un Rêve; Hymne; Barcarolle; Au Bord de l'Eau; La Rançon; Ici-bas; Nell; Le Voyageur; Automne; Poème d'un Jour; Les Berceaux; Notre Amour; Le Secret; Chanson d'Amour; La Fée-aux-chansons; Aurore; Fleur Jetée; LePays des Rêves; Les Roses d'Ispahan; Noel; Nocturne; Clair de Lune; Larmes; Au Cimetière; Spleen; La Rose;* 5 *Mélodies de Verlaine; La Bonne Chanson* (Verlaine); *Le Parfum Impérissable; Arpège; Prison; Soir; Dans la Forêt de Septembre; La Fleur qui va sur l'eau; Accompagnement; Le Plus Doux Chemin; Le Don Silencieux; Chanson; Le Chanson d'Éve; Le Jardin Clos; Mirages; C'est la Paix; L'Horizon Chimérique.*

FOSTER, STEPHEN C. Songs: *Beautiful Dreamer; Camptown Races; Come Where My Love Lies Dreaming; Down Among the Cane Brakes; Ellen Bayne; Gentle Annie; I Would not Die in Spring Time; Jeanie with the Light Brown Hair; Laura Lee; Lou'siana Belle; Maggie by My Side; Massa's in de Cold, Cold Ground; Melinda May; My Old Kentucky Home; Nelly Bly; Nelly Was a Lady; Oh! Boys, Carry Me 'Long; Oh! Susanna; Old Black Joe; Old Dog Tray; Old Folks at Home; Old Uncle Ned; Open Thy Lattice, Love; She Was All the World to Me; Sitting by My Own Cabin Door; There's a Good Time Coming; Virginia Belle; Way Down in Ca-i-ro; Willie, We Have Missed You;* and others.

FRANCK, CÉSAR. For the Theatre: *Le Valet de Ferme; Hulda; Ghisèle.* Orchestra: *Symphony* in D Minor; *Psyché; Variations Symphoniques; Les Djinns; Les Eolides; Le Chasseur Maudit.* Chamber Music: *Trois Trios Concertants; Quatrième Trio Concertant; Andante Quietoso; Piano Quintet in F Minor; Sonata for piano and violin; String Quartet in D Major.* For Voice and Orchestra: *Ruth; La Tour de Babel; Les Béatitudes; Paris, chant Patriotique; Rédemption; Rebecca; Psyché; Psaume CL; Le Vase Brisé; Nocturne; La Procession; Les Cloches du Soir.* Voice: *Souvenance; Ninon; L'Émir de Bengador; Le Sylphe; Robin Grey; L'Ange et l'Enfant; Le Mariage des Roses; Roses et Papillons; Lied; Les Trois Exilés; Ave Maria; Domine non Secundum; Quasi fremuerunt gentes; Panis Angelicus; Veni Creator; Hymne; Le Premier Sourire de Mai;*

Cantique; and others. Piano: *Églogue; Grand Caprice; Souvenirs d'Aix-la-Chapelle; Quatre Melodies de Schubert; Ballade; Fantasies* on Dalayrac's *Gulistan; Fantaisie; Les Plaintes d'une Poupée; Prélude Choral et Fugue; Danse Lente; Prélude Aria et Final.* Organ: *Andantino; Trois Antiennes; Six pièces pour Grand Orgue; 44 Petites Pièces; Préludes et Prières de Ch. V. Alkan; Trois Chorals;* and many others.

FRANZ, ROBERT. Songs: *Die Lotosblume; Schlummerlied; Aus Meinem Grossen Schmerzen; Auf dem Meere; Mädchen mit dem Rothen Mündchen; Gute Nacht; Vergessen; Wie des Mondes Abbild; Bitte; Für Musik; Stille Sicherheit; Mutter, O sing mich zur Ruh; Ein Friedhof; Widmung; Marie am Fenster; Wonne der Wehmuth; Mein Schatz ist auf der Wanderschaft; Es hat die Rose sich Beklagt;* and others.

GERSHWIN, GEORGE. Musical Comedies: *La La Lucille; Our Nell; Sweet Little Devil; Lady Be Good; Tip-Toes; Song of the Flame; Oh Kay; Strike Up the Band; Funny Face; Treasure Girl; Show Girl; Girl Crazy; Delicious; Of Thee I Sing; Let 'em Eat Cake; An American in Paris.* Symphonic-Jazz: *Rhapsody in Blue; Piano Concerto in F; Second Rhapsody.* Opera: *Porgy and Bess.*

GLINKA, MICHAEL. Operas: *A Life for the Tsar; Russlan and Ludmilla.* Orchestra: *Jota Aragonesa; Night in Madrid; Kamarinskaya; Valse-Fantaisie;* Incidental music to *Prince Kholmsky.* Chamber Music: *String Quartet* in F; Minuet for string quartet; *Trio* for piano, clarinet and bassoon; *Sextet* for piano and strings. Piano: Five *valses;* seven *Mazurkas;* eight sets of *Variations;* four *Fugues*, *Polkas*, *Nocturnes*, *Polonaises*, etc. (about 40 pieces). Voice: Polish Hymn, *Great is Our God;* Memorial Cantata; *The Midnight Review;* 85 songs, duets, and quartets.

GLUCK, CHRISTOPH W. Operas: *Artaserse; Demétrio; Demofoonte; Tigrane; Sofonisba; Ipermestra; Poro; Ippolito; La Caduta dei Giganti; Artamène; Le Nozze d'Ercole e d'Ébé; Semiramide Riconosciuta; La Contesa dei Numi; Ezio; Issipile; La Clemenza di Tito; Le Cinèsi; L'Innocenza Giustificata; La Danza; Antigono; Il Re Pastore; Tetide; Orféo ed Euridice; Il Trionfo di Clelia; Telemaco; Il Parnaso Confuso; La Corona; Prologo; Alceste; Le Feste d'Apollo; Paride ed Elena; Iphigénie en Aulide; Orphée; Alceste; Armide; Iphigénie en Tauride; Echo et Narcisse.* Opéras Comiques: *L'lle de Merlin; La Fausse Esclave; Cythère Assiégée; L'Arbre Enchanté; L'lvrogne Corrigé; Le Cadi Dupé; La Rencontre Imprévue.* Ballets: *Don Juan; Semiramide; L'Orfano della China.* Church Music: *De Profundis.* Vocal Music: Klopstock's Odes. Chamber Music: 9 Symphonies; 6 Sonatas.

GOUNOD, CHARLES. Operas: *Sapho; La Nonne Sanglante; Le Médecin Malgré Lui; Faust; Philémon et Baucis; La Reine de Saba; Mireille; La Colombe; Roméo et Juliette; Cinq-Mars; Polyeucte; Le Tribut de Zamora.* Oratorios: *La Rédemption; Mors et Vita; Tobie.* Cantatas: *Marie Stuart; Fernand; Les Sept Paroles du Christ; Jésus de*

Nazareth; Jésus sur le Lac de Tibériade; A la Frontière; Gallia; Le Vin des Gaulois et la Danse de l'Épée. Church Music: 9 Masses; three *Requiems; Stabat Mater; Te Deum; De Profundis,* etc. Orchestra: Symphonies in D and in E-Flat; *La Reine des Apôtres; Marche Romaine; Le Calme.* Piano: *Marche Pontificale; Convoi Funèbre d'une Marionette; Dodelinette; Romances; Morceaux.* Miscellaneous: *Méditation sur le Prélude de Bach* (known as the *Air on the G String*), etc.

GRANADOS, ENRIQUE. Orchestra: 4 Suités *Elisenda, Navidad, Arabe, Gallega; Marcha de los Vencidos; La Nit del Mort* (poem). Stage Works: *Maria del Carmèn; Goyescas; Petrarca; Follet; Picarol; Gaziel; Liliana; Miel de la Alcarría.* Voice and Piano: *Coleccion de Canciones Amatorias; Coleccion de Tonadillas; Elegia Eterna; La Boira; L'Ocell Profeta.* Piano: Twelve *Spanish Dances;* two *Spanish Dances; Danza Gitana; Danzas Para Cantar y Bailar; A la Cubana;* Six Pieces on Spanish Popular Songs; Rapsodiá Aragonesa; *Capricho Español; Morisca; Canciòn Arabe; Escenas Romanticas; Escenas Poeticas; Libro de Horas; Valses Poeticos; Valses de Amor; Carezza; Allegro de Concierto;* two *Impromptus; Romeo y Julieta; Fantasia; Goyescas,* Parts I and II; and many others. Twenty-six unpublished sonatas by Scarlatti transcribed for the piano by Granados. Chamber Music: *Serenata* for two violins and piano; *Madrigal; Trova,* for cello and piano; Trio; *Oriental* for oboe and strings. Choral: *Cant de les Estrelles* for chorus, organ and piano.

GRIEG, EDVARD. Orchestra: Concert Overture *In Autumn; Peer Gynt* Suite, No. 1; *Romance* with Variations; *Peer Gynt* Suite, No. 2; Three Numbers from *Sigurd Jorsalfar;* Lyric Pieces; Piano Concerto in A Minor. Various works for String orchestra, and for chorus and orchestra. Chamber Music: Sonatas for violin and piano, No. 1, F Major, No. 2, G Major, No. 3, A Minor; String Quartet, G Major; Sonata for cello and piano, A Minor. Piano: *Four Pieces;* Six *Poetic Tone Pictures;* Three *Humoresques; Sonata* in E Minor; *Lyric Pieces,* 10 Books; *Sketches of Norwegian Life; Ballade* in G Minor; Four *Album Leaves; Holberg* Suite; *Cradle Song; I Love You; When Once She Lay;* Twenty-five *Northern Dances* and *Folk Tunes; The Princess; To Spring; Norwegian Peasant Dances; Moods; Funeral March for Nordraak;* Many others. Also, for four hands: Concert Overture, *In Autumn;* Two *Symphonic Pieces;* Four *Norwegian Dances;* Two *Waltz Caprices; Symphonic Dances.* Songs: *Closely Wrapped in Murky Vapors; I Stood in Gloomy Musing; The Miller Maiden; What Shall I Say?; Parting; Morning Dew; The Old Song; Hunting Song; Where Have They Fled?; The Orphan; The Poet's Heart; I Love You; My Mind Is Like a Snow-Crowned Peak; Two Brown Eyes; At Sunset; Outward Bound; Cradle Song; The Harp; Thanks; Forest Song; Language of the Flowers; Song of the Crag; Love; Margaret's Cradle Song; A Mother's Grief; Folksong from Langeland; The Poet's Last Song; Woodland Wanderings; Autumn Storm; The Hut; Poesy; Rosebuds; She Is So Pure; The Young Birch Tree;* Three Songs from *Peer Gynt; In the*

Summer Evening; Autumn Thoughts; The First Primrose; Hope; At the Bier of a Young Woman; When to That Song I Listen; 'Neath the Roses; Hidden Love; From Monte Pincio; From Fjeld and Fjord; Prologue; Joan; Ragna; Ragnhild; Ingelborg; Epilogue; Have You Seen the Brave Peasant Lad?; Waft, O Waters; At Your Service, Ladies!; Lo! the Evening Light; Christmas Snow; Spring Showers; The Return Home; From the Fatherland; Hendrik Wergeland; The Dairy Maid; The Wanderer; The Mountain Maid etc.; *The Odalisque; The Princess; Ave Maria Stella;* Many others.

HANDEL, GEORGE F. Operas: *Agrippina; Rinaldo; Radamisto; Ottone; Giulio Cesare; Tamerlano; Rodelinda; Admeto; Tolomeo; Ezio; Serse;* and many others, totaling 46 in all. Oratorios: *Saint John Passion; La Resurrezione; Trionfo del tempo; Saul; Israel in Egypt; Ode to Saint Cecilia; L'Allegro, il Pensieroso ed il Moderato; Messiah; Samson; Semele; Joseph; Belshazzar; Hercules; Judas Maccabaeus; Alexander Balus; Joshua; Solomon; Susanna; Theodora; Alceste; Choice of Hercules; Jephtha; Triumph of Time and Truth; Acis and Galatea; Esther; Deborah; Athalia; Saul;* totalling 32. Cantatas: 100 Cantatas and 20 duets. Instrumental Music: *Water Music; Forest Music; Fire Music;* 5 orchestral concerti; 12 concerti grossi; 3 concerti a due cori; Sinfonie diverse; ouvertures; 6 organ concerti; 15 chamber sonatas; 2 sonatas for oboe; 12 sonatas for flute; 22 trio sonatas; Sonata for viola da gamba, etc. Also, for Harpsichord: 16 Suites de Pièces; 6 Fugues; Various detached suites and pieces not dated. Church

Music: Psalms; Utrecht *Te Deum* and *Jubilate;* various *Anthems* etc.

ORCHESTRAL WORKS: *Andante; Andantino; Symphony "1933"; Chorale for Strings; Johnny Comes Marching Home; Farewell to Pioneers; Second Symphony; Prelude & Fugue for Strings; "Time" Suite; Third Symphony.*

CHAMBER MUSIC: *Concerto* for piano, clar. & string quartet; Piano Sonata; First String Quartet; String Sextet; Three Var. on Theme; Quintet for piano and wind instr.; Piano Trio; Poem for Violin and Piano; Passacaglia, Cadenza and Fugue for Piano Quintet; and others.

CHORAL WORKS: *Song for Occupations; Symphony for Voices; Whitman Suite; Story of Noah; Sanctus; He's Gone Away;* etc.

HAYDN, FRANZ JOSEPH. Stage Works: *Der neue krumme Teufel; La Marchesa Napola; La Vedova; Il Dottore; Il Sganarello; Acide e Galatea; La Cantarina; Lo Speziale; Le Pescatrici; L'Infedeltà delusa; L'Incontro impromiso; La vera costanza; Il Mondo della luna; L'Isola disabitata; La Fedeltà premiata; Orlando Paladino; Armida;* and others. Symphonies: *Le Matin*, D Major; *Le Midi*, C Major; *Le Soir*, G Major; *Horn Signal*, D Major; *Surprise*, G Major; *Military Symphony*, G Major; *The Clock*, D Minor and Major; *Drum Roll*, E-Flat Major; *London*, D Minor and Major; The *Farewell*, F-Sharp Minor; Oxford, G Major; and many more, totaling over a hundred. Other Orchestral Works: About 70 Cassations, Divertimenti, Nocturnes and Serenades. About 80 Marches, Minuets and German dances. About 50 Concertos, Concertinos, etc., for various instruments. About 200 Pieces for baryton and for lyra viol. *Feld-Partien* for wind instruments. Chamber Music: 61 string quartets; about 38 Piano trios; 30 trios for strings; 15 trios for various combinations. Sonatas for piano and violin. Several Quintets and one Sextet. *Echo* for 4 violins and 2 cellos; and many more. Oratorios and Cantatas: *Il Ritorno di Tobia; Mare Clausum; The Creation; The Seven Words of the Saviour on the Cross; The Seasons; Birthday Cantata* for Prince Nicolaus Esterhazy; *Festival Cantata;* etc. Church Music: 12 Masses; *Stabat Mater;* Motets. Miscellaneous: Songs for solo; for several voices; pieces for Clavier, for musical clock, for glass harmonica, etc.

HERBERT, VICTOR. Operettas: *Prince Ananias; The Wizard of the Nile; The Gold Bug; The Serenade; The Idol's Eye; The Fortune-Teller; Cyrano de Bergerac; The Singing Girl; The Ameer; The Viceroy; Babes in Toyland; Babette; It Happened in Nordland; Miss Dolly Dollars; Wonderland; Mlle; Modiste; The Red Mill; Dream-City; The Magic Knight; The Tattooed Man; The Rose of Algeria; Little Nemo; The Prima Donna; Old Dutch; Naughty Marietta; When Sweet Sixteen; Mlle. Rosita; The Lady of the Slippers; The Madcap Duchess; Sweethearts; The Debutante; The Only Girl; Princess Pat; Eileen;*

Her Regiment; The Dream Girl. Operas: *Natoma; Madeleine.* Instrumental and Choral Works.

HINDEMITH, PAUL. Orchestra: *Concert music* for strings and brass; *Philharmonic* Concerto; Symphony, *Mathis der Maler; Concerto* for orchestra; *Philharmonic Dances; Concertos* for cello and piano. With Chamber orchestra: 4 *Concertos*, for piano, violin, cello, and viola; 2 *Concertos*, for viola d'amore, organ; *Concert Music* for solo viola; *Der Schwanendreher* for viola; *Trauermusik* for viola. Chamber Music: *Three Pieces*, cello and piano; 4 *string quartets;* 16 *sonatas;* 1 *quintet;* string *trio; Chamber music* for five winds; *Trio* for viola, heckelphone and piano; many more. Piano: *In einer Nacht; Dance-pieces; 1922 Suite;* Three *Studies;* Three *Sonatas; Small Pieces.* Voice: Eight *Songs with Piano; Die Junge Magd; Das Marienleben; Die Serenaden; Des Todes Tod;* and others. Wind Instruments: *Concert Music* for wind orchestra; *Concert Music* for piano, brass, and harp. Gebrauchsmusik, etc.: *Spielmusik* for strings, flutes, and oboes; *Songs for Singing Groups; Music to Sing or Play*, for amateurs or music-lovers; *The Lindbergh Flight*, for radio; *Let's Build a Town*, play with music for children; *Plöner Musiktag;* and many more. For the Theater: *Mörder, Hoffnung der Frauen; Das Nusch-Nuschi; Santa Susannah; Mathis der Maler* (opera); *Nobilissima Visione* (ballet); *Hin und Zurück;* and more.

HUMPERDINCK, ENGELBERT. Operas: *Hänsel und Gretel; Dornröschen; Die Heirat wider*

Willen; Die Königskinder; Die Marketenderin; Gaudeamus. Incidental Music: *The Merchant of Venice; The Winter's Tale; the Tempest; As You Like It; Lysistrata; The Blue Bird; The Miracle.* Voice: *Das Glück von Edenhall; Die Wallfahrt nach Kevlaar; Kinderlieder*, etc.

INDY, VINCENT D'. For the Theatre: *Attendez-moi sous l'orme; Le Chant de la cloche; Karadec; Fervaal; Medée; L'Étranger; La Légende de Saint-Christophe; Le Rêve de Cynias.* Orchestra: *Jean Hunyade; Antony and Cleopatra; La Forêt enchantée; Saugefleurie; Symphonie Cevenole* for orchestra and piano; *Sérénade et Valse;* Fantaisie for orchestra and oboe solo; *Tableaux de Voyage; Istar; Medée;* Second Symphony in B Flat; *Jour d'éte á la montagne; Wallenstein trilogy; Souvenirs; La queste de Dieu; Symphonie sur un chant montagnard français;* and others. Chamber Music: 3 String Quartets; 2 Trios, 1 Sonata, 1 piano Quintet, 1 piano quartet; 1 Sextet; and others. Piano: *Trois Romances sans paroles;* Petite Sonate; *Poème des Montagnes;* Quatre *Pièces; Helvètia; Saugefleurie; Sarabande et Menuet; Nocturne; Promenade; Schumanniana; Tableaux de Voyage; Sonata* in E; *Menuet sur le nom de Haydn; Pour les enfants de tout age; Conte de fées; Fantaisie sur un vieil air de ronde française;* and others. Voice: *Attente; Madrigal; Plainte de Thecla; Clair de Lune; L'Amour et le Crane; Lied maritime; La première dent;* Ninety *Chansons populaires du Vivarais; Mirage; Les Yeux de l'Aimée; Vocalise.* Miscellaneous: Vocal Works; works for organ; literary works.

IVES, CHARLES E. Orchestra: Fourth Symphony; First Orchestral Set; Second Orchestrai

Set; *Symphony Holidays;* Overture No. 3; *Tone Roads* No. 3; Scherzo No. 2; *Barn Dance; In the Night; General Booth Enters Heaven; 67th Psalm.* Chorus: *An Election; The Masses; Lincoln—The Great Commoner; 67th Psalm.* Chamber Music: Fourth Violin and Piano *Sonata; String Quartet* No. 2; *Aeschylus and Sophocles*, for string quartet, piano, voice; *Concord, Massachusetts, 1840–60*, piano sonata. Also songs and song cycles.

KERN, JEROME. Popular Musical Productions: *Very Good, Eddie; Have a Heart; Oh, Boy; Sally; Stepping Stones; Sunny; Show Boat; Sweet Adeline; Music in the Air;* and others.

LASSO, ORLANDO DI. Sacred Music: *Sacrae Cantiones 5 vocum* (25 numbers); *Seven Penitential Psalms; Madrigals;* Chansons; Motets. A great many compositions, totaling 1,250.

LEONCAVALLO, RUGGIERO. Operas: *Chatterton; Pagliacci; Zaza; Der Roland; Maia; Malbruk; I Zingari; La reginalla delle rose; Are You There?; La Candidata; Gioffredo Mameli; Prestami tua moglie; Edipo Re.* Ballet: (*La Vita d'una Marionetta.*) Symphonic Poem: *Serafita.*

LISZT, FRANZ. Orchestra: Symphonic Poems: *Ce qu'on entend sur la montagne; Tasso; Les Préludes; Orpheus; Prometheus; Mazeppa; Festklänge; Hungaria; Hamlet; Hunnenschlacht; Die Ideale;* and others. Also *Faust Symphony; Dante Symphony;* Two Episodes from Lenau's *Faust; Les Morts; Goethe Festmarsch;* and others. Piano: *A la Chapelle Sixtine; Album d'un Voyageur; Ap-*

paritions; Années de Pèlerinage; Ave Maria; Consolations; Élégies; Études de Concert; Mazurka Brillante; Mephisto-Waltz; Les Funérailles; Mephisto-Polka; Sonata in B Minor; Grande Valse de Bravura; Valse Impromptu; Transcendental Études; Liebestraüme; 20 *Hungarian Rhapsodies; Czardas* (2); *La Marseillaise; God Save the Queen; Napolitana; Rhapsodie Espagnole; Trois Airs Suisses; Rakoczy March; Roumanian* Rhapsody; and many others, including transcriptions. Piano and Orchestra: 2 concertos, in E-flat and A-flat; *Hungarian Fantasia; Todtentanz;* and others. Songs: Fifty-five collected songs; and others. Transcriptions from Operas: *Grande Fantaisie sur La Sonnambula* (Bellini); *Fantaisie sur des motifs de Dom Sebastien* (Donizetti); *Reminiscences de Lucia di Lammermoor* (Donizetti); *Robert le Diable* (Meyerbeer); *Le Prophète* (Meyerbeer); *L'Africaine* (Meyerbeer); Many others from works of Auber, Glinka, Gounod, Halévy, Lassen, Mozart, Busoni, Raff, Tchaikovsky, Verdi, and Wagner. Religious Works: *The Legend of Saint Elizabeth,* oratorio; *Christus*, oratorio; *Natus est Christus*, hymn; *Hymne de l'enfant;* Mass for four male voices; *Missa choralis* in A Minor; *Graner Mass;* Hungarian *Coronation Mass;* Motets; and others. Miscellaneous: Many Transcriptions of instrumental works and songs; Works for Organ; Secular Choral Music; instrumental and literary works.

LOEFFLER, CHARLES M. Orchestra: *La Mort de Tintagiles; La Villanelle du Diable; A Pagan Poem; Poem; Memories of My Childhood; Canticum Fratris Solis; Evocation;* Five *Irish Fantasies.*

Chorus: Opus 3, *By the Rivers of Babylon; For one who fell in battle; Beat, beat, drums.* Chamber Music: Two *Rhapsodies* for oboe, viola, and piano; Music for Four Stringed Instruments; *Quintet* in One Movement for 3 violins, viola and cello. Songs: Four Melodies for voice and piano; Four Poems for voice, viola and piano; Four Poems for voice and piano; *The Wind among the Reeds; The Reveller;* and others. Miscellaneous Works: Violin studies, etc.

LULLY, JEAN BAPTISTE. Operas: *Cadmus et Hermione; Alceste; Thésée; Atys; Isis; Psyché; Bellérophon; Proserpine; Persée; Phaëton; Amadis de Gaule; Roland; Armide et Renaud; Les Fêtes de L'Amour et de Bacchus.* Comedy-Ballets: *Le Mariage forcé; L'Amour médecin; La Princesse d'Élide; Le Sicilien; Georges Dandin; Monsieur de Pourceaugnac; Les Amants magnifiques; Psyché; Le Bourgeois Gentilhomme.* Pastorales and Divertissements: *Les plaisirs de l'île enchantée; La pastorale comique; Les festes de Versailles; La Grotte de Versailles; Idylle de Sceaux ou de la Paix.* Ballets: *Ballets d'Alcidiane; Ballet de la raillerie; Ballet de Xerxès; Ballet de l'Impatience; Ballet des saisons; Ballet de l'Ercole amante;* and many others. Instrumental: *Danses,* for various instruments; *Suites de Symphonies et Trios,* etc. Religious: 5 *Grands Motets,* 12 *Petits Motets,* and many more.

MACDOWELL, EDWARD. Orchestra: *Hamlet and Ophelia; Lancelot and Elaine; Lamia; The Saracens; First Suite; Second (Indian) Suite.* 2 Piano Concertos: No. 1, A Minor; No. 2, D Minor. Piano: First Modern Suite; Prelude and Fugue; Second Modern Suite; *Serenata; Two Fantastic Pieces* (1) *Legend* (2) *Witches' Dance;* Two Pieces, *Barcarolle, Humoresque; Forest Idyls;* Four Pieces (1) *Humoresque* (2) *March* (3) *Cradle Song* (4) *Czardas;* Six Idyls after Goethe (1) *In the Woods* (2) *Siesta* (3) *To the Moonlight* (4) *Silver Clouds* (5) *Flute Idyl* (6) *The Bluebell;* Six Poems after Heine, (1) *From a Fisherman's Hut* (2) *Scotch Poem* (3) *From Long Ago* (4) *The Post Wagon* (5) *The Shepherd Boy* (6) *Monologue;* Four Little Poems (1) *The Eagle* (2) *The Brook* (3) *Moonshine* (4) *Winter*; Étude de Concert, F Sharp; *Les Orientales; Marionettes*, Eight Little Pieces; *Twelve Studies; Twelve Virtuoso Studies; Sonata Tragica;* Air and Rigaudon; Sonata No. 2, *Eroica; Woodland Sketches*, incl. *To a Wild Rose, To a Water Lily, Told at Sunset; Sea Pieces;* Sonata No. 3, *Norse;* Sonata No. 4, *Keltic; Fireside Tales; New England Idyls*, (1) *An Old Garden* (2) *Midsummer* (3) *Midwinter* (4) *With Sweet Lavender* (5) *In Deep Woods* (6) *Indian Idyl* (7) *To an Old White Pine* (8) *From Puritan Days* (9) *From a Log Cabin* (10) *The Joy of Autumn; Technical Exercises*—2 Bks. Songs: Two Old Songs (1) *Deserted* (2) *Slumber Song;* Album of Five Songs (1) *My Love and I* (2) *You Love Me Not* (3) *In the Sky Where Stars are Glowing* (4) *Night Song* (5) *The Chain of Roses;* From an Old Garden (1) *The Pansy* (2) *The Myrtle* (3) *The Clover* (4) *The Yellow Daisy* (5) *The Bluebell* (6) *The Mignonette;* Three Songs (1) *Prayer* (2) *Cradle-song* (3) *Idyl;* Two Songs after Robert Burns (1) *Menie* (2) *My Jean;* Six Love Songs; Eight Songs (1) *The Robin Sings in the Apple-tree* (2) *Midsummer Lul-*

laby (3) *Folksong* (4) *Confidence* (5) *The West Wind Croons in the Cedar Trees* (6) *In the Woods* (7) *The Sea* (8) *Through the Meadow;* Four Songs (1) *Long Ago* (2) *The Swan Bent Low to the Lily* (3) *A Maid Sings Light* (4) *As the Gloaming Shadows Creep;* Three Songs (1) *Constancy* (2) *Sunrise* (3) *Merry Maiden Spring;* Three Songs (1) *Tyrant Love* (2) *Fair Springtide* (3) *To the Goldenrod.* Miscellaneous: Part-Songs; Piano Duets; Arrangements; Poems.

MAHLER, GUSTAV. Symphonies: No. 1 in D Major ("Titan"); No. 2 in C Minor ("Resurrection"); No. 3 in D Minor; No. 4 in G Major ("Ode to Heavenly Joy"); No. 5 in C Sharp Minor; No. 6 in A Minor ("Tragic"); No. 7 in E Minor ("Song of the Night"); No. 8 in E Major ("The Symphony of a Thousand"); No. 9 in D Major; No. 10 (unfinished). Song-Cycles and Songs: *Lieder eines fahrenden Gesellen; Lieder und Gesänge aus der Jugendzeit; Kindertotenlieder;* Five Songs from Rückert; *Das Lied von der Erde.* Cantata: *Das Klagende Lied.*

MASCAGNI, PIETRO. Operas: *Cavalleria Rusticana; L'amico Fritz; I Rantzau; Guglielmo Ratcliff; Silvano; Zanetto; Iris; Le Maschere; Amica; Isabeau; Parisina; Lodoletta; Il Piccolo Marat; Si; Nerone.* Other Compositions: Cantata for the Leopardi centenary; Requiem in Memory of King Humbert; *Rapsodia Satanica,* etc.

MASSENET, JULES. Operas: *La Grand'tante; Don César de Bazan; Les Erynnies; Le Roi de*

Lahore; Hérodiade; Manon; Le Cid; Esclarmonde; Le Mage; Werther; Le Carillon; Thaïs; Le Portrait de Manon; La Navarraise; Sapho; Cendrillon; Phédre; Grisélidis; Les Rosati; Le Jongieur de Notre Dame; La Cigale; Cherubin; Ariane; Thérèse; Espada; Bacchus; Don Quichotte; Roma; Panurge; Cléopatre; Amadis. Voice and Orchestra: *David Rizzio; Marie-Magdeleine; Éve; Narcisse; La Vierge; Biblis; La Terre Promise.* Orchestra: Overture de Concert; First Suite; *Scènes Hongroises; Scènes Dramatiques;* Overture to *Phèdre; Scènes Pittoresques; Scènes Napolitaines; Scènes de Féerie; Scènes Alsaciennes; Parade Militaire; Visions*, symphonic poem; *Devant la Madone; Marche Solennelle; Fantaisie* for cello and orchestra; *Brumaire*, overture; Concerto for piano and orchestra. Other Works: Choruses, duets, and about 200 songs.

MENDELSSOHN, FELIX BARTHOLDY. Orchestra: Symphony No. 1, in C Minor; *A Midsummer Night's Dream*, Overture in E Major; *Overture in C Major* for wind instruments; *Die Hebriden Overture* in B Minor; *Meeresstille und Glückliche Fahrt Overture* in D Major; *Märchen von der Schönen Melusine Overture* in E Major; Symphony No. 2; Symphony No. 3, in A Minor (Scotch); Symphony No. 4 in A Major (Italian); Overture *Ruy Blas* in C Minor; Overture in C Major, *Trumpet; Trauermarsch* in A Minor; Symphony No. 5 in D Minor (*Reformation*); *March* in D Major. Piano and Orchestra: Concerto No. 1 in G Minor; Concerto No. 2 in D Minor; Rondo Brillant, in E-Flat Major, and others. Violin and Orchestra: Concerto in E

Minor. Chorus: Oratorio, *Elijah; Lauda Sion*, Sacred Cantata; *Glory to God in the Highest; Grant us Thy Peace; Hear My Prayer*, Hymn; 6 Motets; many Psalms; and others. Chamber Music: *Octet*, E-Flat Major, for four violins, two violas, two cellos; *Sextet*, D Major; two *Quintets* for strings; seven *quartets* for strings and three with piano; two *trios* for violin, cello and piano; a *sonata* for violin; two *sonatas* for cello; 2 *concertstücke;* and others. Piano: *Rondo Capriccioso*, E Minor; *Songs without Words* (8 books); Six *Preludes and Fugues; Variations sérieuses*, D Minor; *Variations*, E-Flat Major; *Variations*, B-Flat Major; Sonatas; *Capriccio; Albumblatt;* Many others. Songs: *On Wings of Song; Winterlied; Sonntagslied; Volkslied; Gruss; O Jugend; O Schöne Rosenzeit; Venezedianisches Gondellied;* and others totaling 74 in all. Organ: Three *Preludes and Fugues;* Six *Sonatas; Allegro*, B Flat Major; *Andante and Variations*, D Major; *Fugue*, F Minor; *Praeludium*, C Minor. Miscellaneous: Partsongs; Songs for Voice and Organ; Works for the theater.

MEYERBEER, GIACOMO. Operas: *Jephthas Gelübde; Alimelek; Romilda e Costanza; Semiramide riconosciuta; Eduardo e Cristina; Emma di Resburgo; Margherita d'Anjou; L'esule di Granata; Das Brandenburger Thor; Il crociato in Egitto; Robert le Diable; Les Huguenots; Das Feldlager in Schlesien; Le Prophète; L'Étoile du Nord; Dinorah ou Le Pardon de Ploermel; L'Africaine.* Oratorio: *Gott und die Natur;* and Cantatas. Miscellaneous: church music; songs for voice and piano; three dances for brass band; *Grand*

March for orchestra; *Overture* in the form of a March; *Coronation March*, etc.

MILHAUD, DARIUS. For the Theatre: *La Brébis Égarée; Les Euménides; Agamemnon; Les Choëphores; Salade*, ballet; *Le Pauvre Matelot; Christophe Colomb; L'Annonce fait à Marie; Protée; Le Boeuf sur le Toit; Le Train Bleu; La Création du Monde;* and others. For Orchestra: 2 Symphonic Suites; 5 symphonies for small orchestra; *L'Homme et son Désir; Le Tango des Fratellini; Fantaisie sur le Boeuf sur le Toit; Caramel Mou*, shimmy, for jazz band; *Serénade; Saudades do Brazil; Deux Hymnes;* 3 *Rag Caprices; Actualités;* 6 *Préludes Dramatiques;* and others. Chamber Music: Sonatines and Sonatas; 9 string Quartets; *Le Printemps*, violin and piano; etc. Piano: *Suite; Sonata; Printemps; Caramel Mou, shimmy; Saudades do Brazil;* 3 *Rag Caprices.* With Orchestra: *Concerto; Le Carnaval d'Aix;* 5 *Études; Ballade.* Voice and Piano: 7 *Poèmes de la Connaissance de l'Est;* 3 *Poèmes de Lucille de Chateaubriand;* 4 *Poèmes de Léo Latil;* 4 *Poèmes de Paul Claudel;* 2 *Poèmes d'Amour; Poèmes Juifs; Les Soirées de Petrograd;* 3 *Prières Journalières;* and others. Other vocal and miscellaneous works.

MONTEVERDI, CLAUDIO. For the Theatre: *Orfeo; Ballo delle Ingrate; Tirsi e Clori; Il Combattimento di Tancredi e Clorinda; Il Ritorno d'Ulisse in patria; L'Incoronazione di Poppea; Lament of Arianna.* Also 13 lost works. Sacred Works: Masses and Psalms in great numbers. Madrigals: 8 Books for 5 voices; 1 Book for 2 or 3 voices. Miscellaneous Works: Scherzi Musicali; Canzonettas, etc.

MOUSSORGSKY, MODEST. Operas: *The Marriage; Boris Godunoff; Mlada; Khovanschchina; The Fair At Sorotchinsk.* Songs: *Little Star, Where Art Thou?; Why, Tell Me, Maiden?; The Merry Hour; The Leaves Rustled Sadly; Why Speak of Love?; King Saul; The Harper's Song; Could I but Meet Thee; I Own Many Palaces; The Winds Blow Wild; Night; Kaltistrat; A Prayer; The Outcast; The Peasant's Lullaby; Why Should Your Eyes?; Longing; Hopak; My Tears Give Birth to Flowers; Savishna; You Drunken Sot; Jewish Song; Tell Me, Maiden; The Magpie; Gathering Mushrooms; The Banquet; The Ragamuffin; By the Don; The Classic; The Orphan; Yeromushka's Lullaby; A Child's Song; The Nursery; The Peep-Show; Evening Song; You Saw Me Not in the Crowd; Sunless; He Lies Forgotten; The Wanderer; The Song of the Flea;* many others. Choral Works: *The Rout of Sennacherib; Joshuah; Four Russian Folksongs.* Orchestral Works: *A Night on Bare Mountain*, and others. Piano: *Souvenir d'Enfance; Scherzo C Sharp Minor; Memories of My Childhood; Pictures from an Exhibition;* and others.

MOZART, WOLFGANG AMADEUS. Operas: *La Finta Semplice; Bastien und Bastienne; Mitridate, Re di Ponto; Ascanio in Alba; Lucio Silla; La Finta Giardiniera; Il Re Pastore; Zauberflöte, Idomeneo, Re di Creta; Die Entführung aus dem Serail; Le Nozze di Figaro; Don Giovanni; Cosi fan tutte; La*

Clemenza di Tito; Die Schuldigkeit des ersten Gebotes; Apollo et Hyacinthus seu Hyacinthi Metamorphosis; Il Sogno di Scipione; Zaïde; Thamos, König in Aegypten; Der Schauspieldirektor; Lo Sposo Deluso; and others. Church Music: Many Masses, *Offertories, etc.; Requiem, D Minor.* Vocal Music: About 54 arias with orchestra; Many Songs with piano; *Choral Works with Orchestra; Unaccompanied Music for Several Voices; Other Miscellaneous Vocal Works.* Orchestra: Nearly fifty symphonies; Concertos for piano, violin, bassoon, harp and other instruments with orchestra,—about 60. Chamber Music: 7 String Quintets; 23 String Quartets; 5 String Trios and Duets; 2 Piano Quartets; 8 Piano Trios; 35 Violin and Piano Sonatas. Piano: about 60 works, including 16 piano sonatas; works for 4 hands, for 2 pianos, etc. Miscellaneous Works: Sonatas for organ and orchestra; organ and strings; voice with different instruments; choral works with orchestra; too many to mention.

OFFENBACH, JACQUES. Operettas: *Orphée aux Enfers; La Belle Hélène; Barbe-Bleue; La Vie Parisienne; La Grande Duchesse de Gerolstein; Madame Favart; La Périchole; Romance de la Rose; Voyage dans la Lune;* and many more.

PALESTRINA, GIOVANNI PIERLUIGI DA. Masses: Many for 8, 6, 5, and 4 voices,—including *Ecce Sacerdos Magnus; Missa Papae Marcelli; Illumina Oculos Meos; De Beata Virgine;* and many more. Motets: For 12, 8, 7, 6, 5, 4 voices. Many sacred cantatas, magnificats, hymns, offertories, psalms, litanies, sacred madrigals, lamentations; also a few secular madrigals and cantiones profanae.

PERGOLESI, GIOVANNI BATTISTA. Operas and Oratorios: *Il maestro di musica; La Sallustia; La Serva Padrona; Adriano in Siria; L'Olimpiade; Il Flaminio;* and others, including fragments. Instrumental: 26 sonatas for 2 violins and bass; violin concerto; symphony; many more cantatas and sacred music; many masses and other works; *Stabat mater.*

PROKOFIEFF, SERGE. Operas: *Magdalene; Gambler; Love for Three Oranges; The Flaming Angel.* Ballets: *Buffoon (Chout); Le Pas d'Acier; L'enfant Prodigue; Sur le Borysthène; Romeo and Juliet.* Orchestral Music: *Scythian Suite; Classical Symphony;* 4 symphonies; *Peter and the Wolf; Lieutenant Kije; Eugen Onegin; Boris Godunoff Suite; La Dame de Pique; Egyptian Nights; Marches for Military Orchestra; Russian Overture;* 2 violin concertos; 5 piano concertos; 1 cello concerto. Piano Works: Five piano *Sonatas; Sarcasms; Visions fugitives; Pensées;* many others. Choral Works: *The Swan and the Wave; Seven, They are Seven; Mass Songs; Cantata for the 20th Anniversary of the October revolution; Songs of our Days;* etc. Chamber Music: *Ballade; Overture on Hebrew Themes; Quintet* for Wind and Strings; *Quartet; Sonata* etc.

PUCCINI, GIACOMO. Operas: *Le Villi; Edgar; Manon Lescaut; La Bohème; Tosca; Madama Butterfly; La Fanciulla del West; La*

Rondine; Il Trittico; Il Tabarro; Suor Angelica; Gianni Schicchi; Turandot.

PURCELL, HENRY. Opera: *Dido and Aeneas.* Other stage works: *The Fairy Queen; The History of Dioclesian; King Arthur; The Tempest; The Indian Queen;* incidental music for many plays. Songs: 108 solo songs, 60 anthems; 3 services; 24 psalms, canons and hymns; 22 sacred songs; 53 catches; 43 duets; *Ode on St. Cecilia's Day; Orpheus Brittanicus; From Rosy Bow'rs; Song to Welcome Home His Majesty from Windsor; My Heart is Inditing; They that Go Down to the Sea in Ships; Thou Knowest, Lord, the Secrets of our Hearts;* 25 Odes and Welcome Songs; Many secular cantatas; etc. Instrumental: for strings, without continuo: *Chaconne* in G Minor, 4 parts; Three *Fantasias*, 3 parts; Nine *Fantasias*, 4 parts; *Fantasia* upon 1 note, 5 parts; *In Nomine*, 6 parts; *In Nomine*, 7 parts; *Pavan* in G Minor, 4 parts. For strings with continuo; *Fantasia* on a ground in D Major, 4 parts; *Overtures* in G Major and D Minor (4 parts), and G Minor, 5 parts; Twelve *Sonatas*, 3 parts; Ten *Sonatas*, 4 parts; *Sonata* G Minor and Suite G Major for Violin. Miscellaneous: Pieces for wind; harpsichord; organ.

RACHMANINOFF, SERGEI. Operas: *Aleko; The Miserly Knight; Francesca da Rimini.* For Orchestra: *The Rock; Caprice Bohémien;* 3 Symphonies; *The Isle of the Dead; Four Piano Concertos; Rapsodie.* For Chorus with Orchestra: *The Spring; Liturgy of St. John Chrysostcmus; The Bells; Vesper Mass; Three Russian Folksongs.*

Chamber Music: *Sonata for Cello and Piano; Trio Élégiaque*, and others. Piano Solo: *Five Pieces, Op. 3; Seven Pieces Op. 10; Two Piano Sonatas; Études Tableaux; Moments Musicaux; Variations*, etc.; *Preludes;* also works for two pianos and for piano with other instruments. Songs: 77 in small collections.

RAMEAU, JEAN PHILIPPE. Operas: 17, including *Castor et Pollux; Daphné et Eglé; Zoroastre; Les Sybarites; Hippolyte et Aricie.* Ballets: 10, including *Les Indes Galantes; Les Fêtes d'Hébé; La Princesse de Navarre; Anacréon*, etc. Harpsichord pieces, some with violin or flute. Books on harmony and composition, etc.

RAVEL, MAURICE. Theater Works: *L'Heure Espagnole; Daphnis et Chloé; Ma Mère L'Oye; Adelaide ou le Langage des Fleurs; L'Enfant et les Sortilèges; Boléro.* Orchestral: *Pavane pour une Infante Défunte; Rapsodie Espagnole; Une Barque sur l'Océan; Alborado del Gracioso; Daphnis et Chloé; Ma Mère L'Oye; Le Tombeau de Couperin; La Valse; Boléro; 2 concertos* for piano. Chamber Music: String quartet in F; Piano trio in A minor; sonata for violin and piano; sonata for cello and piano; and others. For Piano: *Menuet antique; Jeux d'Eau; Miroirs; Sonatine; Gaspard de la Nuit; Valses Nobles et sentimentales; Le Tombeau de Couperin;* and others. Songs: *Sur l'herbe; Quatre chants populaires; Ronsard à son âme; Rêves; Deux mélodies hébraiques; Trois Poèmes de Mallarmé*, for voice, piano, string quartet, 2 flutes, 2 clarinets; and others.

RIMSKY-KORSAKOFF, NICOLAS. Operas: *The Maid of Pskov; May Night; Snow Maiden; Mlada; Christmas Eve; Sadko; Mozart and Salieri; Boyarina Vera Sheloga; The Tsar's Bride; Tsar Saltan; Servilia; Kashchey The Immortal; Pan Voevoda; Kitezh; The Golden Cockerel.* Orchestra: *Overture on Three Russian Themes; three Symphonies; Sadko; Fantasia on Serbian Themes; Sinfonietta on Russian Themes; Skazka; Piano Concerto on a Russian Theme; Scheherazade; Easter Overture; On The Tomb; Dubinushka; Spanish Capriccio.* Miscellaneous: Chamber music; cantatas; choruses; duets; piano pieces, etc.

ROSSINI, GIOACCHINO. Operas: *La Cambiale di matrimonio; L'equivoco stravagante; La pietra del paragone; Tancredi di Siracusa; L'Italiana in Algeri; Elisabetta, Regina d'inghilterra; Barbiere di Seviglia; Aureliano in Palmira; La Gazetta; La Cenerentola; Otello; La Gazza Ladra; Armida; Mosè in Egitto; La Donna del lago; Maometto II; Semiramide; Guillaume Tell; Il Figlio Per Azzardo; Il Turco in Italia; Sigismono; Adelaide di Borgogna; Ricciardo e Zoraïde; Ermione; Edoardo e Cristina; Bianca e Falliero; Matilde de Shabran; Zelmira; Il viaggio a Reims; Le Siège de Corinthe; Moïse; Le Comte Ory; L'Occasione fa il ladro; Il Signor Bruschino; L'inganno felice; Ciro in Babilonia; La scala di seta; Torwaldo e Dorliska.* Miscellaneous: *Stabat Mater;* Cantatas; Pasticcios; Juvenilia; and many others.

RUBINSTEIN, ANTON. Operas: *Dmitri Donskoi* and many others; also sacred operas: *Das verlorene Paradies* etc.; also ballet *Die Rebe.*

Songs: About 125. Orchestra: *Six symphonies; Four overtures;* Symphonic Poem *La Russie; Suite in E Flat;* Portraits *Faust, Ivan IV, Don Quixote; Fantasia Eroïca;* 5 piano concertos; 1 violin concerto; 2 cello concertos. Chamber Music: 10 string quartets; 5 trios; octet; piano quintet; string quintet; and many more. Piano Works: *Konzertstück; Fantasia in C; Caprice Russe;* 6 *Soirées de St. Petersburg; Kammenoi Ostrow; Le Bal;* 6 barcarolles; preludes and fugues; études; dances; many shorter pieces; Cadenzas for Beethoven's 5 piano concertos and for Mozart's in D Minor; many more. Miscellaneous: Piano duets; two-piano works; vocal duets; literary works.

SAINT-SAËNS, CHARLES CAMILLE. Operas: *Le Timbre d'Argent; Samson et Dalila; La Princesse Jaune; Henri VIII; Ascanio; Les Barbares; Déjanire; Proserpine; Phryne; Hélène; L'Ancêtre; Étienne Marcel;* Ballet, *Javotte.* Orchestra: *Three symphonies; Five piano concertos; Two cello concertos; Three violin concertos; Danse Macabre; Africa; Le Rouet d'Omphale; Phaëton; La Jeunesse d'Hercule; Le Déluge; La Lyre et la Harpe; Suite Algérienne;* and many more. Piano Music: *Variations on a Theme of Beethoven; Scherzo; Caprice Arabe; Feuillet d'Album; Études; Albumblatt;* and many more. Chamber Music: Sonatas; *Le Carneval des Animaux;* duets; trios; septet; many more. Miscellaneous: Much Organ Music; Incidental Music to plays; Literary works.

SCARLATTI, DOMENICO. Harpsichord: *Esercizie per gravicembalo; Pièces pour le clavecin*

(32 pieces); *Collection* by Alexander Longo (545 pieces); probably others lost. Operas: *Narciso; Orlando; Fatide in Sciro; Ifigenia in Aulide; Ifigenie in Tauride;* etc. Masses; *Stabat Mater;* 2 *Salve Reginas;* 15 *cantatas;* 12 *concertos;* organ fugues, etc.

SCHÖNBERG, ARNOLD. For the Theater: *Erwartung; Die Glückliche Hand; Von Heute auf Morgen;* etc. Orchestra: *Pelleas und Melisande; Chamber Symphony; Five Pieces* for Orchestra; *Variations* for Orchestra; *Pierrot Lunaire;* Violin *concerto.* Choral Works: *Friede auf Erden; Gurrelieder,* and others. Chamber Music: *Verkärte Nacht* Sextet; four *string quartets; Suite* with piano; *Quintet* for wind instruments; and others. Piano Works: *Klavierstücke; Six Pieces; Five Pieces; Suite;* and others. Songs with orchestra: *Nature; The Coat of Arms; Longing; Never was I, O Lady, Tired; Full of that Sweetness; When Little Birds Make their Plaint; Seraphita; All that Seek Thee; Make Me Thy Guardian; Premonition.* With piano: *The Forest Sun; Jane Grey; The Lost Crowd; Das Buch der Hängenden Garten;* and others. Miscellaneous: Arrangements; choruses; songs with other instruments.

SCHUBERT, FRANZ. Songs: *Hark, hark, the lark; Who is Sylvia; Die Mondnacht; Heidenröslein; Fischerweise; Der Wanderer an den Mond; Der Tod und das Mädchen; Erlkönig; Totengräberweise; Der Abend; Am See; Irrlicht; Der Leiermann; Ständchen; Die Post; Der Wegweiser; Das Wirtshaus; Der Doppelgänger; Am Meer; Die Stadt;* and others totalling over 600. Song Cycles: *Die Schöne*

Müllerin; Winterreise; Schwanengesang. Chamber Music: 15 *String quartets;* 1 string, 4 piano Trios; 2 *quintets*, "The Trout" and 2-cello; *Nonet* and *octets; Sonatas* for various instruments. Piano Works: *Valses Nobles; Sonatas; Moments Musicaux; Impromptus;* Many more. Also for four hands. Orchestra: 8 *Symphonies*—D Major; B-Flat Major; D Major; C Minor ("Tragic"); B-Flat Major; C Major; C Major; B Minor ("Unfinished"). Overtures: B-Flat Major; C Major; D Major; *Rosamunde;* and others. *Concertos: Concertstück* for violin; 5 *German Dances;* and others. Choral Works: for mixed voices with orchestra, with piano, unaccompanied; for male voices ditto; for female voices. Miscellaneous: Incidental music; Melodrama; Operas; Operettas.

SCHUMANN, ROBERT. Opera: *Genoveva.* Orchestra: Symphony No. 1, B-Flat Major, "Spring;" Symphony No. 2, C Major; Symphony No. 3, E-Flat Major, "Rhenish"; Symphony No. 4, D Minor; Overture to *Manfred;* other overtures. Concertos: Piano and orchestra, A Minor-Major; cello and orchestra, A Minor; 4 horns; and others. Chamber Music: 3 string *quartets;* piano *quintet;* piano *quartet;* 3 *trios;* 2 violin and piano *sonatas;* and others. Piano Solo: *Abegg* variations; *Papillons; Davidsbündlertänze; Carnaval; Fantasiestücke; Kinderscenen; Kreisleriana; Novelletten; Nachtstücke; Faschingsschwank; Albumblätter;* and many more. Also piano duets and two-piano pieces. Songs: Cycles—*Myrthen; Frauenliebe und Leben; Dichter-Liebe. Liederkreis; Liede und Gesänge; Romanzen und Balladen; Liederalbum für die Jugend;* and many more. Miscellaneous: Trios; duets; part songs; Choral works with orchestra; many Literary Works.

SCRIABIN, ALEXANDER. Orchestra: *Three symphonies; Poem of Ecstasy; Prometheus; Reverie.* Piano: 24 Etudes; 85 Preludes; 10 Sonatas; impromptus, mazurkas, waltzes, fantasias, and many others.

SHOSTAKOVITCH, DMITRI. Orchestra: Seven Symphonies, including No. II, "October" and No. III, "Mayday"; Concerto for piano, trumpet, strings. Operas: *The Nose; Lady Macbeth of Mzensk.* Ballets: *The Golden Age; Bolt; The Limpid Stream.* Piano: *24 Preludes; Piano Sonata; Aphorisms; Three Fantastic Dances.* Chamber Music: Two *pieces for string octet;* one *string quartet;* piano quintet; cello sonata. Films: *Maxim's Youth; The New Babylon; Alone; Golden Mountains; Passerby; Tale of a Priest; His Dumb Hired Man; Girl Companions; Maxim's Return; The Days of Volotachaevo; Vyborg District; A Great Citizen; The Man with a Gun; Silly Little Mouse.* Incidental Music: *The Bed-bug; The Shot; The Virgin Soil; Rule Brittania; Conditionally Killed; Hamlet; The Human Comedy; Salute to Spain.*

SIBELIUS, JAN. For Orchestra: *En Saga; Four Legends; Karelia;* 7 Symphonies: E Minor; D Major; C Major; A Major; E-Flat Major; D Minor; C Major; *Finlandia; Romance in C Major for String Orchestra; Valse Triste; Pelléas et*

Mélisande; Concerto in D Minor for violin and orchestra; Incidental Music to Shakespeare's "The Tempest"; Tapiola; Pohjola's Daughter; and many more. Chamber Music: 2 string quartets, including *Voces Intimae.* Songs: 85 songs, including *Black Roses; Ingallil; Tennis at Trianon; On a Balcony By The Sea; Echo Nymph; A Hundred Ways;* and others. Choral Works: 20 including *Song of the Athenians; Hast Thou Courage; The Origin of Fire;* and others. Instrumental: More than 50 compositions for solo violin; more than 130 for piano; pieces for cello; for organ. Miscellaneous: chamber music without opus nos.; recitations; songs; choruses.

SMETANA, BEDŘICH. Operas: *The Bartered Bride; The Brandenburgers in Bohemia; Dalibor; Libuše; Two Widows; The Kiss; The Secret; The Devil's Wall; Viola.* Songs: *Erste Lieder; Our Song; Evening Songs.* Choral: *The Renegade; The Three Horsemen; The Farmer; Czech Song; Sea Song; The Dower;* and others. Chamber Music: *String Quartet in E Minor* "Aus Meinem Leben"; *Second String Quartet in C Minor; Piano Trio in G Minor.* Piano: *Six Characteristic Pieces; Album Leaves; Sketches;* and others. Orchestra: *Wallenstein's Camp; Hakon Jarl; Mà Vlast; Festival March; Prague Carnival; Richard III.*

SOUSA, JOHN PHILIP. Marches: *The Stars and Stripes Forever; Semper Fidelis; The Washington Post; King Cotton; The High School Cadets; Hands Across the Sea; Liberty Bell; Manhattan Beach; El*

Capitan; Thunderer. Light Operas: *El Capitan; The Charlatan; The Bride-Elect; The Smugglers; Desirée; The Queen of Hearts; Chris and the Wonderful Lamp; The Free Lance; The Glass Blowers; The American Maid; Victory.* Orchestral Suites: *Chariot Race; The Last Days of Pompeii; Sheridan's Ride; Three Quotations; At The King's Court; Looking Upward; Impressions at the Movies.*

STILL, WILLIAM GRANT. Orchestra: *Dismal Swamp; Africa; Afro-American Symphony; Kaintuck* for piano and orchestra; *Lenox Avenue*, for announcer, (radio) orchestra and chorus; Ballets *La Guiablesse; Sahdji;* and others. Opera: *Blue Steel.* Chamber Orchestra: *From the Land of Dreams; Levee Land; From the Black Belt; Log Cabin Ballads.*

STRAUSS, JOHANN. Waltzes: *Künstlerleben; Geschichten aus dem Wienerwald; An der schönen blauen Donau; Wiener Blut; Bei uns z' Haus; Tausend und eine Nacht; Man lebt nur einmal;* and many more. Operettas: *Indigo und die vierzig Raüber; Der Karneval in Rom; Die Fledermaus; Cagliostro; Prinz Methusalem; Blindekuh; Das Spitzentuch der Königin; Der lustige Krieg; Eine Nacht in Venedig; Der Zigeunerbaron; Simplicius; Ritter Pasman; Fürstin Ninetta; Jabuka; Waldmeister; Die Göttin der Vernunft.* Ballet *Aschenbrödel.*

STRAUSS, RICHARD. Orchestra: Symphony F Minor; *Burleske; Aus Italien; Don Juan; Macbeth; Tod und Verklärung; Till Eulenspiegel's Lustige Streiche; Ein Heldenleben; Don Quixote;*

Also Sprach Zarathustra; Sinfonia Domestica; Eine Alpensinfonie; Concertos for violin and for horn. Operas: *Guntram; Ariadne auf Naxos; Intermezzo; Feuersnot; Salome; Elektra; Der Rosenkavalier; Die Frau ohne Schatten; Arabella; Die aegyptische Helena; Die schweigsame Frau; Daphne; Der Friedenstag.* Ballets: *Eine Joseph-Legende; Schlagobers.* Songs: *Ständchen; Heimliche Aufforderung; Cäcilie; Morgen; Traum durch die Dämmerung; Ein Heldenleben; Zueignung; Allerseelen; Ruhe, meine Seele; Schlagende Herzen; Ich Schwebe;* and others totaling over 100. Chamber Music: String quartet; piano quartet; sonatas for cello and piano, violin and piano. Miscellaneous: Piano pieces; songs with orchestra.

STRAVINSKY, IGOR. For the Ballet and Theater: *Rossignol; Petrouchka; Renard; Les Noces; Histoire d'un Soldat; Pulcinella; Mavra; Oedipus Rex; Sacre du Printemps; The Fire Bird; Apollon Musagète; Le Baiser de la Fée; Persephone; Card Party.* Orchestra: *Concerto in E-Flat Major; Two Suites for Small Orchestra; Symphony of Psalms; Ragtime; Symphonies of Wind Instruments;* and others. Chamber Music: *Suite Italienne; Three Poems from the Japanese; Three pieces for String Quartet; Octet* for wind instruments; *Berceuse du Chat,* for female voice and three clarinets; *Concertino* for string quartet; and others. Miscellaneous: Compositions for voice and piano; chorus; solo piano; two pianos; literary works.

SULLIVAN, SIR ARTHUR. For the Theater: *Thespis; Trial by Jury; H.M.S. Pinafore: The*

Sorcerer; The Pirates of Penzance; Patience; Iolanthe; Princess Ida; The Mikado; Ruddigore; The Yeomen of the Guard; The Gondoliers; Cox and Box; The Grand Duke; Utopia Limited. Oratorios and Cantatas: *Kenilworth; The Prodigal Son; On Shore and Sea; The Golden Legend;* and others. Miscellaneous: Incidental music; ballets; operettas with librettos not by Gilbert; orchestral works; anthems; hymn tunes; piano pieces; songs.

SZYMANOWSKI, KAROL. Operas: *Hagith; King Roger; Prince Potemkin.* Orchestra: *Three symphonies; Concert Overture.* Violin Works: *Notturno e Tarantella; Mythes;* Two *Violin Concertos; Romance: Berceuse; Les Fontaines d'Aréthuse;* etc. Chamber Music: Two *String Quartets; Trio; Sonata* for violin and piano. Songs: *Songs of the Foolish Muezzin; Songs of Kurpie; Children's Rhymes; Slopiewnie; Love Songs of Hafiz; The Swan; Bunte Lieder; Vocalise-Étude;* and many more. Ballets: *Harnasie; Mandragora.* Vocal Works: *Stabat Mater; Veni Creator; Litania* etc.

TCHAIKOWSKY, PETER ILICH. Operas: *The Voyovoda; Undine; Mandragora; The Oprichnik; Vakula the Smith; Eugen Onegin; Joan of Arc; Mazeppa; The Enchantress; Pique Dame; Iolanthe.* Ballets: *The Swan Lake; The Sleeping Beauty; Casse-Noisette* "Nut-cracker." Orchestra: Symphony No. I, G Minor (Winter Dreams); Symphony No. II, C Minor (Little Russian); *The Tempest;* Symphony No. III, D Major, (Polish); *Marche Slave; Francesca da Rimini;* Symphony No. IV, F Minor; *Capriccio Italien;*

Festival Overture "1812"; Manfred Symphony; Symphony No. V, E Minor; Overture *Hamlet;* Symphony No. VI, B Minor, (Pathétique); and others. Concertos: 3 for piano, B-Flat Minor, G Major, E-Flat Major; Violin concerto in D Major; *Sérénade Mélancolique;* etc. Songs: 92 songs in various collections, including *None but the Lonely Heart.* Miscellaneous Works: Much piano music, choral works, chamber music, duets, etc.

VAUGHAN-WILLIAMS, RALPH. Stage Works: Incidental music to *The Wasps; Riders to the Sea; Job; Old King Cole,* a ballet; *The Shepherd of the Delectable Mountains.* Operas: *Hugh the Drover; The Poisoned Kiss; Sir John in Love.* Orchestra: *London Symphony; Academic Festival Overture; Pastoral Symphony; Symphony No. 4;* Three *Norfolk Rhapsodies; Bucolic Suite;* and others. Choral Works: *Willow Wood; A Sea Symphony;* Five *Mystical Songs;* Five *Tudor Portraits; Flourish for a Coronation;* and others. Chamber Music: Piano Quintet: *On Wenlock Edge;* String quartet; String Quintet (*Fantasy*). Miscellaneous: Numerous songs and cycles; hymns; organ and piano pieces.

VERDI, GIUSEPPE. Operas: *Oberto; Un Giorno di regno; Nabuco; I Lombardi; I Due Foscari; Luisa Miller; I Vespri Siciliani. Ernani; Macbeth; Rigoletto; Il Trovatore; La Traviata; Simon Boccanegra; Un Ballo in Maschera; La Forza del Destino; Don Carlos; Aïda; Otello; Falstaff;* and many more. Miscellaneous: Chamber music; sacred music; songs.

VILLA-LOBOS, HECTOR. Orchestra: *Légende Indigène; Suite Paulista; Carneval de Brazil; Le Centaura d'Or; Danses Africaines.* Orchestration of *Rude Poêma; Bachianas Brasileiras* for piano and orchestra; several *Chôros* for piano and orchestra; Suites, *Descrobimento do Brasil.* Other Compositions: Operas *Femina, Jesus, Isaht;* three ballets; an Oratorio; Two Masses; Sonatas; three piano trios; a nonet; chôros in various settings; four string quartets; many piano pieces; songs.

WAGNER, RICHARD. Operas: *Rienzi; Die Feen; Die Hochzeit; Das Liebesverbot; Der fliegende Holländer; Tannhäuser; Lohengrin; Der Ring des Nibelungen,* including *Das Rheingold, Die Walküre, Siegfried, Die Götterdämmerung; Tristan und Isolde; Die Meistersinger von Nürnberg; Parsifal.* Orchestral Works: *Symphony in C Major; Siegfried Idyll; nine overtures; Huldigungsmarsch;* and others. Miscellaneous: Choral works; songs; piano music; arrangements; incidental music to plays; Literary works.

WEBER, CARL MARIA VON. Operas: *Peter Schmoll und seine Nachbarn; The Girl of the Forest; Silvana; Die Drei Pintos; Der Freischütz; Euryanthe; Oberon; Abu Hassan.* Many dramatic works. Piano Works: *Four Sonatas; Polacca brillante; Aufforderung zum Tanze; two piano concertos;* Variations; *Allemandes;* and many more. Also pieces for 4 hands. Orchestral: *Overture to The Ruler of Spirits; two Symphonies* in C Major; *Six concertos;* several for clarinet, one for bassoon, one for horn; *Konzertstück* for piano; many more.

Miscellaneous: many Lieder; masses; cantatas; part songs; concerted pieces.

WOLF, HUGO. Songs: *Lieder nach verschiedenen Dichtern* (31); *Mörikelieder* (53); *Eichendorff-Lieder* (20); *Goethe-Lieder* (51); Spanisches Liederbuch (Vol. I, 44, Vol. II, 24); *Italienisches Liederbuch* (22). Instrumental Works: *String Quartet in D Minor; Penthesilea*, symphonic poem; *Italienische Serenade* for small orchestra or string quartet. Stage Works: *Der Corregidor; Manuel Venegas; Das Fest auf Solhaug*. Choral Works: *Christnacht; Elfenlied; Der Feuerreiter; Dem Vaterland;* and others. Miscellaneous: Literary works.

2 5050 00626132 1